Super Skills,
Super Reading

Super Skills, Super Reading

Literacy and Television Superheroes

Perry Dantzler

McFarland & Company, Inc., Publishers
Jefferson, North Carolina

This book has undergone peer review.

LIBRARY OF CONGRESS CATALOGUING-IN-PUBLICATION DATA

Names: Dantzler, Perry, 1982– author.
Title: Super skills, super reading : literacy and
 television superheroes / Perry Dantzler.
Description: Jefferson : McFarland & Company, Inc., Publishers, 2021. |
 Includes bibliographical references and index.
Identifiers: LCCN 2020044357 | ISBN 9781476678351
 (paperback : acid free paper) ∞
 ISBN 9781476641577 (ebook)
Subjects: LCSH: Literacy on television. | Superhero television programs—
 United States—History and criticism.
Classification: LCC PN1992.8.L57 D36 2020 | DDC 791.45/653—dc23
LC record available at https://lccn.loc.gov/2020044357

BRITISH LIBRARY CATALOGUING DATA ARE AVAILABLE

ISBN (print) 978-1-4766-7835-1
ISBN (ebook) 978-1-4766-4157-7

© 2021 Perry Dantzler. All rights reserved

*No part of this book may be reproduced or transmitted in any form
or by any means, electronic or mechanical, including photocopying
or recording, or by any information storage and retrieval system,
without permission in writing from the publisher.*

Front cover illustration by Martin Malchev (Shutterstock)

Printed in the United States of America

*McFarland & Company, Inc., Publishers
 Box 611, Jefferson, North Carolina 28640
 www.mcfarlandpub.com*

To Harris, Libby, and Kennedy—
my three mini superheroes.

Table of Contents

Preface   1
Introduction   10

1. How Does a Superhero Read?   33
2. *Arrow* and Specialized Literacies   48
3. Scientific Literacies as the Scientific Method in *The Flash*   67
4. *Gotham* as a Place Mired in Print-Privileged Literacy   85
5. Literacy as Agency and Equality in *Jessica Jones*   100
6. How Ethnicities and Local Communities Shape Literacy in *Luke Cage*   117
7. *Daredevil* and Disabilities   136
8. Literacies for Evil Purposes: Villains and Antiheroes   151
9. Sidekicks and Mentors: Literacies from the Sidelines   168
10. Places for Literacy Development: Caves and Workshops   185
11. How the Average Citizen Reads in Superhero Worlds   201

Conclusion   217
Chapter Notes   221
References   229
Index   243

Preface

The Scope of This Project

> Superheroes are about wish fulfillment. They're about imagining a better world and creating an alternate version or yourself—bigger, brighter, bolder than the real thing—to patrol and protect it [11].
> —Will Brooker, "We Could Be Heroes"

This book is the first monograph to examine the literacy practices and events of superheroes in current and recent TV superhero shows. By discussing different literacy representations (such as events, metaphors, and myths), I analyze the fictional manifestation of literacies and multiliteracies that shape superheroic abilities and identities. So much has been written and researched about superheroes with theoretical approaches (politics, gender, nationalism, sexuality), but the index of literacies as a means of assisting and empowering superhero endeavors has not received attention so far. Superheroes usually have advanced intelligence and detection skills, but this monograph argues that their multimodal literacy practices not only aid superheroes, but they become vital in establishing and developing their detective skills, combat powers, and expansive capacities to learn and do more.

Over the last eighty years, superheroes have appeared in other modes—film, video games, novels, comic runs, graphic novels, audio dramatizations, and plays. In *Superheroes on World Screens*, Rayna Deinson et al. define the superhero as "an emphatically transmedia phenomenon; or, at very least, needs to be conceptualized as a genre whose wide-ranging manifestations are hard to pin down to an original or even dominant sources" (4). Within this genre of superheroic characters and actions, the medium of TV extends superhero narratives through longer storylines and character arcs. The average superhero film is about two hours, and there are often sequel films to explore characters further, but the average season of a superhero TV drama is usually a cumulative seventeen hours. Because of lengthy screen time, TV superheroes have many more literacy events, participate in broader literacy practices, and work to further their multiliterate capacities. Therefore, viewers can witness patterns of reading and comprehension that superheroes use to facilitate their endeavors. Much written and admired about superheroes focuses on their physical attributes and daring feats: Daredevil employs a blend of martial arts, Green Arrow works through parkour and free running, and Jessica Jones and Luke Cage use their advanced strength to crush foes. Even *Gotham* shows a superhero at his beginning as Bruce trains himself to fight, withstand pain, and counteract incoming threats. Behind these impressive actions resides an undercurrent of the mind and cognitive processes, repetitively sifting through and evaluating new and complex information, reading and critiquing, evaluating, collecting, and discarding new pieces of data as the superhero's mind links together pertinent information in logical patterns.

The shows I've selected for analysis are *Arrow, Daredevil, Flash, Gotham, Jessica Jones,* and *Luke Cage*. These six shows represent a range of superheroes across a spectrum of age, gender, ethnicities, disabilities, socioeconomics, and education.[1] I explore the corresponding range of literacy practices and developments by analyzing how a superhero read, comprehends, and compiles data, and I connect those literacy activities to further student engagement with students' literacy activities. This monograph acts not only as a connection between academia and pop culture but also as a resource for developing strong multiliterate skills for student reading and learning. The representations of literacy from superheroes in TV shows are exaggerated—through futuristic technology, hyper-realistic skillsets, and dramatic stakes—but they have potential for representing ideological versions of literacy that a range of literacy scholars sanction. This project will answer two central questions regarding literacy representations in superhero TV shows: what are the apparent assumptions inherent in the representations? How do they frame literacy and multiliteracies?

As I explore superhero stories, I emphasize two significant concepts: the importance of literacy in the shaping and formation of each superhero story and how we see our own cultural values in the literacy elements as grounding our identities as intelligent, cultivated people with a range of expansive literacy practices. By identifying these representations of literacy, we hold a mirror up to and arrive at better understandings of our culture and its time and place in American history. As overarching depictions of American values, these representations of literacy are exaggerated in their skills, capacity, abilities, and rate of success; the fact that literacy practices are so ingrained in the superheroes demonstrates the extent to which we desire to have similar methods of comprehension, memorization, and pattern formation. It becomes important that we recognize their exaggerations and their prominence in our culture and media because they reflect our ideas and ideals of perfection.[2] By critiquing those desires through enacted representations of our culture, students in writing and in the larger fields of the humanities cannot only develop larger, broader, more complicated views of literacy, NLS authors, and representations of literacy elements, but they can develop richer skills through critical thinking and academic writing that seek to explain human communication and knowledge through concepts of reading and comprehending.

Subjects Beyond the Scope of This Study

Because this is a summation and overview of six TV shows, each with multiple episodes in multiple seasons, this project does not perform close readings on any single episode or character extensively. As I aim to establish an understanding of literacy practices and events for the entirety of each show, my examination remains broad and macro-focused. Although I address different literary and critical theories such as feminism, ethnic studies, and disability studies, the focus remains on the link between theoretical lens and literacy studies, mainly in the manifestations in which literacy practices influence or result from these theoretical readings. Further research in literacy studies could certainly perform close readings of individual episodes or scenes in superhero media as a microcosmic instance of performed literacy events.

This project focuses only on superhero TV shows from the last decade. Superheroes have rich histories and mythologies that span comics, graphic novels, movies, video games, and multiple franchises of merchandise, art, and fan-discussion, but this project does not give an overview of or bring into discussion other modes of superhero media. Mainly, this is for the sake of brevity and concentration as superhero stories have infiltrated all areas of media and story-telling, and covering literacy events and practices of all superhero modes could fill several volumes. Many of the literacy representations and theories in this project have potential in exploring literacy, learning, and education foundations in superhero media: films through decades of American life, videogames, comics, graphic novel standalones, cartoons, anime, and manga. Further research on superhero literacies could even tease out literacy distinctions between superhero origin films (*Captain America* 2011, *Batman Begins* 2005) and superhero ensemble films (*Avengers* 2012, *Justice League* 2017).

This project does not present historical summations of superhero mediation and remediation, and it does not present analysis on writers, creators, or artists that contributed the superhero media. The problem here lies in the extensive history of the superhero genre: the TV shows I explore all have creators, writers, directors, and actors who interpreted the superhero characters for the medium of TV, but a long history of comics and other modes preceded the TV shows. For example, the character Daredevil was created in the 1960s by Stan Lee, but over the next decade, nine writers wrote and/or designed 180 comic issues. Each writer interpreted Daredevil through their own preferences: Gerry Conway's issues had Daredevil pair up with Black Widow, a pairing that does not happen the current MCU. More writers followed in the following forty years, and the task of tracing these superheroes back to their roots could fill up several books at this point. The original versions of most of the superheroes are products of their times: cultural and historic representations of these superheroes that did not age well and do not reflect current perspectives of the characters or their literacy events. Many of the male superheroes reflect misogynic and hyper-masculine attitudes of the 1960s that saw women characters mainly as damsels in distress; Luke Cage, the first black superhero protagonist, was created by four white men who created the character at the height of Blaxploitation in 1972; most of the early comics feature main characters from white, middle-class, heteronormative backgrounds with access to resources and privilege; and almost all early superheroes were simplistic, one-dimensional, near-perfect models of American idealism. If I were to examine only the writers of the TV shows, they are often not one person repeatedly: the first season of *Daredevil* had Douglas Petrie, Steven DeKnight, Luke Kalteux, Christos Gage, Ruth Gage, Joe Pokaski, Marco Ramirez, and Drew Goddard each writing an episode independently or pairing up together. It becomes nearly impossible to draw authorial influence from such a diverse group of people who contributed to one season of the TV show.

This project assumes basic literacy (the ability to read and comprehend alphabetic texts) as a standard for college students and fictional superheroes. Almost all superheroes have advanced literacy skills involving print, alphabetic texts and employ these skills as literacy events regularly into larger patterns of literacy practices. Therefore, this project does not address literacy deficiencies in K-12 education or the endeavor to improve adult literacy.

Why This Project Matters

While other academic research on superheroes examines identity and physical performance, this project focuses on the learning, comprehension, and knowledge-making mental processes of superheroes. Students in college should invest in the development of their literacy events as part of a larger educational literacy practice, and this project shows elevated, hyper-intelligent literacy practices of superheroes. Through evaluation, comparison, critical observations, and lesson-planning through examinations of superhero TV shows, this projects establishes the following points throughout:

- Expansive definitions of literacy should be used, considered, examined, and identified in superhero TV shows as implications for establishing understandings of ourselves and our reading/learning processes in this age of digital multimodality.
- New knowledge and meaning-making lessons arise by applying NLS scholars' theories of literacy (myths, sponsors) to narratives of TV superheroes who exaggerate American ideals and culture.
- Representations of literacy appear in superhero media and connect to larger theories of literacy, and their extraordinary use in superhero stories reflect our cultural values regarding the uses of multiliteracies.
- The teaching of these representations of literacy change, affect, broaden, and redefine students' attitudes towards and understandings of literacy and multiliteracies by examining these representations.
- Literacy lessons are presented to effectively change attitudes towards literacies in the academic classroom to facilitate higher-quality, analytical writing and critical thinking.
- Students learn through observing literacy events, critiquing them, and then establishing their literacy events as part of a large communal practice.

The opportunity for studying literacy at the intersections of pop culture studies and composition has great potential past the research and theories of my research and those of superhero TV shows. Regardless of the medium for telling the stories, superhero narratives exhibit exaggerated expectations of art: higher stakes (the dark elves want to plunge the world into eternal darkness in *Thor: The Dark World*; Bane wants to detonate an atom bomb in Gotham in *The Dark Knight Rises*), higher performances of bodies (Supergirl must learn to train her alien abilities in *Supergirl*; Captain America launches a series of parkour/marital-art attacks in the Marvel films), higher special effects (physical stunts combined with advanced CGI to make superhero fly, flip, fight, interact with machinery, and battle multiple foes; the Batmobile turning into the Batpod motorcycle in *The Dark Knight*). Throughout their stories, the presence of American culture, morality, capitalism, and ideology is understood and reflected through the storylines and the characters (Stark

Enterprises sells missiles to the U.S. military fighting the Middle East and Tony Stark uses the company to fund his Iron Man suits and build Avenger's Tower to house his fellow superheroes in the *Iron Man* and *Avengers* films). Most of the superheroes serve as models for American conformity: white, middle/upper class, heteronormative, gender-specific, educated, and literate as a given baseline and then everything after as superheroic features such as superbodies, super-movements, super-tech, and/or super-skills. Current superheroes are flawed so viewers identify with them, but they have some aspect that they have advanced and perfected to the point of audience admiration as the (im)possible pinnacle of human conditioning: the body, speed, intelligence, fighting styles, supernatural ability, and/or technological advancements. We as audiences see those markers of perfection coupled with American culture/ideals, and therefore superheroes become perfected embodies of what we ourselves would like to be. Any of these primary sources regarding superheroes could be utilized through the lens of literacy, pop culture studies, and composition to facilitate higher student engagement and critical thinking.

Different types of multimodalities involve the merging of texts on platforms across different types of meaning and information to please, entertain, or interest various audiences as well as presenting different modes of learning opportunities. With these multimodalities, we see an influx of learning opportunities that speak to multiple audiences through new methods and means of learning and efforts. My aim of this project is to open up avenues of future research, first starting in literacy studies and then moving into other areas that speak to students' needs for analytical thought and better theoretical approaches to writing, composing, and research. Much like our understandings of multimodal multiliteracies, educational skillsets should traverse wide areas and arenas of interaction, participation, self-reflection, and personal understanding. By creating this study which examines representations of literacy in superhero narratives and then correlate to them to actions that students can take, I emphasize the important connection between the information learned in composition and the outcomes of its effect on students' lives, learning process, communication models, and literate activities, reflecting Patrick Sullivan's understanding of deep reading and learning: "an active, generative process of intellectual inquiry built around reading and sustaining engagement with complex, ill-structured problems" (145). My intent in this project is to begin conversations about literacy, TV superheroes, critical thinking, student innovation, and new teaching methods. These conversations offer other emerging scholars opportunities to work at the intersections of literacy studies, pop culture studies, and composition, opening up new spaces of critical thinking for students and expansion of new studies for instructors.

Research and Methodology

My dissertation, *With Great Literacy Comes Great Responsibility: Rethinking Popular Culture and the Literacy Practices of Superheroes* (2016), surveyed superhero literacy practices across multimodalities: film, TV shows, video games, comics, and books. This wide focus only let me glimpse over superheroes in TV shows as a part of the larger emphasis of superhero media. Superheroes in TV shows are permitted more time and space to demonstrate their literacy practices and individual events, activities that speak to the detective and intellectual work that grounds superheroes' decisions and evaluations.

For primary texts, I look at major superhero TV shows from the last decade; those shows reflect current trends in digital technologies and therefore digital literacies. I narrow the selection by longevity and critical acclaim: *Legends of Tomorrow* has an ensemble superhero cast, but it does not have as many episodes as *Arrow*. *Iron Fist* disappointed fans and critics who preferred Daredevil and Luke Cage as titular heroes. To limit these primary texts to manageable criteria, I examine only the first two seasons of each show. Usually, the first season develops the primary superhero to a point of self-recognition or communal acknowledgment, and new growth occurs in the second season. Further seasons of these shows have literacy events and practices that develop characters towards a wider utilization of literacy activities.

Examining TV shows superheroes in their third and fourth seasons complicates the discussion of literacy, and I would be simply retelling multiple plot lines to reach any understanding of literacy events. At the time of this writing, *Gotham* is in its 5th season; *Arrow*, its seventh; *the Flash*, its fifth; and so on. The characters Jessica Jones and Luke Cage have both appeared in the first season of the *Defenders*, and several characters in *Jessica Jones* and *Daredevil* appeared in *Iron Fist*.

For secondary sources to support my claims, I include work on superheroes and literacy studies.[3] I blend together these two fields of research to argue for new definitions of multiliterate comprehension as cognitive processes with reading across print and digital modes of information. This examination results in discoveries of a more-nuanced characterization of the roles and affordances of literacy in the construction of superheroes as agents with ethical aspirations and altruistic endeavors. I demonstrate through this extended study of superhero TV shows and literacy studies the fact that these literacy practices embody exaggerated portrayals of our culture and ideals. By bringing the discussion of representations of literacy in superhero media into the writing classroom, students can see literacy studies scholars' theories in action.

Organization of the Book

The Preface, Introduction, and Chapter 1 present an overview and collective understanding of TV superheroes and their literacy skills. Chapters 2–7 identify one or two TV shows and present the reader with new information on literacy elements: terms that identify perspectives, angles, definitions, or limitations of literacies. These chapters identify literacy practices and events that define particular superheroes and ground their identity through their intelligence, learning patterns, and comprehension that span multiple modes of information and data. Chapters 8–11 assemble together TV shows to trace literacy patterns through collective groups of characters such as the villains or sidekicks. These chapters use previously learned literacy terms to expand on perspectives of reading and comprehension. All chapters include New Literacy Studies (NLS) and digital media (DM) authors that shape the field and contribute to current perspectives of literacy and multiliteracies in and out of academia. All chapters end with short lessons for instructors, students, and readers to encourage deeper discourse and study in the field of multimodal multiliteracies.

The Preface introduces the topics for discussion and narrows the scope of research to the six TV shows selected. The Introduction presents modes, multimodalities, literacy, and multiliteracies as key concepts for understanding literacy representations and gives a brief explanation of the goals and objectives of this project, mainly centering on establishing why studying and understanding superhero multiliteracies are important in this age of digital information and labor. Chapter 1 summarizes common literacy traits of TV superheroes and the ways those traits empower superheroes to react with superhuman responses. Specialized alphabetic and multimodal literacies are shared by most superheroes, and connective networks of literacy practices empower superheroes to become detectives. Chapter 2 reviews multimodalities in *Arrow*, mainly through its protagonist, Oliver Queen, and his broad range of multiliteracies that allow him to navigate the many digital and hardcopy modes in his narrative: online maps, emails, business records, historical documents, blueprints, and legal records. Chapter 3 highlights the scientific literacy methods—biogenetic, forensics, physics—that empower the hero, Barry Allen, and the other scientists to fight villains that have been modified through hyper-sci-fi mutations. Chapter 4 surveys the main characters of *Gotham* and their dependencies on written, alphabetic modes; because of the severe lack of digital information, characters have advanced skills of traditional literacy in which print and written documents are of utmost importance but limit their detective work in uncovering evidence of crimes. Chapter 5 discusses the literacy practices of female superheroes that often become catalysts for their agency and autonomy. Jessica Jones has a superhuman body, but her job depends on analysis and observation of multiple modes of data. Chapter 6 scrutinizes how ethnicities shape literacy practices in *Luke Cage* and notes the ways that dominant hegemony has suppressed, censured, and monitored minorities' access to literacy development. Chapter 7 examines disabilities and literacy practices through a blind superhero who develops different literacy events to aid him in his work. Netflix's *Daredevil* sets a precedent for exploring a disabled superhero whose blindness encourages viewers to reevaluate the ableist culture of America in general. Chapter 8 analyzes the "bad guys" of the shows and their literacy practices and events. Villains frequently have multiliterate skills that rival the heroes', and villains work to improve those skills to aid their nefarious plans. Chapter 9 looks at literacy practices of the sidekicks and mentors of the main superhero. Usually, supporting characters do not have as developed a range of multiliteracies as the superheroes but have advanced literacy in specialized areas such as data-mining or engineering. Chapter 10 examines the spaces where superheroes work, train, surveil, gather data, and heal, spaces that reflect the literacies of the heroes and sidekicks. Chapter 11 moves beyond literacies of superheroes, villains, and secondary characters to present literacy practices of the average citizen in superhero TV shows, citizens that live in communities of heightened tension and global threats. The Conclusion wraps up the discussion and provides additional information about other sources and media to supplement this project.

Introduction

> Superhero literature has become much too large for [confines of comics books], and the nature of multiple continuities necessitates taking a broad view of what the superhero gene encompasses [189].
> —Alex Romagnoli and Gian Pagnucci,
> *Enter the Superheroes*

    This project came out of a simple question about superhero media: how do superheroes read? As I deliberated on the question, I asked other questions that expounded upon my initial query. Superheroes by definition have advanced skills in combat, agility, detection, surveillance, and protection; shouldn't they have advanced literacy skills as well? What does the study of literacy offer in terms of understanding superheroes' identity, knowledge, research detection, and plan formation? Why should college students study superheroes and their literacy activities: how superheroes collect information through reading, how they employ a range of multiliteracies across digital platforms, and how they transition between literacy events? These questions directed the research and production of this book as I triangulated three areas of interest: superhero TV shows, representations of literacy events and practices, and composition pedagogy.

    I learned about superheroes in my early twenties between semesters of college classes, working part-time, and preparing for grad school. In my sophomore year, the first *Spider-Man* (2002) arrived in theaters on the heels of 9/11, ushering in a new era of media with the modern superhero. The following years saw more Spider-Man films, Nolan's Batman trilogy, the launch of the Marvel Cinematic Universe, and finally the infiltration of superheroes in all avenues of modalities: a rich tapestry of characters larger than life infused into various modes of storytelling. In her research on the attributes of heroes, Jane Gordon states that creators of current-day renditions of superheroes worked within real constraints so that their protagonists could only defy some but not all social and physical rules. The results were lovable and fascinating, because they combined being extraordinary with having real and profound limitations. They were also often carefully contextualized in historical and political moments, inviting readers and viewers to explore the relation of the actors' agency to what the circumstances would and could not permit [254].

Many young people have admired superheroes with their feats of strength and fighting styles; I admired the intelligence and detective skills of superheroes that rely on sharp cognitive processes. They were so confident in their perceptive magnitudes, effortlessly learning and expanding their knowledge bases while practicing exceptional discernment in moments of chaos. While I attempted to learn the complexities of French post-modernism theory, superheroes learned in multiple areas of dispersed information with relative ease. I pieced together a master's thesis with painstaking effort, and Tony Stark build an Iron Man suit in a cave. I learned about representations of literacy by plodding through linguistic analyses, and the Flash could read at super-speed.

By the time I started my PhD in rhetoric and composition and began studying for the comps, superhero films dominated the box office as blockbuster goliaths that earn fans' appreciation, critics' approval, and (most importantly) giant revenues. According to Charles Hatfield, Jeet Heer, and Kent Worcester in the introduction to *The Superhero Reader*, "Superheroes thus occupy a magical position in contemporary popular culture" (xiii). This magical place allows for "a seemingly inexhaustible resource for commercial artists, publishers, moviemakers, animators, radio and television dramatists, videogame designers, and other cultural entrepreneurs" (xiii) to create complex, intricate stories that speak to a human need for meaningful moments of superheroic endeavors. The rise of technologies and digital media aided the rise of superhero narrative through effective story-telling in various modes: according to Louis Rosen in his analysis of superheroics, "For the last twenty years, superheroes have been enjoying a crest of popularity due to a seemingly never-ending series of movies and television shows that mine decades of comic book source material for action and drama" (380). New avenues of storytelling in superhero media allowed for new studies about their detective work, intellectual capacities, and methods of expanding mental and logistical processes. Superheroes reflect the exaggerated ideals of our culture as feats of human accomplishment and potential, spun out through suspension of disbelief to its utmost conceptualization. With these superheroic achievements, literacy skills of multiple uses have been honed, coupled, created, and perfected inside their stories. What I argue for, in terms of this project, is that superheroes have advanced forms of literacy which have been overlooked by other scholars.[1] However, representations of literacy in superhero narratives have been overlooked, ignored, or simplified. When literacy is connected with superheroes, it is often in using their stories to encourage interest in reading from students.

When most Americans think about superheroes, super bodies and superpowers are the first criteria to come to mind: Superman's invincibility, Hulk's gigantic body, Spiderman's web-swinging, and the endless possibilities of the X-Men whose mutations imagine natural and supernatural contortions of the human body. With their wildly-fantastica mediations and remediations, superheroes have become models of altruism and goodwill by their endeavors to protect others. While more recent films show supervillains reaching an untimely end, usually due to their miscalculations and greed, the original superheroes were careful to rescue all those in danger, including villains who started skirmishes in the first place. Superheroes of the Golden Age (1930s–50s) had two goals: thwarting devilish plans and saving as many lives as they could (Thomas et al. 1990). The Silver Age (1960s–70) of comics saw the growth of superheroes into flawed, realistic characters. Today, in the age of digital media, superheroes also strive to save lives, but their storylines and histories have grown complex, riddled with trickery and coded with ambiguity in a world of post-modern grayness. Yet, despite their complex histories, moral ambiguity, and endless conflicts, the allure of the superhero holds fast: many of us want to be superheroes mainly for the amount of personal control and agency that most superheroes can access. This control and agency facilitate superheroes to make effective and deliberate decisions with altruistic intentions as appositive changes that unite superheroes' mental and physical proficiencies.

Determining what makes a superhero superheroic usually reflects on the type of work that the superhero does—sometimes physical, sometimes mental, but always aware. Regardless of the "edgier" narratives, heighten gore and violence, and stark terror of the superhero's dilemmas, the first step of the superhero's work has remained relatively the same. Whether poor like Spider-Man, rich like Batman, indestructible like Hulk, or vulnerable like Daredevil, superheroes perform a vast array of detective work. Jessica Jones in particular has the title of Private Investigator on the door of her office; one of Batman's aliases is the World's Greatest Detective.[2] The purview of the detective work may be narrow (Daredevil stays primarily in the Hell's Kitchen) or broad (characters on Team Flash have traveled to other universes), but their work requires investigation, research, data assimilation, and final analysis to pinpoint the villain, the villain's plan, and a plan of counterattack. All of these actions, regardless of the modalities used, require advanced literacy skills. Superheroes must move beyond the limits of defined and institutionalized literacy (traditional and autonomous) with its socially-sanctioned spaces (courtrooms, libraries, media centers, boardrooms); they must utilize the activities of multiliteracies for its expanded opportunities in superheroic endeavors: reaching new heights of achievement in physical combat, digital intel, citywide surveillance, scientific experimentation, and weapon manipulation. This move towards new understandings of literacies allows us to better understand our current attitudes towards literacy in our culture and higher education by studying a range of representations of literacy in superhero TV shows.

Modes

> Clearly, the concept of *mode* is crucial in a multimodal theory of literacy, and so are associated concepts such as inherent and culturally made *affordance, modal specialization, functional load,* and *materiality* [36].
> —Gunther Kress, *Literacy in the New Media Age*

Before I begin my discussion of how superheroes read and how their reading informs and shapes their identities, I define four terms used through this project: modes, multimodalities, literacy, and multiliteracies. Due to continued advancements in technology, digital learning, and mass media, we have moved our knowledge access and cognitive formation into multiliterate methods, texts, communications, and discourses across a range of modes and platforms. In "The Future of 'Social Literacies,'" Brian V. Street asks pertinent questions about how modes work in our current lives: "What is a mode, how do modes interact, how can we best describe the relationship between events and practices, and how do we avoid becoming the agents producing the new constraints of newly described and impose grammars?" (31). In its simplest definition, modes refer to any artifact—printed, digital, hand-drawn—that contains a message or idea which conveys information to a reader.[3] A mode could include grocery receipt, a video-game, an atlas, an advertisement on a bus, a novel, or a podcast; the list has almost endless possibilities in its inclusion of modes. Furthering Street's discussion, Carlota Smith in *Modes of Discourse* defines modes as linguistic features, as "grammatical form with consistent interpretations," having "characteristic patterns of distribution and of interpretation" (1). These patterns, she argues, depend on their usage and identification within particular discourses. In *Modality*, Bob Hale and Aviv Hoffmann argue, "Modal notions—notions of necessity and possibility—are implicit in our understanding of a wide class of fundamental concepts" (1). Many of the studies, intent on the examination of forms that create meaning through language, emphasize the expression of modality over the modes: Hieko Narrog's *Modality, Subjectivity, and Semantic Change* (2012) examines cross-linguistics through claims regarding truth and discourse while Joseph

Melia's *Modality* (2003) explores realism and skepticism through language formation and expression; other scholars regard multimodality as context such as Alex Linge and Henrik Muller, stating that "modality is not directly coded in linguistic expressions but arises through interpretation in a context of utterance, be that through conventional indirectness, metaphorical mapping, enrichment procedures, non-demonstrative inference or other context-bound mechanisms" (1). Defining of modality is not as important as understanding that the expression of the mode can shape or alter the information it contains.

Against particularities of modality across disciplines, I stress the importance of understanding the affordances of individual modes because the information they hold frequently impacts readers more than the modality itself.[4] Deborah Brandt and Katie Clinton in "Limits of the Local" stress the influence of modes:

> Objects are animated with human histories, vision, ingenuity, and will, yet they also have durable status and are resilient to our will. Our objects are us but more than us, bigger than we are; as they accumulate human investments in them over time, they can and do push back at us as "social facts" independent and to be reckoned with [345].

In unison with Brandt and Clinton's approach, Gunther Kress and Theo van Leeuwen (*Reading Images* 1996) emphasize that the different modes of representation do not exist in solidarity because marginalized entities "are not held discretely, separately as autonomous domains in the brain, or as autonomous communicational resources in a culture, nor are they deployed discretely, either in representation or in communication; rather, they intermesh and interact at all times" (39–40). Instead, modes intersect, network information, influence readers, and disseminate knowledge. An example would be Batman who, as a fictional character, has more cultural gravitas than any singular mode he appears in: comics, movies, TV shows, or video games. Even as a collective part of American culture, the idea of Batman exists as larger and more significant than his simple presence or artistic interpretation through any mode. Through this project, the term mode refers to any text that holds, correlates, and/or alters messages or data that humans or superheroes can read and comprehend.[5]

Multimodalities

> The social semiotic multimodal world shapes our social and semiotic actions, our engagement, and it shapes the possibilities of our meaning-making in responses to prompts [51].
> —Jeff Bezemer and Gunther Kress,
> *Multimodality, Learning, and Communication*

What Multimodals Are

The networking of singular modes into multiple modes or multimodality has interested scholars in the humanities, especially with the foundational shift from traditional, print-privileged learning and writing into digital learning composition. In *Before Writing: Rethinking the Paths to Literacy* (1997), Gunther Kress explores potentials of multimodal expression by looking at children's drawings. Against the narrow perspectives of modality (traditionally limited to print and alphabetic forms), he argues for wider perceptions of communication that cross genres and modalities to infer new types of meaning: "Modes of communication, other than language, are becoming increasingly prominent and even dominant in many areas of public communication in which language was formerly used exclusively or dominantly" (xvii).[6] Kress's *Literacy in the New Media Age* (2003) also expands on digital modes by moving away from the hardcopy book and the page to the screen and the image because he states that limitations on views of knowledge in modes—especially confining it to print, alphabetic texts—deprive higher education opportunities to delve deeper into more-intrinsic understandings of human communication in all its modalities. Kress defines his use of the term multimodality and its functions in creating and portraying meaning, message, and tone by claiming, "The digital media of representations/production/communications facilitate the use of many such technologies of transcriptions: modes such as speech, moving image or still image, writing, colour, layout all appear and are available to be used" (97). Much like the pen, the typewriter, and the computer, new tools of technology allow users to access audiences with larger outreach, advancing human communication and aptitudes as networked, interconnected, and multifaceted.

In pop culture studies, new research in the ways that digital media interlinks, remediates, and continues narratives, even across multiple modalities, has grown significantly. Primarily the influence is evident across digital modes that network and complicate meaning across media. For example, *Daredevil*, *Jessica Jones*, and *Luke Cage* are extensions of the MCU (Marvel Cinematic Universe) films started by *Iron Man* (2008), but whereas the MCU films premiered in theaters, these other shows were released as an entire season on Netflix. The digital and technological revolution remains a central draw for the discussion of multimodals, offering new opportunities for discourse, pedagogy, and praxis, but the terms are conflated; the differences between multimodality, multiliteracies, digital composing, and technical writing are lost in the depth of scholarship that examines them and seeks to define them within and outside the context of academia. Rather than examine literacy usage in only one or two modes inside superhero TV shows, I present a wide selection so that the multimodal aspects focus on the literacy elements rather than on particularities of the mode. Throughout my discussion of superhero TV shows and their literacy practices, I examine literacy/multiliteracies activities primarily, and multimodality, while important to understanding the means of communicating those activities, remains a secondary concern. For the sake of clarity, here is the simple rule of definitions: **multimodalities** refer to the study of various modes across platforms; **multiliteracies** reflect how we read and comprehend these multiple modes.[7]

How Multimodals Lead to Digital Learning

Learning can take place across a variety of contexts, situations, and outcomes; digital learning is grounded in multimodalities that can support knowledge and data gathering on screens. Gunther Kress and Theo van Leeuwen in *Multimodal Discourse* argue, "In the era of multimodality, semiotic modes other than language are treated as fully capable of serving for representation *and* for communication. Indeed language, whether as speech or as writing may now often be seen as ancillary to other semiotic modes" (46). Information still has potency in hard-copy, printed, alphabetic modes, but the transition of this information onto digital platforms lead to greater access, further collaboration, and wider dissemination. Personally, I have lived the digital revolution: I was a freshman in college in 2000; the hand-written, 5-paragraph essay ruled English Composition 1 in my school; and almost all information was limited to whatever the local library or college collection offered. This class taught grammar and form over content and expression, rooted in pedantic rules that led to correctly-written prose that was dull and lifeless.[8] The class felt outdated, especially at the turn of the millennium, and fellow students complained about the irrelevance of handwritten prose at the dawn of the digital revolution. Fast-forward twenty years, not only does my research take place as digital learning, but my pedagogy and praxis in the classroom are grounded in the usage and mastery of digital tools of learning. Similarly, those of us teaching in higher education need to stay current because writing as a process changes to fit the task at hand in expressing meaning, and therefore writing relies on technology for its best, most capable production.[9]

While digital learning sounds appealing to most Americans, a subset of the population doubts the usefulness that multimodality can have in higher learning. Michael Henderson et al. comment on the concerns of making learning mobile: "digital technology continues to be talked about (especially by those not involved immediately in university teaching and learning) in portentous terms of systematic change and reform" (308). Detractors of multimodal teaching might object that the writing, research, and knowledge-gathering data in college work will become more about the coolness of the tools used rather than the challenging, strident work of higher education that pushes critical thinking and new innovations of learning. After all, in a culture obsessed with digital devices, amok with a near ADHD-level of distraction towards short bursts of messaging and entertainment via texting and YouTube, the long process of higher education that values deep reflection and methodical research might suffer in return. The pushback against digital pedagogy and instruction is understandable, on a basic level at least. Many Americans see all multimodalities and digital media as a conglomeration of sparkly, shallow narratives and tropes that provide mindless entertainment and do not foster critical thinking past simple comprehension of information and fictional storylines.

To this possible objection, I emphasize the role that digital multimodality should have in the college classrooms: a balance of introspective, active learning enhanced by digital tools rather than solely focused on them. In the same way that a teacher's pedagogy remains only as effective as his or her actual teaching, the teacher's utilization of tools cannot rise above the teacher's level of expertise in the classroom. An ineffective teacher will stay an ineffective teacher no matter how many tools, toys, or marvels he or she has at hand. (In much the same way, a collection of cool tools does not make a character a superhero; the character must use those tools in superheroic activities to become a superhero.) Because of the focus on the quality of teaching, multimodality—whether in production, research, or process—should serve as an opportunity to provide deeper connections to students' lives and their understanding of their culture. The focus of this project centers on the instructor and the scholar developing new forms of literacy events and practices across modes that supplement robust learning in this digital age.

Literacy

> Literacy is based upon a system of symbols. It is a symbolic system used for communication and as such exists in relation to other systems of information exchange. It is a way of representing the world to others [35].
> —David Cole and Darren Pullen,
> *Multiliteracies in Motion*

Brief History of Literacy Studies as an Academic Discipline

The history of literacy studies as an academic discipline coincided with movements in technology over the last sixty years, and many scholars working in the field acknowledged how new digital and communicative advancements shaped not only social literacy events and practices but also understandings of those events and practices. Gunther Kress in *Before Writing: Rethinking the Paths to Literacy* puts forth "some thoughts about the paths into the new literacy which, as far as one can read the runes, is likely to be the state of the world communication over the next few decades" (146). Research on literacy—its definitions and its uses, its limitations and its expansions, its simplicities and its complexities—has garnered scholarly attention as a study from the 1950s and 1960s. In "The Consequences of Literacy" (1963), Jack Goody and Ian Watt put forth the theory that a great divide exists between literate and illiterate/oral communities.[10] This great divide, they argued, could act as a separation to categorize multiple cultures across the globe as the lack or presence of literacy has direct consequences on the mental processes of the people in those cultures. In subsequent decades, literacy scholars saw the social impact of literacy as more complicated and diverse: Walter Ong's "Writing Is a Technology that Restructures Thought" (1986) examined mental processes of reading; James Paul Gee (*An Introduction to Discourse Analysis*, 1999) focused on discourse communities; Harvey Graff (*The Literacy Myth*, 1979) explored myths in literacy acquisition; and Linda Flower (*Community Literacy and the Rhetoric of Public Engagement*, 2008) researched literacy as community practices. Literacy studies currently occupies a place of interdisciplinary research, and a significant portion of its researchers focus on literacy outreach, improvement, and foundations in the K-12 years of schooling.

For this project, I include literacy scholars involved with the study of literacy across academic disciplines and college writing, a collective body of work called the New Literacy Studies (NLS).[11] In his research of literacies across cultural contexts, Brain V. Street explains that the NLS is research "that for the last 20 years has approached the study of literacy not as an issue of measurement or of skills but as social practices that vary from one context to another" (2017, 4). In *Travel Notes from the New Literacy Studies*, Kate Pahl and Jennifer Roswell observe "New Literacy Studies represents a tradition of considering the nature of literacy not as a neutral set of skills that we acquire, in school or in other learning contacts, but instead is how people use literacy in different context for different purposes" (3–4). Rather than a set definition for a cognitive process, NLS saw literacy as a fluid tool able to change depending on the task at hand, contextualized for recognizing and responding to information in texts.

Within the structure of NLS's expanding and networked perspectives of literacy as a social and logistical tool, I stress the fact that superhero TV shows' representations of literacy (alphabetic and multimodal) embody exaggerated forms of our culture and ideals: superheroes have superheroic literacy practices as well as superheroic skills, abilities, and bodies. In their study of literacy events in film, Williams and Zenger stress that

> the literacy practices displayed on the screen and consumed by the public are part of the ideological construction of what is considered literacy, what social goals it serves in what institutions, how it is perpetuated, how it shapes concepts of identity, and cultural power is determined by who is considered literate [2007, 6].

I select certain exemplifications from the chosen superhero TV shows as representative of larger literacy practices, but by no means have I exhausted the supply of literacy activities in any one superhero narrative. In fact, a closer reading of any single superhero TV show or character would provide an exhaustive list of activities and uses of literacy from small background activities to the imposing and significant movements of reading that affect the plot. Watching someone read silently is a dull task. Although literacy activities guide the superhero's detective work, the visual moments of actual reading are often skipped in visual superhero media: the superhero discovers information in a file, a report, a letter, or even on a scrap of paper, and then the story jumps forward in time to when the superhero has read, comprehended, and discerned the important information contained within that specific text.

Literacy events are specific, personal uses of reading and comprehending texts and are dependent on a person's needs: reading an email for work, reading a numerical table for filing taxes, or reading a story to a child at bedtime. Just because the viewer does not see the literacy events on-screen does not mean that these events do not have great significance for understanding representations of literacy in superhero TV shows. Often literacy events onscreen escape our notice, acting as what Barton and Hamilton (1998) described as "hidden literacies" which are literacy events so ordinary and commonplace that they have a tendency to be "devalued and overlooked" (xvi). Literacy activities may be hidden, implied, or regulated to the background, but that does not lessen their importance or alter "the fact that these images [of literacy] recreate and reinforce pervasive concepts and perceptions of literacy, perceptions that inevitably influence both how we teach reading and writing and how our students respond to print literacy and to writing classes" (Williams and Zenger 5). These concepts and perceptions remain the focus of this project, providing new grounds for understanding and studying literacy events as characters read texts on screens, on pages, and on multimodal platforms. From these new grounds of understanding ordinary literacy events and observing superheroes' literacy, new opportunities arise to better understand our literacy events and create new activities to hone, broaden, or extrapolate meaning from the events.

Here I caution against slapping the term "literacy" haphazardly on all human activities as a means of studying human behavior and activities. The temptation may be to name any setting or scene as a text to be read, and the emerging scholar might feel compelled to stick "literacy" on activities as a method of meaning: body literacy, fighting literacy, or weapons literacy. But that would mean using literacy as a catchall for any object or motion in reality. For activities that rely on the body as a means of accomplishing a goal—fending off random thugs, showdowns with supervillains, or scaling up a building—I use the term "process": body processes, fighting processes, or weapons processes. Superheroes do train their bodies to act and react with rote precision, but activities of the hands, legs, or whole body do not require the mental comprehension and analytical procedures of the mind that literacy events do. The superhero might pause in the middle of a fight to engage with texts—reading a note or cell-phone message dropped by an opponent—but a clear distinction exists between physical combative events and literacy events. The physical activities definitely look cooler than reading activities, and TV shows have upped the drama and effects of hero/villain fights, but the process behind literacy events requires higher mental capabilities. As average viewers (red-blooded Americans immersed in violent media), we can be impressed and excited by what we see in superhero TV shows: Daredevil's hallway fight in Season 1, Oliver Queen's parkour/free-running styles, and Jessica Jones's guerrilla street moves. Literacy activities that cannot be seen but take place in the mind—the interworking between the eyes and mind, the mental in-taking of information, and the brain power to construct meaning and methods into new knowledge—are the emphasis of my study.[12]

Literacy Events in Superhero TV Shows

The study of new literacies—their perspectives, practices, formation, expansion, and fundamentals—not only has implication and application for rhetoric and composition but also answers an immediate need in composition: the need to expand views of literacy and multimodal multiliteracies that students can correlate into more complex writing and deeper critical thinking. In "Interpretive Communities and Variable Literacies," Janice Radway argues that previous theories of literacy have assumed that "the character of print itself determines what can be done with it, and thus what it means to be literate" (467). These theories, narrowing perspectives about literacy acquisition and usage, result in viewpoints that limit reading to print-privileged, academic texts: "a singular, skilled process, which many readers only partially master and some texts do not fully require" (467). Radway's definition of literacy aligns with Mark Warschauer's explanation of the tendency to simplify literate activities: "Literacy is frequently viewed as a set of context-neutral, value-free skills that can be imparted to individuals. [...] Rather, being literate has always depended on mastering processes that are deemed valuable in particular societies, cultures, and contexts" (1999, 1). Superheroes' literacy activities reflect their values and their needs, especially when those activities involve technology to improve their detective work or surveillance. However, Warschauer cautions against making technology a separate entity with its literacy: "Rather, technological change intersects with other social, economic, cultural, and political factors to help determine how literacy is practiced" (1). Both literacy and technology serve as tools for the superhero and depend on the superhero's cognitive ability, mental processes, and logical calculations to be effective.

For examination of the reading, detective work, and learning in superhero TV shows, I have chosen the term literacy as opposed to intelligence, knowledge, or memorization because literacy suggests a process of intake for the individual rather than output.[13] The intake of information through literacy events allows the superhero to then act from a place of mental certainty because of the information learned. In the first season of *Daredevil*, Ep. 1.3, Daredevil enters a hallway where Russian mobsters who have kidnapped a diplomat's child. As the camera lens roams through the hallway voyeuristically, Daredevil fights against the thugs, bashing them into doors, walls, and the floor. While this scene is spectacular in its cinematic effects and physical stunts, the activity on Daredevil's part relies on his martial art and boxing skills to crush on-coming foes. However, his literate skills were in high demand earlier in the episode when he tracked the location of the kidnapped boy by engaging in detective work that required highly-specialized literacy skills to collect information, process it in a logistical framework, and then react appropriately.

Despite the current trend in digital learning to refocus attention on multimodal literacies, traditional autonomous forms of literacy appear in superhero TV shows, and these forms play strident roles in shaping current portrayals of superheroes and their respective worlds. Julia Gillen in "Virtual Spaces in Literacy Studies" argues, "What is 'new' about New Literacies is not a hard and fast binary distinction between the offline and online for the recognition of new practices with enhances interactivity and new ways of combining writing and reading" (369). With wider inclusions of multimodal multiliteracies, views of literacy (traditional, visual, multimodal) demonstrate our identification with the ideology of American culture and its significance in these narratives on all levels of literate understanding. For instance, if we look at Oliver Queen's identity only through traditional, alphabetic print, his status as a superhero has less gravitas and ideological perfection then if we widen his skills to those of multimodal multiliteracies; under this wider perspective, his status of superhero becomes greater, more effective, closer to godlike status for a human. Oliver's reading alphabetic texts and memorize them quickly is skill worthy of admiration and approval from audiences (most of us wish we could read faster and remember more), but Oliver building shooting devices, remotely surveying Starling City, creating computerized databases, mastering body performance, and observing criminal patterns of behavior all elevate admiration and approval to adoration and amazement as he becomes superheroic. The abilities of multiliteracies are exaggerated with superhero TV shows, buffed up to their utmost potential, honed and sharp, and the significance of these literacies serves as a reflection of the ideals we hold for ourselves as Americans. By studying these literacy activities, we can understand the mental processes and cognitive abilities that shape human learning and knowledge formation on personal and communicative levels.

Literacy Practices

The NLS defines literacies in action usually as events within a larger, social literacy practice of particular communities: literacy events refer to the individual usages of literacy that fit a person's personal, career-oriented, and idiosyncratic procedures for comprehending and interpreting messages across modes. In *Ways with Words* (1983), one of the first ethnographic studies on communal literacy practices, Shirley Brice Heath used "literacy events" to define situations in which people interact with reading or writing for a multitude of purposes and needs. Heath claims that, to fully understand the methods and functions of traditional orality and literacy in modern communities, scholars should examine literacy events happening in everyday interactions, indicative of local literacies as "community literacy activities" (200), both public and social. Because these local literacies reflect their community's historical, political, educational, and geographical happenstances and complexities, Heath demonstrates that older academic characterizations of community literacy often become unreliable because oral and literate traditions are deeply intertwined through necessity rather than acting as distinct events achieved through educational dictation from the powers above (7). Whether socially-imposed or personal preferences, literacy events tend to be modeled from larger literacy practices of particulars from one's time, place, group identification, education, and socioeconomic class.

Literacy practices are the patterns of use, a collective of literacy events, which determine the way groups of people read and approach literacy and knowledge-gathering purposes in and through their communities. While literacy events are individual uses of literacy, literacy practices refer to the larger systems of reading and comprehension which these events create within social groups and larger communities. For example, a student reading instructions for an online quiz, then forming answers in a Word doc, and finally uploading the doc to a college database like D2L are all separate literacy events; the literacy practice of college students refers to the collective of all students reading, writing, and uploading, ignoring personal reading and writing styles to observe the whole of the activities as a specific, defined literacy practice.[14] The distinction between events and practices applies to superheroes as most superheroes have highly-advanced literacy skills as part of a literacy practice, but the literacy events of each superhero depend on their particulars: their jobs, their missions, their relationships, and their superpowers.

Understanding the difference between events and practices allows students to see individual events—acts of literacy indicative of the individual—as part of larger literacy practices in particular communities, locations, and time periods. Brandt and Clinton note, "Literate practices are not typically invented by their practitioners. […] Literacy in use more often than not serves multiple interests, incorporating individual agents and their locales into larger enterprises that play out away from the immediate scene" (338). Much like discourse communities that James Paul Gee researches extensively, literacy practices arise out of communities that need these practices to meet their intellectual and textual activities.[15] Brandt and Clinton expound upon their ideas by explaining that "literate practices depend on powerful and consolidating technologies—technologies that are themselves susceptible to sometimes abrupt transformations that can destabilize the functions, uses, values, and meanings of literacy anywhere" (338). As digital information and accessible technology grow and expand, so must literacy practices develop as users interact with information and technology. In *Literacy as Involvement*, Deborah Brandt argues that

> for some, literacy is a technology; for others, a cognitive consequence; for still others, a set of cultural relationships; yet for others, a part of the highest human impulse to think and rethink experience in place. Literacy is a complex phenomenon, making problems of perspective and definition inevitable. Literacy is also something of real value, making struggle around it unlikely to end [1].

Precisely this struggle around literacy cements it as a function of superhero narratives as superheroes struggle to learn more, do more, and become more than their initial states allow at the beginning of their stories.

Other NLS scholars have a range of perspectives about the fundamentals of literacy: Jenny Cook-Gumperz in "The Social Construction of Literacy" argues, "The historical view of literacy begins in early modernity when literacy became regarded as a virtue, and some elements of such moral virtue still seem to attach to its use" (191). In "Literacy Practices," David Barton and Mary Hamilton extrapolate on this perspective because "the notion of literacy practices offers a powerful way of conceptualizing the link between the activities of reading and writing and the social structures in which they are embedded and which they help shape" (7). As a mediation between individuals in a culture and the culture itself, literacy practices are the patterns of literacy events in a society; different domains may have different literacy practices, as literacy has various functions within a society, across fields, between groups, and out of particular cultural demands, just as a superhero's literate needs arise from different demands on his or her detective and cognitive skills. For the most part, superheroes follow their culture's literacy practices; they just have better, more comprehensive literacy events insides those practices.

Brain Street defines literacy practices as the "broader cultural conception of particular ways of thinking about and doing reading and writing in cultural contexts" (2003, 79). Like most NLS scholars, Street perceives literacy as social practices that are intermeshed and fortified through the individuals and groups that use them. Rather than a narrow, static activity for superheroes, literacy activities remain a complex compilation of multiple possibilities; depending on the user's need, literacy can exist as low levels of basic reading like those taught in early elementary schooling as well as highly-integral networks of merging literacies. The purpose of defining literacy practices is not to set forth a definitive description, but rather to observe the growth and expansion of the field as it incorporates new perspectives of language and reading that speak to the real needs of more diverse populations in a digital age. In the same way, superhero literacy practices speak to the needs of the situations, dilemmas, missions, and careers of superheroes who direct all their literacy events towards a purposeful activity.

An ordinary person's literacy events usually blend into larger literacy practices of the community and immediate setting: a college student's literacy events include reading and memorizing sections of textbooks, composing essays, and engaging with texts in the classroom, all of which reflect a larger culture of literacy practices across the campus. Yet, the circumstances of the campus itself (a large university, a small college, an online school) necessitate particular practices that determine personal events. Brian Street (2013) elaborates on the expansion of literacy practices, calling for "the move away from a narrow, cognitive, and decontextualized approach to teaching reading and writing as social practices" (61). He stresses that this need in higher learning is mainly due to "the recognition that students these days are familiar with a variety of literacy practices, multiple literacies including those emergent literacies associated with the Web and the Internet" (61). The overall perspective of how we view literacy shapes events and practices, and without some consideration of context—what shapes literacy practices across geographical, socioeconomic, racial, political, and educational spheres—too narrow approaches to literacy can manifest. These narrow approaches often lead to autonomous views of literacy: treating "literacy as if it were a decontextualized skill, neutral, self-contained, portable, a skill that can be acquired once and for all and used and measured transparently without regard to contextualized conditions" (Brandt, 2001, 3–4). Superhero literacy practices, like many elements of the superheroic life, are exaggerated past all aspects of practicality or possible human achievement, and this endeavor to idealize what we want to be provides us with the opportunity to explore the possibilities of literacy achievements rather than the practicalities. Since many superheroes share the same literacy events (Jessica Jones and Oliver Queen both perform close readings of police reports to gain in-depth knowledge about villains' histories, combative methods, and specific threats), I focus instead on the extensity of unique events rather than the repetition of shared events.

Literacy events can have a presence at the forefront of the action, but they usually remain in the background; identifying them allows us to identify the power of written and digital texts in superhero worlds that reflect the needs of social groups and communities which perform them. In *Literacy and Literacies: Texts, Power, and Identity*, James Collins and Richard Blot define social control as forces that attempt to link "political, economic, and religious power and the desire to regulate literacy as a means of regulating conduct more generally" (67). Despite the importance of physicality in superhero narratives (hand-to-hand combat, weapons usage, body performance), these narratives portray Americans institutions that enforce ideology and social control through written, alphabetic texts, primarily documents that have legal and financial significance. Gee argues the discrepancies and variations that meaning takes across modalities by stating, "When we write or read, speak or listen, we coordinate and are coordinated by specific identities, specific ways of using language, various objects, tools, technologies, sites and institutions, as well as other people's minds and bodies" (1996, 6). These individual uses of texts direct and influence the literate practices of superheroes. Students studying pop culture should recognize the dichotomy between literacy and those employing literacy events and practices as there is not a one-to-one correlation of invention or use. Not all people will share literacy events or participate in a larger communal practice, but superheroes consistently use literacy events in their work, moving multimodally across a range of texts in digital and alphabetic platforms.

Much like writing, literacy for the superhero is first and foremost a tool, a means to an end of comprehending and analyzing the eternal world. According to Mary Kalantzis and Bill Cope in "Changing the Role of Schools," "Literacy represents a kind of symbolic capital in the two senses: as the preeminent form of symbol manipulation that gets things done in modern times and a symbolic marker of being educated" (121). Those inside large communal literacy practices control their events to fit the task at hand, altering their personal literacy applications to accommodate texts and messages across modes and through genres, replete with complications and new forms of knowledge assimilation. Due to this fluctuation, literacy does not appear as a set, singular practice, even for superheroes, and superheroes thus develop specialized literacy events that fit their particular needs for progression.[16] When facing off against villainous metahumans who threaten citizens in Central City, Barry has literacy events as a forensic analyst and as the speed-runner Flash. His literacy events differ from Oliver—a privileged club owner with no superpowers—but both are superheroes who aim to protect their team, family, and city from destruction, and both engage in literacy practices of detective work and logical processing through multimodal research.

My overview of superhero literacy—their individual literacy events and larger literacy practices—depends on the understanding that superheroes, much like ordinary people, participate in literate activities to fulfill objectives, not just to develop literacy as a goal in and of itself. Print literacy does play an important role in superhero media; we might feel tempted to focus on multimodal multiliteracies because those are the elements which have excited audiences and have contributed to the recent popular appeal of superhero media. Limiting views of literacy to that of alphabetic print offers a unique perspective of literacy uses in superhero media, especially as a means of grounding and establishing the high intelligence levels of superheroes. Regardless of whether superheroes engage in traditional literacy activities or multimodal multiliterate activities, they all perform detective work that relies on traditional literacy practices. In their detective work, we can see the connections between reading, thinking, connecting, learning, and assessing as a model for making new discoveries and creating new branches of knowledge. Reading acts as an intermediate activity between the superhero and the outside world, a bridge that lets the superhero create meaning from the chaos and confusion of his/her fictional worlds.

Multiliteracies

> As digital technologies enable and make desirable new kinds of human capital, school systems, schools and teachers are faced with mandates for teaching to encompass an expanding range of skills and capacities. Chief among the new desirables are student capacities and multimodal literacies [112].
> —Anne Cloonan, "Integrating by Design"

Introduction 27

In 2000, a group of scholars who called themselves the New London Group coined the term "multiliteracies": a word they chose "because it describes two important arguments we might have with the emerging cultural, institutional, and global order. The first argument engages with the multiplicity of communications channels and media; the second with the increasing salience of cultural and linguistic diversity" (5). This project presents a range of multiliteracies, in various modalities and utilization, to establish a perspective to facilitate wider, more nuanced networking of print and digital modes, what they are, and how their fictionalized uses in superhero TV shows reflect current trends and attitudes about literacy in the age of new media. In their discussion about literacy trends in pop culture, Williams and Zenger note, "Much has been written about the ways in which digital technologies have changed the perceptions and engagement with popular culture. There has been a great deal of attention paid to the ways in which new media are changing the concepts and practices of reading and writing" (2007, 5). These concepts and practices, direct results of changes in literacy practices over the last two decades, are only possible because of the impetus to move into digital communication and story-telling. Therefore, "new technologies make it all but impossible to discuss literacy practices without also confronting the complexity of interpreting and composing texts that have been created by new media and online technologies" (5). The movement from narrow autonomous views of literacy into larger, digitally-infused views of multiliteracies is a undertaking that has redefined the field of NLS overall, but more research is needed to address new effects of literacy practices as learned, specialized, adaptive, and internetworked activities such as those occurring in superhero TV shows.[17]

In their "Introduction" to *Multiliteracies in Motion*, David Cole and Darren Pullen define an academic perspective of multiliteracies that has informed research in NLS:

> in terms of multiliteracies, the questions inherent within reading comprehension exercises are expanded beyond a dualistic notion of reading and writing, and include aspects such as visual literacy if images are involved in the source material, and critical literacy, that is the purposeful questioning of text for prejudice or silences and that might determine the political or social usage of the text in question [2].

This change also has contributed significantly towards the study of writing in its movement towards an inclusion of multimodalities as a significant shift towards broader, more complex, more intricate forms of both critical thinking and expressions through writing and reading.[18] Gunther Kress emphasizes the inverse relationship between visual, digital texts and print, alphabetic texts because, in the last few decades, American culture has promoted the former and diminished interest in the latter;

therefore, we can no longer "think about literacy in isolation from a vast array of social, technological, and economic factors" (2003). Because these factors influence our culture through communication and production, Kress argues that "language-as-speech will remain the major mode of communication; language-as-writing will increasingly be displaced by image in many domains of public communication" (1), moving us from a world-as-told culture into a world-as-shown culture. Sue Nichols in "Ecological Approaches to Literacy Research" notes that a written text in a literacy event "can be considered a part of an assemblage which also comprises human actors who select, carry, handle, process, talk about and otherwise interact with the book and with each other" (109). Most superheroes work to expand their literacy events of detection, reaction, combat, digital manipulation, and physicality across multimodalities, and our understanding of multiliteracies in these fictionalized spaces should also shift to include broader, more diverse multiliteracies as culture reflects fluid progression and digital advancements of new media throughout the disciplines.

My emphasis on literacy activities and superhero narratives correlates to a fundamental shift in students' perspectives of literacy: recognizing fictional, superheroic specialized and advanced literacy practices empowers students to recognize and improve their literacy practices. In that recognition comes a deeper understanding of literacy as complex and nuanced, a broad collective of more thoroughly, more intrinsically, and better reflective methods of our literacy practices that span multiple modes and platforms. In their discourse about the connections between multimodality and learning, Pahl and Roswell argue, "Students no longer simply decode, skim and scan, but they move across and among texts, design texts, create mark-up code, render images, and so on" (27). Throughout their narratives, superheroes have wide literacy activities, but those activities are always put into actualization by being performed, by being utilized, by being done. To state it simply, superheroes don't sit around talking about what they can do; they go out and do it. They are superheroic by their actions. Therefore, this project aims not just to change thinking in regards to literacy but to improve actual literacy events and larger learning practices for students across print, digital, and moving texts. Literacy as a skill and a tool requires users to engage its events, to recognize its affordances, and to work to improve its functions through deliberate, informed activities.

In the same vein, the literacy activities I discuss throughout this book center on the students performing literacy events rather than simply reflecting on them. Mary Kalantzis and Bill Cope in "Changing the Role of Schools" stress the gap between learning and doing:

> The problem for institutionalized education, and the problem for the teaching and learning of literacy, is that students bring with them different life experiences. What they know, who they feel themselves to be, and how they orient themselves to education vary because their lifeworlds vary [121].

This mirrors the intent of rhetoric and composition as a field which aims to facilitate better writing and critical thinking by having students engage with actual concerns. Theories on composition also imply that students will not just understand what better writing looks like after engaging with theories of composition; they will become better writers through doing it. Comparatively, literacy events prove the same philosophy: literacy skills improve when the act of reading in performed deliberately and consciously. To this end, each activities section at the end of each chapter lays out new criteria for understanding literacy, objectives for students perform, and finally a learning outcome. This layout authorizes students to change their literacy understandings, usage, and events to reach new levels of literacy activities that push the boundaries of their abilities and their current state of literacy activities towards broader, more complex states of comprehension and learning.

How to Teach the Literacy Activities

> If it seems that everything is a "literacy," that is largely because we can no longer be sure which literate practices will be the ones that matter most a generation from now [322].
> —Jay Lemke and Caspar van Helden, "Social Design Literacies: Designing Action Literacies for Fast-Changing Futures"

Each activities section has a variety of multimodal learning actions that students can perform to explore, understand, research, and analyze aspects of literacy studies. I term these activities as such, rather than as lessons, because they are meant to open up NLS, superheroes, and literacy practices to students, to expand their perspectives of literacy, and to inspire critical thinking and digital learning through literacy studies. The readings for each activity are either an article from an academic journal or a chapter of a book; each citation is followed by a quote for discussion. The first activity of the following chapters is an individual student project that incorporates studying literacy events through questions and suggested readings, tasks that students could complete in or out of class. The second activity is a group project that requires 3–5 students to work through the contents of the chapter and suggested reading to facilitate a presentation. The third activity is a multimodal project with suggested readings which could be created individually or collaboratively and is meant to be displayed on a digital portal or website.[19] The activities present possible methods of teaching literacy studies and pop culture studies as well as rhetorical theory to students by having them

- demonstrate what they have learned about superheroes and literacy events;
- study their own culture through literacy practices;
- recognize superheroic detective and research skills;
- incorporate multimodal learning and reading in their work; and
- engage in a variety of multimodal activities: writing exercises, group discussions and presentations, multimodal webpages, and self-reflections.

As a professor who spends a good deal of time in front of students teaching college-level reading and writing, my pedagogy and praxis rely heavily on active learning. Moving away from the "sage on the stage," traditional approach to teaching, I follow a pattern of explanation, demonstration, complication, and then pedagogy and praxis; this reliance on showing and then repeating, of identifying and then doing, creates a model for the teaching in both literacy studies and composition as well as other areas of study in the humanities. This pedagogy has potential in composition with the merging of cultural icons and literacies as all evidence and examples (film, television, video games etc.) discussed in the following chapters can be brought into composition as teaching methods, literacy instruction, and/or calls for more research in multiliteracies, current culture, and an amalgamation of both areas. We currently live in the YouTube age: we all can watch an activity being done before we attempt it ourselves. Rather than simply reading about theoretical abstracts of college-level material, students want to see visual representations to clarify complex ideas and complex activity. If students examine the extent of superheroes literacy events and practices, both those of traditional perspectives and those of multimodal multiliteracies, they can see the exaggeration of literacy activities as well as limitations and possibilities that superheroes reading, writing, and achieving knowledge formation have.

Superheroes and their stories have grown more complex, more intricate, more dramatic, and more sensational in their narrative modalities in terms of effects, complex plots, and realistic depictions as well as the modalities the superheroes build and use. Just as digital technology infiltrated all aspects of culture (educational, social, capitalistic, and professional), so did the digital revolution change the space of superheroes. Alex Romagnoli and Gian Pagnucci argue that, in this age of digital, technical spaces that now thrive throughout American culture, our superheroes have produced "definitions of heroism that evolve with audiences and that reaffirm what is important to the collective, cultural consciousness. The heroes in these stories have conquered death, censorship, relegation, and creative strife only to come out stronger and more socioculturally relevant than ever" (185). This change in definition reflects the current movement and understanding about the capacity and ability of human communication and reading that have changed in the last few decades. When studying superhero TV shows, we can better understand the ways that general communication and multiliterate skills have changed for the average citizen, indicative of the way that most college students learn multimodally today than they did twenty years ago.

By bringing the discussion of representations of literacy in superhero TV shows into a college-level writing and research class, students can see NLS scholars' theories in action. Through the findings, theories, disparities, and objectives of NLS scholars, students can work through complex literacy questions: how do definitions of literacy shape our understandings about current and fictionalized literacy practices? Why do we consistently uphold literacy acquisition and skills as a means of success rather than other activities of human life (social networking, personal development, religious association)? The application of representations of literacy first to superhero TV shows and then to other areas of pop culture encourages students to develop deeper understandings of current American values and perspectives of literacies, emphasizing how literacy affects all areas of life in complex, yet sometimes hidden ways. Views and understandings of literacy and multiliteracies are not just objectives of knowledge to check off (much like objectives on a standard composition syllabus); these perspectives should facilitate critical thinking, analysis, deeper understanding of human communication, and ultimately sharper insight into one's own literacy events and practices, inside and outside of higher education.

While the recognition of these events allows students to better understand themselves and our current culture, I take this project a step further past recognition and understanding of literacy activities; I argue that students should emulate superheroes in expanding their literacy practices, moving towards those of great power and great responsibility. In *Literacy and Education*, Kate Pahl and Jennifer Rowsell note, "Literacy is not a neutral set of skills that we have in our heads and develop through language teaching and learning. Rather, literacy is always and everywhere situated and, what is more, literacy is inseparable from practices" (3). Throughout performing these practices and making them our own, with each subsequent study of literacy, possibilities of what literacy can encompass, achieve, enable, and promise increase, not decrease. Educational practices reflect this expansion as students' knowledge within various disciplines increased exponentially, some with the emergence of technology and digital tools in higher education, but all with the expectations that students can learn more, can expand their knowledge in a variety of specializations, and can develop their unique literacy practices which speak to their own needs for literacy and learning. When developing their events and practices, students create procedures of literacy acquisition and advancements, skills needed for success in the workplace and for democratic participation in citizenship.

♦♦ 1 ♦♦

How Does a Superhero Read?

> Superheroes may be literate in their daily lives, but then they are also impotent. It is only when they get away from institutionalized literacy that they become powerful [70].
> —Bronwyn Williams and Amy Zenger, *Popular Culture and Representations of Literacy*

Common Superhero Reading Patterns

The following scene is familiar across visual superhero stories: the superhero stands staring at information on some platform or mode—a book, page, cellphone, computer screen, TV, newspaper, or even handwritten note. The superhero's eyes dart back and forth, frantically searching for meaning in the words or images. The camera focus may zoom in on the hero's face, the music may mount dramatically, and the background noises may fade as the hero's concentration builds. Then the moment of understanding, a dawning of connection and knowledge. The superhero may smile in triumph or frown in determination, but the message to the viewer is clear: the superhero has figured the mystery all out and knows the truth about the situation, the responsible parties, and the remedy to solve the problem.

This scene conveys a superheroic literacy event: an occurrence of someone reading symbols and messages, then comprehending information from reading, and finally reacting to the gathered information, all with the intent of serving the greater good to protect humanity. Literacy events occur multiple times within an average person's day, but what the superhero has comprehended in his or her literacy event requires more than usual literacy activities from the average person.[1] The superhero's work requires elevated literacy skills that often demonstrate a blend of specialized literacies across multiple modes of meaning through various platforms. Moreover, the information that the superhero reads usually has been seen and read by other characters first. In the cases of *Daredevil* and *The Flash*, that information is often produced by secondary characters (Ben Ulrich and Iris West) who work in mass media, implying that most likely hundreds, if not thousands, of ordinary citizens in their respective cities have already witnessed the information via newspapers, broadcasts, or online sites. However, the superhero must put all the pieces of various information together to solve the mystery or figure out the villain's nefarious plans, halting world destruction or countless deaths of others. Literacy, for the superhero, means more than simply reading words, symbols, or images; literacy means in-taking those words, symbols, and images, understanding their importance, and then filtering all the information into a complex network of significant surveying of the world. When we recognize the superhero's literacy events as a part of the larger literacy practices of superheroes, we can better understand our literacy practices as a part of cultural influences and can explore the ways that we should improve, develop, or alter them to in-take more ourselves.

The role of the superhero—as a stereotype, an archetype, or a symbol—has occupied a significant portion of superhero research throughout the humanities. In her exploration of superheroes as figures for delivering justice, Nicole Maruo-Schroder argues that "superhero narratives are immensely influential in shaping our everyday ideas, norms, and values although they depict the fictional and fantastic world of superheroes" (1). In his comparison of superheroes to enduring mythic heroes, Armond Boudreaux notes, "Superhero mythology also has the same kind of applicability or adaptability. Different writers and artists can reinterpret familiar superhero stories so that they can use them to speak to the relevant questions of their time" (xvi). It may be tempting to lump superheroes with the larger collection of action heroes, but the superhero as an archetype differs from the action hero. Most superheroes have labs and workplaces where they perform research, investigation, and chronicling of their heroic activities, performing more literate activities than other action heroes perform in their narratives. The levels of sophisticated literacy skills for TV superheroes' human jobs do vary: Matt Murdock is a lawyer; Jessica Jones is a private investigator; Barry Allen is a forensic scientist; Luke Cage is a police officer-turned-janitor and later a club entrepreneur. Their individual literacy skills and developed specialized literacies allow them to work in different areas of American capitalism (all with different salary scales), but they share similar superheroic literacy practices: the ability to piece together bits of information and data collected from a range of modes. Superheroes have advanced literacies of detection, surveillance, and scrutiny on micro and macro levels. Their abilities to master specialized literacies also include intersecting literacies that enable them to perform a variety of tasks using multimodal texts and evidence, both for their human personas and their superheroic alter-egos. Because the superhero in a TV show has longer screen-time to improve their skills over an action hero who is usually thrust into combat immediately, we can see the literacy events of superheroes at work: a slow, methodical calculation of critical reading and critical thinking that allows maximum oversight and control in a vastly unpredictable world.[2]

As either their human personas or their superhuman alter-egos, superheroes have literacy skills that authorize them not only to decipher and network information from ordinary texts of current-day American culture such as newspapers, emails, text, websites, and books, but they also have enhanced, improved memorization skills greater than we ourselves possess. Most TV superheroes can comprehend vast arrays of convoluted texts (and create them, alter them, and improve them through digital modes) and can also recall the information from those texts with near-photographic memory. For the superhero, multiliterate skills mean being able to perform elevated literacy events: gathering information from multiple modes, having instant realization of important data while reading, later recollecting the information read. Like most superheroic skills, their literacy activities must be better, more comprehensive, more in-depth, and more fantastic than those of the educated American.[3] Superheroic literacy events and practices, though exaggerated to the extreme, follow traditional implementation and growth of literate activities through hierarchies of access and implementation: superheroes (Oliver Queen, Barry Allen, Bruce Wayne) develop the skills first and they trickle outward to sidekicks (Felicity, Iris West, Alfred Pennyworth) and other secondary characters (John Diggle, Joe West, Jim Gordon) as well as villains (Slade Wilson, Eobard Thawne, Edward Nigma). The collective appropriation of literacy events for characters demonstrates patterns of advanced literacies that fit a range of heroic needs and objectives. These patterns link the superhero to higher forms of reading, thinking, and detection work, all activities that make the superhero the next step up the evolutionary chain of advanced thinking and mental processing. By studying these patterns, we arrive at more intrinsic realizations about the complexities of our learning processes: a continual fluctuation of in-taking information, arranging it into logical structures, and responding appropriate with new data.

For the superhero, advanced literacy skills mean machine-like recall, instant transference of the alphabetic text itself into meaning, pattern formation, and extraordinary reading speeds. A byproduct of these literacy skills is the developed reliance on one's memory to have remembered information correctly and extensively; this skillset makes the hero super because most of us cannot recall what we have read with perfect recollection.

Having ordinary, proficient literacy is never enough for the superhero; their world and the demands on them require that they master an exhaustive list of literacy skills and then put those skills to work at their utmost capacity for the greater good. In "The Very Real Work Lives of Superheroes," Gary Burns and Megan Morris state that

> most superheroes have a strong need for achievement, which in this context refers to an individual's desire to make a significant accomplishment, to master skills, and to have high standards of accomplishment. In stories, superheroes are often shown with a need for achievement as well as a desire to seek meaningfulness in work, both of which combine new theories and cognitive theories of motivation [147].

Before I examine multiliteracies that superheroes have mastered, I emphasize their engagement with traditional literacy events: the moments when superheroes read, comprehend, and respond to alphabetic, print texts that contain information relevant to their missions. These moments, all traditional literacy events, remain essential elements of superhero media, and more importantly, they empower us to understand how fictional superheroic worlds embellish and exaggerate these events. As Gee emphasizes in *Social Linguistics and Literacies*, "Literacy has no effects—indeed, no meaning—apart from particular cultural contexts in which it is used and it has different effects in different contexts" (90). We want to understand our contextualized values and beliefs about literacy as fundamental elements of our civilized, educated, and highly-textual culture; we have to first observe the range of representations in which traditional literacy takes place, affects fictional narratives, defines superhero characters, and provides ideology in their superheroic worlds. Once we observe these representations, implications of literacy have significance through multiliterate understandings of current culture, and we can better understand their potential for effective teaching of writing and literacy and into the larger field of the humanities.

The evidence of literate activities appears through superhero TV shows: in *Daredevil*, folders of law briefs occupy prestigious places on desks and Karen is coerced into signing a non-disclosure agreement (the representative from Union Allies waves a handful of stapled papers in front of her as he makes veiled threats about her future). Ben Ulrich, who works for a newspaper, has an office where mock-ups of the next issue of the newspaper hang on work-boards and bold headlines flash on computer screens. Throughout *The Flash*, S.T.A.R. Labs features computer screens blinking in the background, and papers on the desks and walls show handwritten and printed blueprints of evolving technology, physics formulas, and new designs for machinery and weaponry. In the first episode of *Arrow*, Oliver looks at newspaper articles onscreen and has in his hand a hard-copy clipping of a newspaper. In the other hand, he has his father's book; he scans down the list of names until he finds the one that corresponds with the research that he is doing. The maid comes in and comments, "You are different. Not like you to read a book." He does not reply, but the scene implies that, because he now identifies as a superhero, he has developed literacy events fitting into the larger practices of superhero literacy. These literacy practices, however covert or obvious on the screen, inform and support the mental processes and detective abilities of TV superheroes; literacy practices often seem invisible or taken for granted, much like our literacy practices. In the real, non-superhero world, we have literacy events of reading texts such as emails, social media posts, news articles, traffic signs, grocery lists, calendar appointments, etc.

The values in popular TV shows usually reflect the culture, time, and place from which the media was made, and literacy activities in superhero TV shows are a part of this reflection. In *Literacy: An Introduction to the Ecology of Written Language*, David Barton notes, "People make sense of literacy as a social phenomenon, and their social construction of literacy lies at the root of their attitudes towards literacy and their actions" (47). In the same manner, our cultures' values and definitions of what constitutes literacy, knowledge-forming, and communication appear in superhero narratives; however, these attributes have not been researched or explored in-depth as they tend to disappear into the background of the stories, overshadowed by the intensity of action and heightened drama. As with most research on multimodality and multiliteracies, establishing the evidence of literacy events grounds the superhero's identity, knowledge-gathering, and detective skills. Our culture has sanctioned, explored, exploited, and oversaturated media with the ideal of the superhero because it exists an extreme representation of the pinnacle of possible (though in most cases, impossible) human perfection. While human perfection can never be fully realized or actualized, the possibility of improvement necessitates our desire to see ourselves with potential for greatness and deeper self-realization.

In his linkage of superheroes to modern culture, Jeffrey Brown states, "The spectacular nature of these live-action superhero films is also premised on the technological development of digital special effects that allow fantastical characters to appear believable, and most importantly, to provide a point of identification for viewers" (2017, 2–3). Even for superheroes whose bodies or abilities are enhanced by science, mutation, magic, or supernatural means, their perfection still appeals to modern audiences because the hero fights through escalating challenges that test his or her skillsets. The majority of American culture has embraced superhero media because we see our culture reflected back at us—exaggerated, embellished, and amplified to the extreme. Yet, superheroes all correspond or represent the ideals of American culture (and how we encounter these ideals, are shaped by them, replicate them, and alter them). We often watch and read what we desire to be, and despite their tumultuous lives, numerous flaws, self-doubt, and existential crises, we still desire on some level to be superheroes ourselves—enhanced, capable, intelligent, informed, and endlessly resilient.

Detective Activities

Throughout these early sections, I have referenced detective work as a primary method of gathering information, and the groundwork of starting superhero activities involves detective skills that first begin with literacy practices. Unpacking the detective work in superhero TV shows proves a multilayered task because it reflects the audience's expectation about the superhero's skills and achievements within the confines of the story. Because the superhero must engage in detective work to uncover crimes to stop them, the literacy practices of superheroes first reflect superheroes' preliminary needs. Some superheroes depend on a supportive team such as in *Arrow* and *The Flash* where those with specialized literacies work to gather information, monitor the city, or conduct medical research to provide Oliver or Barry with better data and technology for their quests. Yet, the superhero never acts as just the muscle to carry out physically-demanding tasks. The superhero works equally hard in finding and reviewing data as he or she does in a physical smack-down of villains who often have literacy skills that rival the hero's (see Chapter 8). These detective abilities become a solidified part of the hero's identity, rooted primarily in discerning vital information from unimportant data. In their "Introduction" to *Superhero Synergies,* James Gilmore and Matthias Stork note that

> instead of limiting themselves to certain kinds of iconography and structures, the superhero genre is constantly expanding through technology, finding new ways to speak its ideas, to represent them, through a continued consideration of what technology makes possible on the level of the spectacular, the effective, the intellectual, and any other number of emotional or cognitive registers [4].

In our current age of multimodalities and near-infinite stream of news, opinions, facts, alternative facts, fake news, and commercialization across all media platforms, the skill to narrow important data from tremendous amounts of information has become essential.[4] In this discernment, careful readers must learn to filter through a wide assortment of information, finding patterns of usefulness in the chaos and discarding redundant or useless material.

The breakdown of detective work for superheroes usually follows a pattern: an instinct of something wrong, the gathering of information, an overview of evidence, the planning of an attack/rebuttal, and the gathering of more information after the first attempt. Through all these activities, superheroes network and constantly improve their literacy practices through multiple modes of intertwining data. We, as emerging scholars, thinkers, writers, and learners, must develop methods of reading and learning that speak to a need for "reflexive" pedagogy, a term coined by Bill Cope and Mary Kalantzis. They refer to the constant vigilance that teachers, whether teaching others or teach themselves, need to develop "to gauge which pedagogy move is appropriate at different moments of the learning process, for different students, and for different subject matters" (2015, 16). Reflexive learning and reading usually lead the superhero (and ideally the student) to a place of intersecting knowledge platforms that span multiple social institutions and distinct fields of human and non-human life, requiring the superhero and the diligent learner to participate in literacy networking and training.

For superheroes, the skills of distinction, of selection, and of carefully reducing down overwhelming data into a few vital points prove paramount to their missions. A dual concentration on achievement and meaningfulness with data leads to the superheroes building, controlling, managing, changing, and improving their specialized literacies, all abilities that require reading and comprehending information across several different fields: computer graphics, robotics, technology, physics, weaponized machinery, and defensive strategies. Their work in these fields sometimes relies on the imagination and suspended disbelief of the audience to enter into these hyper-realized worlds through fictional narratives where such feats could be possible. As long as the scene remains compelling or contains measured CGI effects that suggest an aura of realness, most of the audience enters into the story with the assumption that the technology adds to the appeal of the superhero in much the same way that our modern dependencies on technology affect and enhance our own multimodal lives. Even if we in the audience do not understand the technology (how it functions, what type of coding it uses, what types of robotics it controls), we believe that the superheroes do and therefore trust in their multiliterate skills for the story to advance.[5] Regardless of the possibility/impossibility of the superhero's literacy events in reality, we can study these events to better understand the methods by which humans learn.

At the pinnacle of cognitive capabilities, superheroes can access and comprehend information with alert, critical process attributes. Superheroes develop literacy skills effortlessly, and the fact that we do not usually see the hero working to improve these literacies presents an interesting and almost paradoxical situation: we admire the hero for having developed these literacies, yet we do not want to waste time during TV shows to watch the hero improve or master these literacies. As Williams and Zenger explain, although "it may provide important information at a pivotal point in a film, literacy is not usually present at the crucial, climactic moment" (100).[6] The absence of literacy training often reflects the demands of the particular modality of superhero media because training takes time away from the tightly allotted plot of film.[7] Training scenes happen more often in TV where the extended season of multiple episodes can devote time to showing the hero in training: Oliver in *Arrow*, Matt in *Daredevil*, and Bruce in *Gotham* all have various scenes of them honing their detective skills and enhancing their abilities in the quiet moments when they are not in immediate demand to rescue someone or in danger themselves.

Yet, even these TV shows, much longer than superhero movies, cannot show the superhero partaking in all the physical and mental training required to maintain superhero status. Superhero TV shows often shorten the training to clips of a few seconds to indicate the on-going practice of training and improvement.[8] These activities demonstrate superheroic literacy events that are used to achieve an objective, performed on missions to rescue, avenge, combat, and/or survive; according to Lesley Farrell in "Texting the Future: Work, Literacies, and Economies," "This is not so much because people need to be literate to *produce* new knowledge, but more because global economic activity needs people to be literate to *trade* knowledge" (181). Regarding superhero TV shows, we as the audience have come to watch the superhero be superheroic, and therefore he or she must step outside of normal parameters of traditional literacy practices to engage with specialized literacies and superheroic uses of basic literacy.

Some of the data that superheroes access is that of traditional print (police files, legal briefs), but a large portion of it exists in digital and technical storage, messages, modes, and signs. Superheroes parse through these actions with a pattern of research, observation, compilation of evidence, and their own discernment. The superhero has a developed series of events to enable his or her comprehension, analysis, and control of texts through literacy abilities indicative of that hero. Often viewers are shown scenes with the villain that heroes do not have privy to: Wilson Fisk colludes with other criminal syndicates in *Daredevil*, Thawne works with his futuristic computer Gideon hidden in a secret alcove in the first season of *The Flash*, and Mariah Dillard kills her cousin Cottonmouth in *Luke Cage*. Superheroes may not have access to data preliminarily when they begin a mission, but they rely on their instincts and drive to find information to discover more about the crimes the villains commit, all activities that depend on specialized literacy events.

Specialized Literacy Networking and Training

The process of developing and improving specialized literacies is not enough for superheroes; they have to connect literacies into a network of information to help them arrive at the truth, utilizing a practice of gathering, evaluating, and connecting information. After all, if superheroes did not have webbed frames of comprehension, they would be unable to perform as superheroes and would be stuck in one-directional, often singular modes where they cannot use various avenues of information to collect data. According to Cope and Kalantzis, when we move through modes, "New Literacies centered on hybrid and multimodal text emerge. Modes of meaning that were relatively separate become ever-more closely-intertwined" (2010, 95). Perhaps the most compelling superhero narratives involve these types of intersecting multiliteracies because they require an understanding on a deeper level than typically shown in short comic book issues or cartoon episodes, and these stories require the audience to also develop a context for political, socioeconomic arrangements that usually mirror actual social statuses or circumstances in America. The intellectual work of superheroes needs to have a real, actualized sense to it for their stories to have gravitas. When Oliver approaches Felicity to gather information about his mother and Walter (*Arrow* Ep. 1.4), we as the audience understand that he wants to have actual documentation of their crimes to support his suspicions of criminal activities. Oliver's instincts begin the missions; concrete evidence will prove his hunches correct.

Using multiple modes of surveillance, superheroes collect massive amounts of information and draw out only vital, important, truthful, or relevant information they need. This skillset utilized literacy in a specific directive: scanning collection of data to find small pieces of truth. In his reflection on current life in a densely-literate, digitally-informed America, Malcolm Gladwell's best-seller, *Blink* (2005), identifies endless input of data as "an enormous frustration with the unexpected cost of knowing too much, of being inundated with information. We have come to confuse information with understanding" (264). The difficulty of determining the validity of information (the significant vs. the unnecessary, repetitive, or untrue) hinders the average person, but superheroes have developed such high cognition that they do not worry that they might miss or overlook vital data. They know what evidence they are looking for and when they have found it, a desirable learning trait we all wish we could have or develop (and which both students and instructors performing secondary research would like to have).[9] Yet, much like all of the steps in the learning process, literacy as a progression exists in a state of needing active participation for improvement and complexity; the superhero who does not train his/her literacy skills cannot remain effective or relevant.

Often, superheroes step into the middle of criminal power plays where interacting schemes involve networking of political, social, financial, and governmental language, texts, and literacies. Some of this networking includes various uses of traditional literacy; the use of written and print texts matter in schemes for power and prestige as law documents, political slogans, emails or letters, newspaper articles, web documents, and other written works all impact the political systems, creating important information and then enforcing ideological restriction through social hierarchies. Messaging to the vast public becomes vital for understanding the multiliteracies of political arenas as the bodies and the technology have less impetus than the intent and meaning behind all signs and symbols. The superhero not only has to engage with the print texts, steeped in institutional jargon, but he or she also has to be able to read the social signs and messages behind modes of behavior, language, and intent. This perhaps becomes the defining point of multiliteracies for the superhero: the fact that these literacies blend together, embed in new knowledge forms, continually are reprocessed, and produce new perspectives of literacy across multiple platforms and information bases. The preliminary steps of reading—the process of intake, comprehension, and assimilation—do not reflect the vast possibilities of literacy activities where the superhero overviews immense amounts of information. Their dedication to all-consuming work may account for our current attraction to superhero narratives: the brilliancy of superheroes' abilities to comprehend and filter through the mountainous piles of information of the digital age and derive not only new knowledge but certainty from the data.

Superheroes in training consistently demonstrate the act of testing and improving human potential in both physical and mental capacities. In "The MCU and the Organized Superhero," Adrian Acu reflects on the attraction of superhero narratives: "As depictions of individuals accomplishing fantastic feats, the superhero genre uniquely manifests the greater culture's conception of an individual's potential: the limits of what one can realistically—and unrealistically—do" (197). For example, *Arrow* has flashbacks to the island where Oliver was marooned for five years, and to prepare for guerrilla fighting with the arms smugglers, he designs a series of obstacles that force him to run, jump, and shoot arrows simultaneously to develop the ability to master his own body in the heat of action. The narrative implies that the move from overindulged playboy to prepared warrior is possible as long as one believes in the virtue of training and applies oneself to the activities. As the Flash, Barry Allen uses both his speed and his mental capacity to force himself to work faster and comprehend more information than his teammates. In *Gotham*, after witnessing and failing to stop the deaths of his parents, Bruce subjects himself to a series of fearful and painful activities that include standing on the edge of the roof of Wayne Manor to conquer his fear of heights, holding his hand over an open candle flame to master his control over pain, and staying underwater for minutes at a time to expand his breathing capacity. When Selina Kyle questions Bruce's choice to undertake such activities, he responds, "I'm developing self-discipline and will power [...] so I can be strong" (Ep. 1.09). Alfred initially disapproves of his training, but we as the audience who know that Bruce grows up to become Batman must believe in this possibility: that the superhero status remains within reach as long as the mind and body are dedicated to an ultimate ideal. The training, whether mentored or self-imposed, always demands an understanding of physical and mental interplay. The mind must direct activities towards improvement and capability in the same way that it directs literacy activities towards greater states of cognitive knowledge and logical processes.

Due to this interplay between the mind and the body, viewers of superhero TV shows find immense pleasure in the training that the superhero endures when improving their physical agility and abilities, so much so that training montages occur frequently across superhero TV shows. Yet, for most superheroes, the training itself often occurs in the early days of the superhero narratives. In flashbacks in *Daredevil,* a recently-blinded child Matt learns to "read" his environment with the help of Stick who teaches him to monitor his immediate surroundings through his remaining four senses. Both blind characters sit in a park and read passersby through smell and sound, deciphering pieces of stimuli that offer pertinent information and learning to ignore any stimuli that do not. The superheroes' abilities to transgress this brave new world and conquer it with a sense of fortitude endear them to our culture as they represent the heights of new mental capacities. We as viewers witness learning taking place, and the next step in developing our superheroic literacies is to begin training ourselves through literacy activities. We have arrived at new heights of mental expectations in regards to digital and multimodal information, a brave new world of cross-specializations, interdisciplinary training, and access to excessive collections of raw, unarchived data as well as processed, published information.

Chapter Conclusion

Most of this chapter focuses on the different methods of reading and comprehension patterns that superheroes develop in general as well as the extensive training that they perform to improve their literacy events. The terms *literacy events* and *literacy practices* are used extensively throughout this chapter, setting up definitions of these terms as they will be utilized in subsequent chapters. Cultural values determine literacy practices for citizens in communities, and superheroes' literacy events, while better than most people in their fictional communities, subscribe to those cultural values. Literacy, as a tool, works to achieving objectives for the reader, and most superheroes use literacy in their detective work especially in coordination with technology that they use and create to monitor the world around them. These literacy events require superheroes to be multiliterate and to have their multiliterate abilities open to change and improvement with training to reach greater heights of performance.

Class Activities

The following activities emphasize a range of literacy actions across multimodalities of superhero TV shows, looking at elements and representations of literacy across modes and platforms to discover new understandings of literacy and design better literacy activities for students. These activities focus on the contrast between the literacy events needed to navigate specific knowledge of various fields against those needed as mainstream average Americans, allowing students to see the difference between different types of events and practices. Students can also connect these perspectives of literacy with Brian V. Street's understanding of literacy events and practices which links "them to something broader of a cultural and social kind" (2003, 78) through their contexts and interlinking patterns. Of course, cultural and social situations in superhero narratives are exaggerated and extreme, but they still explain human psychology and group ideology on a deeper level.

Activity 1: Defining How Superheroes Read

In this activity, students identify how superheroes read traditional, alphabetic, print texts. The first step in this is to watch a short clip of a superhero TV show. I suggest the first half of an episode of *Arrow* or *The Flash* to begin this, filling students in about the storyline and character changes that have taken place in the show. After viewing a portion of a superhero TV show, students should mark when someone reads or engages with texts either printed or digital.

QUESTIONS FOR STUDENTS TO ANSWER:
- How does the superhero read or comprehend differently than other characters?
- What alphabetic texts does the superhero encounter?
- How does the superhero glean knowledge from those texts?

SUGGESTED READINGS AND QUOTES FOR DISCUSSION:
> Henderson, Robyn. "Mobilizing Multiliteracies: Pedagogy for Mobile Students." *Multiliteracies and Diversity in Education: New Pedagogies for Expanding Landscapes*, edited by Annah Healy, Oxford University Press, 2008, pp. 168–200.

"A multiliteracies approach suggests a way of overcoming some of the difficulties of taking up one, possibly narrow, approach to literacy pedagogy" (Henderson 171).

> Boyd, Fenice, and Cynthia Brock. "Reflections on the Past, Working within the 'Future.'" *Social Diversity within Multiliteracies: Complexity in Teaching and Learning*, edited by Fenice Boyd and Cynthia Brock, Routledge, 2014, pp. 1–10.

"A multiliteracies pedagogy views language and other modes of meaning-making as dynamic representational resources. Users constantly remake these representations resources as they work to achieve their various social and cultural purposes, including their goals for literacy achievement and lifelong learning" (2).

Deliverables or Writing Project:

Students create a 300-word sketch of how a superhero reads, using evidence from the TV episode or from another superhero of their own choosing.

Activity 2: Defining Multimodal Multiliteracies

After students have identified actual moments of superheroes employing literacy practices, they then define how multimodal multiliteracies differ from those confined to print, alphabetic texts of information. Students should not create a Great Divide between traditional, autonomous views of literacy and those of digital multimodal, but distinguish how literacies improve and perpetuate new definitions of learning when they are networked and put together. To be able to discern superhero multiliterate events, students can start first with Cole and Pullen's definition—multiliteracies as "a platform for the multiple elements that converge in education practice as it is performed in formal and informal situations" (4). From that broad definition, students can follow up with their expansions of the understanding of multiliteracies by applying them to the TV shows and discussing their understandings of multiliteracies that result. Rather than apply these definitions to broad swaths of the American population, students can observe the literacy events and practices of any superhero TV shows in one or two episodes and then create their definitions that describe the activities.

Group Work:

Students in groups of 3–5 discuss the following questions about an episode of one superhero TV show:

- What types of modes does the superhero use in his or her work?
- How does the superhero read and transfer information between modes?

Suggested Readings and Quotes for Discussion:

Kress, Gunther. "4: Literacy and Multimodality: A Theoretical Framework." *Literacy in the New Media Age*. Routledge, 2003, pp. 35–60.

"The materiality of different modes—sound for speech, light for image, body for dance—means that not everything can be realized in every mode with equal facility, and that we cannot transport mode-specific theories from one mode to another without severe distortions" (Kress 107).

> Domingo, Myrrh, Carey Jewitt, and Gunther Kress. "Multimodal Social Semiotics." *The Routledge Handbook of Literacy Studies*, edited by Jennifer Rowsell and Kate Pahl, Routledge, 2015, pp. 251–266.

"Modes are cultural technologies for making meaning visible or tangible, that is, evident to the senses in some way" (253).

DELIVERABLES:

Student groups present on multimodality, showing how a superhero switches between modes and creates literacy events that empower the superhero to perform his or her work to the maximum effectiveness.

Activity 3: Identifying Personal Literacy Events

Students identify literacy practices in their reading and writing and create a webpage that links different aspects of their multimodal multiliteracy events. The whole point of this exercise is to see how we can improve our literacy: how we can become superheroes in our literacy practices and our learning patterns. Instructors want students to understand that literacy events as multiliterate multimodal practices continue to expand, permitting the user to connect and complement new avenues of information. Developing their literacy skills into new and advanced areas of multimodal learning improves basic literacy skills and new multimodal multiliteracies.

SUGGESTED READINGS AND QUOTES FOR DISCUSSION:

> Tan, Jennifer. "Closing the Gap." *Multiliteracies and Diversity in Education: New Pedagogies for Expanding Landscapes*, edited by Annah Healy, Oxford University Press, 2008, pp. 144–67.

"In the 21st century, cultural hybridity, shifting and multiple identities, and multilingualism are social factors of our everyday life-world, evident on a daily basis and educational, vocational, and recreational contexts" (Tan 146).

> Neville, Mary. "Improving Multimodal Literacy through *Learning by Design*." *A Pedagogy of Multiliteracies: Learning by Design*, edited by Bill Cope and Mary Kalantzis, Palgrave Macmillan, 2015, pp. 210–30.

"Therefore, students must now be taught how to read, view, write and create multimodal texts. These required new navigation concepts, comprehension and design skills alongside highly-valued, customary literacy indicators for improving reading and writing practices in schools" (211).

MULTIMODAL DELIVERABLES:

A web post or blog post that intersects pictures and written text to form a critique of the student's existing literacy practices and ideas for improving those literacy practices.

◆◆ 2 ◆◆

Arrow and Specialized Literacies

This chapter examines the TV show *Arrow* and a range of literacies across modes used and developed by Oliver Queen, the central superhero, and demonstrates the wide range of multimodal, multiliterate activities with digital texts used in his literacy events. While Chapter 1 gives a summation of superhero literacy activities, this chapter emphasizes the particular specialized literacies of an ordinary human who becomes superheroic through training and self-appointed guardianship of a busy metropolis. His extensive array of multiliteracies enables him to navigate digital and hardcopy texts throughout his narrative, including but not limited to online maps, emails, business records, historical documents, blueprints, and legal records. Oliver's detective skills depend on a blend of his multiliteracies and physical skills, but his skills are enhanced through multimodal platforms that he regularly utilizes. For this chapter, I stress the importance of defining specialized multiliteracies to provide new perspectives about task-specific literacies beyond traditional understandings of print and hardcopy literacy practices.[1]

Multiliteracies involve networks of reading and comprehension, indicating the individual reader's needs, usually to accommodate the reader through his or her profession. As early research on specialized literacy events, Lorraine Dagostino and James Carifio argue that we live in an age of "scientific, health and technological related advances in knowledge, as well as with the need to understand how that knowledge affects individuals in everyday society. These advances have created work environments that rely on the development of specialized literacies" (83). With this development, Dagostino and Carifio expand on the ripple effect of engaging with and developing new literacies: "These specialized literacies often permeate the workplace and then filter to open society as communication between the specialists and the general public grows" (83). The disconnection between print, alphabetic literacy and specialized multiliteracies usually results from formal education's focus on the former.[2] Narrow perspectives of literacy often reduce reading activities to events or activities that involve only print, alphabetic texts, and in doing so, these perspectives limit our understandings of the wide range of multiliterate practices which we employ daily. When we study literacy events in a narrative that includes multiple digital modes like *Arrow*, narrow perspectives of literacy give way to broader understandings of multiliterate practices.

How Oliver Queen Reads

At the start of Season 1, Oliver Queen, a rich playboy in his early twenties, is marooned on an island after a shipwreck of his family's yacht. When he returns to Starling City five years later, he has the physical skills and intellectual capacity to become the city's first superhero vigilante. The first two seasons split the narrative between the present day where Oliver hunts criminals and flashbacks from the island where Oliver endures a brutal education of survival tactics under bands of roving mercenaries and militant smugglers. Oliver often resembles comics-canon Bruce Wayne; both are wealthy men who use their family's fortune to fund their superhero endeavors, and both are fully human and must develop their superhero abilities rather than receive them from a spider bite (Spider-Man), alien DNA (Superman), or through gene mutation (X-Men). However, Oliver's disregard for human life and the trail of bodies that he leaves in Season 1 contrasts sharply against Batman's no-kill credence, a motto that spans most Batman narratives. Oliver's nihilistic objective changes in Season 2 when he adopts a creed of life-preservation over killing his enemies, but his intention to rid the city of crime remains his central mission.[3] Oliver becomes a superhero because Starling City's established institutions cannot deliver measured justice and restitution to those mistreated: Oliver's declaration of guilt towards criminals, "You have failed this city!" applies to the personal actions of the criminal individual, but it also fits with the failure of ideological structures to deliver the American Dream that our culture has promised.[4] When social institutions fail to protect vulnerable citizens, a superhero must endeavor to step in as the mediating justice and deliver retribution.

Oliver participates in traditional, alphabetic literacy events throughout his vigilante quest. As a gradual process towards better, more effective technology and equipment, Oliver develops and uses a large range of digital and technical devices, but a traditional text—his father's book of names—starts Oliver on his mission of justice and vengeance. In the pilot episode, after their family yacht sinks in a storm, Oliver escapes with his father and a crew member in a lifeboat; moments before killing the remaining crewman and committing suicide, Robert Queen tells Oliver, "Right my wrongs." Later, while burying his father on the island, Oliver discovers a book with blank pages that, when held up to heat from a fire, reveal a long list of names spanning multiple pages. Each person named in the book has committed some crime against Starling City and its people, and once he returns to the city five years later, Oliver launches into his detective work to find and deliver justice to each name for "failing the city." The List (as Oliver and fans of the show dub it) works as a definitive text that provided Oliver with a concrete undertaking with a repeatable pattern: research each name, verify the crime(s), and then deliver appropriate punishment. The written names—mostly influential associates of his father who used political and underhanded means to gain wealth and power through the subjugation of the poverty-stricken—spur the entire story arc into action as the textual evidence of the book establishes the first step for the superhero: rid the city of the guilty. The List launches him on the quest and then supplies him with future targets to keep his mission moving forward and remaining relevant.

In his introduction to *Literacy, Discourse, and Linguistics*, James Paul Gee defines literacy as "the mastery of or fluent control over a secondary Discourse. Therefore, literacy is always plural" (229). In the first episode of *Arrow* after returning to Starling City, Oliver sits down at his computer with The List and then begins to act on that plurality through various modes of information: he can affirm the language of police reports and business holdings quickly, he can sustain the correctness and legitimacy of the information he reads, and he can draw conclusions about the target's guilt and vulnerability. As he works, the extent of his literacy skills becomes evident: superheroic literacy events are the abilities to read, review, and summarize large amounts of textual data, to establish patterns through an immediate comprehension of the vital information at hand, and to conclude when one has read enough information to proceed with a course of action. Never in superhero media do the superheroes admit that they feel unsure if they have done enough research or that they have read information but did not understand it.

In examining the superheroic journey, Mark Schroll, and Claire Polansky notes, "Through the adventures of the archetypes of success and failure, the superheroes demonstrated how humankind can prevail and overcome adversity" (9). Repeatedly, origin stories about superheroes feature the emerging hero working to improve himself through literacy events and practices—mainly that of research into political, historical, legal, and criminal records. Consistently, superhero media places superheroes in a position where they must have extensive literacy practices yet still be developing new literacy events so they exist in a perpetual dual state: effectiveness that the audience can admire, and frustration with which the audience can sympathize. The superhero's literacy struggles match students' own struggle in learning and cognitive development in higher education: a state of trying something challenging, failing, attempting again with a different approach, adjusting to new data, and so on.

In their comparison of superheroes' worlds to our own, Romagnoli and Pagnucci state, "In fiction, superheroes represent many of our hopes and dreams" (181), hopes and dreams for a better world, one without rampant crime and unpunished perpetrators. With each name he crosses off The List, Oliver uses literacy events to balance out the corruption of Starling City, creating a system to deliver justice and often punishment. The names on The List become judgments, literacy events that let Oliver serve as judge, jury, and executioner. The activities of literacy that Oliver engages in (reading criminals files, tracking down businessmen through their corporate holdings, watching news outlets that report on the targets) all become activities connecting him with his father and reclaiming justice for his father's city. Each name Oliver crosses out makes him feel closer to his father, believing that he is righting the wrongs of his father and improving his family's legacy by enacting the justice his father could not achieve. The List provides him with a tangible task to acquire further knowledge with each name by asking questions to ascertain guilt: who is the person, what crimes has he/she committed, and what resources for justice are available?

Literacy events in this superhero TV show could be seen solely as justice or enacting revenge as they enable the hero in his violent actions on the behalf of a father who cannot act. "Literacy does not take its nature from texts. Rather, texts take their nature from the ways that they are serving the acts of writing and reading" (Brandt, 2011, 13). Oliver's drive to balance out the greed and corruption of his city leads him to interact with a number of multimodal texts as listed below, affirming Gee's emphasis on the activities of texts: "People do not just read and write texts: they *do* things with them, things that often involve more than just reading and writing" (2015, 36). Even after changing his mission at the beginning of Season 2 and deciding to no longer kill, Oliver still uses The List as his moral compass, a text to guide his ever-expanding missions. The punishments he delivers no longer end in death, but his reliance on The List and the detective work that follows persists, aided by a range of multimodal, digital texts.

The List serves as motivation for not only Oliver but other characters as well. Oliver shows Diggle the List in Ep. 1.4, and eventually, Diggle joins the team, although he wants Oliver to help others beyond the scope of just punishing the people named.[5] Oliver's mother, Moira, has a duplicate copy of The List which indicates her involvement in numerous crimes. She arranged for her husband's boat to sink at sea, not realizing her son would also be on board, and she also conspires with Malcolm Merlyn to bomb the Glades, the poverty-stricken area of Starling City where crime, drugs, and homelessness run rampant. When Oliver confronts his mother about her copy of the book, she flings it into the fire, claiming it is useless, but her reaction only solidifies her guilt in Oliver's mind. The book burning in the flames attests the power of the written word in superhero media: the damning evidence remains external, concrete documentation of one's involvement by having one's name written in the book or in the ownership of the book. As Walter Ong (1977) states, written words on a page create a text which has "a rigid visual fixity," a permanence that "assures its endurance and its potential for being resurrected into limitless living contexts by a limitless number of living readers" (271).

The permanence and concreteness of handwritten words are only surpassed by hardcopy, printed words published through commercial venues. Handwritten, printed, and digital writings bring communication into a fixed and exteriorized circumstance where the writer can disappear (or become all-powerful and omnipotent in the mind of the naïve reader) and the text is relegated to a place of admiration and power. According to Paulo Freire, "the human word is more than mere vocabulary—it is word-and-action" (2013, 76). The textual evidence—this small, innocent book—acts as a catalyst for Oliver to unleash his rage and vengeance, and the fact that his father deemed those people guilty enough to write down their names in his book is enough evidence for Oliver to research each of them and then hunt them down.

The range of technical and digital literacies in *Arrow* occupies significant and prestigious places throughout almost every episode; Oliver functions as a superhero by using, enacting, and forming patterns from the information he finds after having developed not only traditional and digital literacies but also technical systems to perform the diverse tasks of surveillance and data collection that he needs to act as the Arrow. When he adds more members to the team, especially Felicity Smoak who serves as his communications and technical genius, the abilities of his digital and technical capabilities and what he can learn, monitor, change, and access become essential characteristics of his superheroic persona. Throughout the TV show during scenes when he discusses cases with Team Arrow, multiple screens blink and monitor data in the background, recording vast amounts of information that he can not only access but also shift through and organize to act with confidence. According to Rahat Naqvi, "To be critically literate is to be able to do more than produce and represent information in the same form it was absorbed. The aim is the development of human capacity to use texts to analyze and transform social relations and material conditions" (50). Though the abilities of the technology are infinitely complex throughout the show, other characters themselves engage in complicated digital activities which suggest that almost every character in the fictionalized world of *Arrow* has technical and computer multiliteracies or at least the ability to believe in the capabilities of the cyber world to shape and reinforce knowledge-making for them and their culture.

Below are listed various modes that Oliver uses to find information, and each mode offers him unique data in his detective work to confirm guilt or innocence, to balance out injustice, or to protect his superhero identity and his team's.

News Media—Reports, Analogs

When launching into investigation with The List, Oliver's first research options are general news media: newspaper articles, broadcast segments, and gossip websites that disseminate broad information to the citizens of Starling City. In the pilot episode, mass media plays an important role in informing the citizens and the viewer as to events that happen around Oliver's return. The broadcast shows TMZ-like clips and pictures of Oliver's earlier life as a playboy and college dropout, and the TV in Laurel's law office continues the story to inform the public about the loss of lives aboard the Queen's Gambit, including her sister Sarah. In the middle of the episode, Oliver looks at newspaper articles on Adam Hunt, the first name he crosses off The List, and this literacy event sets a precedent for subsequent episodes as Oliver goes about collecting information on his targets. He has to sift through data that most of the public has access to, but his focus remains on the detective work of establishing and verifying the crimes of the guilty parties. Although other characters make comments about the untouchable status of those Oliver hunts (usually the powerful and privileged who use crony capitalism and criminal networking to commit acts against those less-fortunate), Oliver as a vigilante can pursue those whom the police cannot. Yet, before he can begin the physical work of tracking and punishing the guilty, he must read and comprehend general information through mass media. Some of the work through these sources require him to question the authenticity of the news, to discern between fact and opinion, and to recognize bribery of public officials as a possible influence in each piece of reporting.

Financial and Business Holdings and Transactions

After the news dispersed to the general public, Oliver's next literacy events usually involve documents that speak to the financial and business reports of companies, collections of holdings and transactions that he must read through to make summations from the data reported and the discrepancies (usually from missing amounts of money) that arise. The complexities of the language and information reported in the reports might confuse the average reader, but Oliver has specialized literacy of business dealings, both as the heir of Queen Industries and as the survivor of mercenary conglomerations. In her analysis of Batman and Green Arrow as humans-turned-superheroes through personal wealth and training, Katherine Marazi states

> Bruce Wayne and Oliver Queen both exhibit dual, albeit secret, identities which allow them to, on the one hand, as Wayne and Queen, belong to and act within the system, but on the other hand, grant them a foothold to the system which they oppose—both at a corporate and government level—when taking on their secret personae. By keeping Batman and Arrow a secret, they offer no access point via which the system can conform or control them, which ultimately leads to them being considered vigilantes by the fictional government and public [71].

After Felicity Smoak joins the team, much of the preliminary research becomes her job to acquire and assimilate, but Oliver still has specialized literacies to navigate the documents she finds. She gathers the data, but he still connects and networks between the information, grounding his detective status in the work he performs by his research into business transactions.

Weapons Calibration and Enhancement

Throughout the first two seasons of *Arrow*, Oliver uses a mix of weapons including whatever objects are present at hand such as chairs, doors, tables, windows, and weapons of his opponents. Although he seems to have some familiarity with guns thanks to his months with Slade on the island, he keeps his preference for a bow and arrow, the weapon with which he trained himself on the island and uses primarily upon his return to Starling City. Oliver gets the name a nickname The Hood from the fact that he wears a hood when fighting but primarily because he, like Robin Hood, uses a bow and arrow. However, the bow and arrow are not just the rudimentary tools one might expect but have been calibrated to perform a number of tasks including lighting a fire, emitting paralyzing electric volts, and acting as a digital transfer, a recording device, a hacking device, and other types of various explosives along with their primary use of penetrating bodies. Cathy Burnett in "(Im) Materialising Literacies," explains a personal literacy event as the relationship between the user and the object in use: "In examining meaning-making then we might zoom in to consider the physical relationship between individuals and equipment—how devices are held and bodies arranged" (525). Oliver's weapon usage serves as a metaphor for literacy as the best superheroes are self-trained through tools that they themselves design, refine, and redesign; like literacy, weapons are tools only for those who put them to use, and weapons have no intrinsic value until they are used, even as only a threat to motivate others into compliance.

Social and Political Media

Beyond the general news, social and political institutions maintain control over texts that influence the public in Starling City and beyond.

2. Arrow *and Specialized Literacies* 55

In *Literacy as Involvement*, Deborah Brandt states that "if we see literacy as a growing metacommunicative ability—an increasing awareness of control over the social means by which people sustain discourse, knowledge, and reality—then social involvement becomes the key model for literacy and literacy growth" (32). As the son of an influential, upper-class family, Oliver learns early that whoever has access to all the information and has developed the ability to interpret and control that information can act with complete impunity and confidence. Once becoming a superhero, he keeps that ideology regarding the relationship between privilege and access to information: he remains the only one with the adequate skillsets to counteract various catastrophes and looming problems because he has arranged his world and team so that he, and only he, has full admittance into information channels and their corresponding literacies. David Barton (*Introduction to the Ecology of Written Language*) states that "people's literacy practices are situated in broader social relations. This makes it necessary to describe the social settings of literacy events, including the ways in which social institutions support particular literacies" (35). Oliver's privileged access to information lets him regulate the information flow of almost every character he encounters, be they teammate, villain, ordinary citizen, or family member. This tight control correlates to elements of control that we see in our culture from institutional restrictions (such as governmental and educational), communal constraints (such as family and local communities), and socioeconomic limitations (such as access to technology and the restrictions of mass media); almost every aspect of our human existence in our current culture features some type of steward who seeks to limit knowledge, access to information, and procedures, both for altruistic and self-serving purposes.[6]

Legal Documents and Written Evidence

While other characters have more specialized literacies involving the language of law, primarily Laurel as a lawyer, the significance of legal documents in the world of *Arrow* points to an understanding of the legality that these documents have, a signifier of meaning and importance in a capitalistic metropolis. Oliver's usage of these documents and how he verifies his information speak to his own literate abilities to understand not only the language of law but its implications and importance in both his work as the head of Queen Industries and his vigilante activities. In Ep. 1.5, after being arrested as a vigilante, Oliver has to go to court to prove his innocence and approaches Laurel about representing him as his lawyer. By the end of the episode, Oliver reveals that he had planned an elaborate scheme: get caught being the Hood on a security camera, be put under arrest, and have Diggle pose as the Hood so to cast suspicion away from Oliver. He asks Laurel to represent him, but Oliver demonstrates throughout the episode that he could represent himself because he can read and interpret legal documents almost as well as she can.

In other episodes, information in written, alphabetic form serves as crucial evidence in proving the innocent to be blameless; in Ep. 1.4, Oliver realizes that an innocent man has been framed by Jason Brodeur, a CEO whose company has been dumping toxic waste illegally and whose name appears on The List. As the Hood, Oliver ties up a business associate of Brodeur to railroad tracks and interrogates him as a train approaches. The man confesses that he has a file with incriminating evidence in his desk in his office, and the Hood frees him right before the train can hit him. Later, the Hood gives the document full of papers to Laurel, and as she reads over it, she notes, "As an attorney, I never would have gotten a file like this." The evidence—a stack of printed, alphabetic text on paper—works to free the innocent man and put Brodeur behind bars, and Oliver's ability to secure and understand the significance of the papers speaks to his multiliterate skills. Small, insignificant literacy events like these often provide impetus into the superhero's missions, giving him or her leverage to act with impunity because of the concrete data found within the texts.

Digital Maps, Blueprints and Grids

Arrow features other digital texts that Oliver must decipher for meanings to perform his missions: digital maps of cities that layout streets and buildings, blueprints of buildings that show him a 3D perspective of rooms, electrical systems, and pipes, and grids of landscape which zoom in and out to give him micro and macro digital representations of physical spaces. Commenting on the hiddenness of literacy activities, Fenice Boyd and Cynthia Brock note, "Literacy teaching and learning occurs through instructions across a variety of spaces and includes moments of interaction that are unmarked and/or unintended literacy acts" (xii). In scenes at the Arrow Cave, digital maps and building grads are on multiple screens; sometimes characters reference or motion towards the screens as a feature of the story, and sometimes the screens remain in the background as an unmarked literacy activity.

Regardless of the mode or platform that he uses, Oliver scans screens and texts with his eyes, looking for possible targets. These types of multiliterate events fit into a wide range of literacy practices that define superhero literacy into larger frameworks of use and development; technology serves different purposes for different superheroes so their abilities to engage with digital texts vary depending on their particular needs. Brandt and Clinton argue in "The Limits of the Local" that "literate practices depend on powerful and consolidating technologies—technologies that are themselves susceptible to sometimes abrupt transformations that can destabilize the functions, uses, values, and meanings of literacy anywhere" (338). Oliver's highly complex multiliterate skills allow him to perform such extreme activities with so many intersecting networks and systems. This level of specialized literate abilities, of superheroic knowledge, and of mastery not only of language but digital systems serves as a pentacle of the intersection between technology, robotics, and knowledge structures, creating for us an idealized superhero who not only engages with digital platforms to seek information but creates new digital platforms to enhance his abilities. Kathy Mills and Barbara Comber in "Socio-Spatial Approaches to Literacy Studies" state that

> spatiality in literacy studies includes the socio-material effects and relations of space-time in relation to literacy practices, including the temporal dimension of flows or connections between literacy practices, textual artifacts, technologies for textual production, locations of literacy practices and texts, networks, social actors, and communities of practice [91].

Moments of literacy work in both the foreground and background of TV shows by connecting the characters' literate abilities to their surrounding world. The instances of specialized literacy are not just for the grand, climactic moments of intensity for the superheroes, but those instances also serve as a constant support to their abilities and knowledge, grounding their literate abilities in a way that reflects the audiences' engagement with literacy: a readied skillset that expands or contracts at will to utilize the needs of the reader to interact with external texts and information.

Pre-Island vs. Post-Island: Multiliteracies and Trauma

The texts that Oliver uses as a superhero require him to train his multiliterate skillsets in Starling City, but his original training took place on the island of Lian Yu where he had to create and enhance his skills to survive. The difference between Oliver pre-island and Oliver post-island offer unique perspectives about the methods by which we learn to cope and adapt to strenuous circumstances and lingering trauma. In the flashback scenes, Oliver aboard the Queen's Gambit is a young, arrogant playboy who relies on his charm and his family's money and prestige to get himself out of hot water unscathed. After getting kicked out of an ivy-league school for the fourth time, he has run off with the sister of his girlfriend in pursuit of hedonistic adventures that suit his jaded, narcissistic personality. After the Queen's Gambit sinks, he witnesses his father's suicide and the murder of fellow seaman, leaving him as the sole survivor of the crash (although later we as the viewers realize that Sarah has also survived). The first season draws out Oliver's early months on the island, at first alone and then at the mercy of rival bands of mercenaries, smugglers, and criminals who use and abuse him for their own purposes. Cold, hungry, and usually hurt in some way, Oliver begins his superheroic training as a desperate plea for survival, a need to endure the hardships of the island.

On the island, Oliver's literacy activities often follow primitive and rudimentary patterns as one might expect in a place where physicality and force overrule social laws and written texts.[7] The training he receives at Slade's discretion focuses on physical improvement, martial arts, and weapon utilization as a first incentive; the more sophisticated, language-heavy literacy activities usually remain a secondary concern. This makes sense as in the early days on the island Oliver works to improve his body and reaction time to cope with the mercenaries, usually engaging in guerrilla, jungle warfare of hide, attack, and hide again with the heavy foliage of the island serving as a defense. Mainly his actions speak to the need to survive until the next day; according to James Iaccino in "The Arrow and His Villainous Counterparts," "It seems as though everyone Oliver meets, friend as well as foe, interacts with him in an aggressive fashion" (49). Oliver learns quickly how to read every new person he meets: the body, their movements, their language, and their intentions. Out of the trauma of his ordeals come sharp, ready multiliteracies that let him respond to threats almost without thinking, body and mind existing in tandem to read and react to oncoming threats. These multiliterate abilities demonstrate his need to first survive his world and then to control and monitor it, a progression of active intention with external texts and messages.

In "The Mark of Cain," John McKnight comments on the significance of marks in *Arrow*: "signs on the body—scars and tattoos—are repeatedly invoked as symbols of both liminality and communitas. From the early scenes in the pilot episode, Oliver's scars are invoked as signs of the extent of the trauma he has suffered in his five years away from home" (120). When Oliver is rescued from the island and taken to a hospital, the doctor informs Moira Queen of the physical damage Oliver has suffered: "Twenty percent of his body is covered in scar tissue. Second degree burns on his back and arms. X-rays show at least twelve fractures that never properly healed" (Ep. 1.1). He also has a dragon tattoo that Slade branded on his skin; as the iron sears the mark in Oliver, Slade comments "In Roman times, a criminal was branded to identify his crime to the world and to remind him of what he'd done" (Ep. 2.17). Sarah Howe in "Beyond Wounds and Words" notes that

> several of *Arrow*'s key characters—most prominently Oliver—are trauma victims. Oliver is traumatized after the five torturous years he spent on the island and in Hong

Kong. He clearly suffers from post-traumatic stress disorder (PTSD): he has nightmares and night terrors, often wakes frightened and ready to fight to the death [100].

The markers of trauma as an indication of history have a significant place in *Arrow* as they indicate that suffering and improvement seem to be tied together in this gritty, human-centered superhero TV show. When reflecting on the extent of Oliver's multiliteracies, students can observe that learning methods and intellectual growth as cognitive processes often result from stress and trauma as a struggle against the outside world.

Certain modalities are afforded more time and space to show the development of body performance than others: throughout *Arrow*, flashbacks and present-day scenes feature Oliver's improving his physical, muscular, kinesthetic, combative, and reactive skills. The skills training starts when he first reaches the island, but they continue into his vigilante quest in Starling City. Throughout each season, he endures sets of brutal, physical feats; some of his own choosing, some because of dire circumstances that thrust him into action, and some under the tutelage of others. Throughout these scenes, the body and its movements, its language of aggression and pain, speak to the character's ability to adapt to his environment or prepare for future dangers. In the pilot episode in the first rendition of the Arrow Cave, Oliver builds and uses a device called the salmon ladder where two parallel metal beams run up about twelve feet vertically with matching hooks of each side. Using a metal pole, he maneuvers his body up and down the hooks sticking, a strenuous exercise that displays his torso with all its muscularity and strength but also shows the abuse he has suffered. Stretched out in exercise, his skin acts as a map of where he has trained and fought, marked with jagged scars and dark tattoos. He performs this type of training to strengthen himself, but it has a larger connotation of realizing social, physical, and kinesthetic cues as a literacy skill: he had learned to read his own body and know the extent of his abilities and how to improve them.[8]

After his rescue from the island, Oliver constantly works to improve his detective, comprehensive, and physical skills; audiences witness his multiliteracies growing and strengthening as he challenges himself both physically and intellectually. Yet, despite his heroic missions, the trauma of what he has suffered remains, ingrained on his body and in his psyche. In Ep. 2.14, Oliver, Diggle, and Sara all spar inside the Arrow Cave with long wooden pools. An errant blow hits Sara on the forehead, but Oliver assures her it is only bleeding a little. The following dialogue ensues between the sparring characters:

> SARA: Good, I can't take any more scars. Speaking of which [she turns to Diggle], mortar round?
> DIGGLE: Yeah, IFD, the Paktika Providence in Afghanistan. Good eye.
> SARA: I know my scars.

They then compare battle wounds: Diggle has mostly bullet scars, Oliver has knife, bullet, and branding scars, and Sara has scars from mostly swords and a spear. Not wanting to be left out, Felicity chimes in that she had injuries, too: stitches in her mouth from her wisdom teeth being removed. Regardless of how they received the wounds, Team Arrow wears the marks of trauma as badges of honor, markers of their actions in superheroic endeavors and reminders of the continual need to improve their skillsets.

While Team Arrow supports Oliver's training and superhero work, other characters in places of authority hinder his mission by acting as stewards of literacy; yet, the most emphatic steward of literacy in *Arrow* as a protector and prohibit of access to information and methods of reading that information is Oliver himself.[9] In the beginning, he works alone, refusing to let anyone assist him in his self-appointed mission to rid Starling City of corruption. Later on, John Diggle, a former Marine, begins to assist the Hood in his vigilante quest, and later Felicity, a rising tech genius with research and digital skills mirroring those of Oracle from *No Man's Land*, joins Team Arrow. Yet despite having a team, Oliver often withholds information from them as much as he does from his mother and sister. He protests that this preservation of information serves as a means of protecting them (and his fear becomes actualized when Slade Wilson comes to Starling City to seek revenge), but for the most part, Oliver's issues of control and knowledge suppression stem from his need to guard the information as the leader of his team. Much like most superheroes in films, Oliver believes that whoever has access to all the data and has developed the ability to interpret and control that information can act with complete self-reliance and confidence; therefore, he remains the only one with the abilities to meet various catastrophes and looming problems. Whether this stems from arrogance or fear—probably both—is not as important as the fact that he arranges his world and team so that he, and only he, has full admittance into information channels and their corresponding literacies.

Consistently, the plots of superhero TV shows place the heroes in a position where they must have extensive literacy practices yet still be developing new literacy events so they exist in a perpetual dual state of effectiveness that the audience can admire and haplessness with which the audience can sympathize. Literacy and intellect merge together in most superheroic TV shows: even without direct confirmation (being shown a scene that establishes the hero's detection skills or having a narrator explain it), the expectation of the superhero's intellect and high-level literacy skills remain defining features of superhero media because the audience expects the superhero to be super in all aspect of human life. Brandt notes, "Skilled literates pull together and maintain *situated meaning*" (2011, 38), and that situated meaning becomes the most significant element when studying superhero literacy practices. Whether we examine an arising hero or an established vigilante, representations of literacy affect them significantly, and their continuous modality gives us to amass greater and more nuanced perspective of what it means to be fully literate and interminably capable. These endeavors require us to consider the superhero in a continual loop of training both the mind and body to be ready to act upon the demands of the next mission.

Training the Mind and the Body

Mary Ryan and Tony Rossi in "The Transdisciplinary Potential of Multiliteracies" put forth a new understanding of literacy with the body: "The term physical literacies has received scant systematic analytical attention.[…] The idea of physical literacy is encapsulated in the rejection of the Cartesian dualistic position of the separation of mind and body" (42). An element that separates superhero media from that of other action-adventure narratives involves the focus on bodies as a part of semiotic language and dialogue; the superhero usually has the background training and developed skills (in scenes either shown or implied throughout the modality) while the action hero seems to act and react from places of pure luck such as the *Die Hard*, *Expendables*, *Indiana Jones*, and *Lethal Weapon* franchises where male bodies leap into action when the need arises but are rarely seen training for such physical demands. The body as text does share some commonalities with combative literacy (in that these bodies are meant for combat), but physical performance requires the skills of the hero to read his own body and environment, namely his ability to adapt to physical spaces through movements, usually aerodynamic, but also kinetic, imposing, and threatening. Physical literacy can apply to both the visual appearance of the superhero's body, both still and in motion, but it can also appear as the superhero reading others' bodies, primarily those in threats or intimidation that the superhero must gauge through his physicality and kinesthetic literacy. John Jennings emphasizes, "The superhero is a symbol of power that is reified as the hyper-physical body, and that body then comes to be a visual representation of that power" (60). For instance, the superhero is often called on to rescue others in distress or physical harm, and he must be able to read the on-coming danger as well as how his body can act and react accordingly to save the day with the least amount of physical harm.

In Ep. 1.5, Oliver sits strapped to a lie detector while Detective Quinton interrogates him, and throughout the questions, Oliver controls his body to the point that he can manipulate the readings of his reactions. The scene is juxtaposed with flashback scenes to the island where Oliver is tied to a pole and tortured with slashes from a machete. In both the flashback and the present-day scenes, his interrogators show him images and demand answers about the images: Quinton shows him a drawing of the Hood, and Edward Fyers (the leader of a group of terrorists on the island) shows him an old photo of Yao Fei in uniform. Spatial literacy has distinctive characteristics that empower the superhero to read bodies and physical surroundings that do not always necessitate some type of fighting. For instance, the superhero is often called on to rescue others in distress or physical harm, and he must be able to read the on-coming danger as well as how his body can act and react accordingly to save the day with the least amount of physical harm. To exist in this state of control, the superhero has to remain vigilant of his or her surroundings, feeding information into their mental process of recognition and response that loops through logistics of the physical world and the superbody.

Chapter Conclusion

By focusing on Oliver Queen's skills and storylines, this chapter identifies different sources of information that Oliver encounters in his detective work. Throughout *Arrow*, flashbacks and present-day scenes feature Oliver's improving his physical, muscular, kinesthetic, combative, and reactive skills as far as his own body is concerned; he endures sets of brutal, physical feats; some at his own choosing, some because of dire circumstances that thrust him into action, and some under the tutelage of others. Many of Oliver's skills for discovering data and uncovering crimes require his mind and body to work in conjunction, processing written, visual, and moving information into networked patterns of knowledge. All of Oliver's skills—literate, physical, interactive—undergo deliberate training as he works to improve and finesse details and sequences of his multiliterate skills.

Class Activities

In "An Introduction to the Pedagogy of Multiliteracies," Bill Cope and Mary Kalantzis stress that "meaning is made in ways that are increasingly multimodal—in which written-linguistic modes of meaning interface with oral, visual, audio, gestural, tactical, and spatial patterns of meaning" (3). Because modes can deliver meaning and messages in so many effective ways, they also argue that "we need to extend the range of literacy pedagogy so it does not unduly privilege alphabetic representations" (3). Much like these skillsets of specialized literacy and quick, accurate memorization, narrations that feature superheroes and their specialized machines rarely show the superhero learning the inner workings of machines whether through textbooks or by taking the machine apart, building the machine, or improving the machine. The machine itself is never a finished product in superhero narratives but is an object in progress, much like the superheroes' bodies, that can be improved and altered in a continuous state of improvement and efficiency. These activities demonstrate to students that the acquisition of more complex multiliteracies still impacts and affects the characters because many of the abilities and feats they develop and perform require not only the use of technology but also the ability to interact with and improve upon technology as a part of their knowledge base.

Activity 1: Multiliteracies in *Arrow*

Students identify multiliteracies in an episode of *Arrow*. Superheroes' multiliteracies reflect our acquisitions of multimodal multiliterate comprehension and understanding because what they can do in the moment of demand—be it using technology, collecting materials, or researching information—results from previous hours of engagement with technology, texts, and multimodal databases that lead to multiliterate states, circumstances which can also be, like Oliver's skills, improved and enhanced.

QUESTIONS FOR STUDENTS TO ANSWER:
- What are several literacy events that Oliver utilizes?
- How do his literacy events encompass multimodal, digital texts past those of alphabetic print?
- How do Oliver's multiliterate activities require the use of his mind and body simultaneously?
- What role do trauma and endurance play in creating his broad multiliterate activities?

SUGGESTED READINGS AND QUOTES FOR DISCUSSION:
> Gee, James Paul. "Where We Are and How We Got Here." *New Digital Media and Learning as an Emerging Area and "Worked Examples" as One Way Forward*. MIT Press, 2010, pp. 9–15.

"Digital media and learning as an emerging area of study is related to, in complex ways, a number of other emerged or emerging areas" (Gee 15).

> Wimmer, Jennifer, and Benjamin Thevenin. "Media Art in the Elementary Classroom." *Arts Education and Literacies*, edited by Amy Jensen and Roni Draper, Routledge, 2015, pp. 99–108.

"A focus on producing media arts also helps students to understand and develop the specialized literacies, skills and techniques necessary to participate in the ever-increasing media world in which they live" (99).

Deliverables or Writing Project:

Students create a map of intersecting multiliterate activities. They then write a short paragraph in which they suggest ways to enhance their connective multiliterate activities that begin to span multiple disciplines.

Activity 2: Literacy of Mind and Body

With each season, Oliver's multiliterate skills improve, letting him create better machines, interact with more complex technology, and access greater stores of information then he had previously discovered. Therefore, students can identify the literacy events of a superhero that grow, improve, alter, and change within the narrative and also create nearly limitless resources for the superhero through activities that train the mind and body to read and react in tandem. Students in groups identify how the mind and body participate in literacy events.

Group Activities:

In groups of 4–6, students take a different episode of *Arrow* and scan through it to identify literacy events that use the mind and body: Oliver or other characters seeing, reacting, interacting, and altering physical and digital conditions. They report back to the group with a short list of all literacy events, and together the group compiles the data.

Suggested Readings and Quotes for Discussion:

> Exley, Beryl. "Communities of Learners: Early Years Students, New Learning Pedagogy, and Transformations." *Multiliteracies and Diversity in Education: New Pedagogies for Expanding Landscapes*, edited by Annah Healy, Oxford University Press, 2008, pp. 126–43.

"This model of learning also values learner differences and stresses the importance of providing time for students to work from their own knowledge platforms, take risks, and be creative and problem-solvers, but within a supported community" (Exley 130).

> Tan, Jennifer. "Closing the Gap." *Multiliteracies and Diversity in Education: New Pedagogies for Expanding Landscapes*, edited by Annah Healy, Oxford University Press, 2008, pp. 144–67.

"The learning principles and processes of multiliteracies provide the lead teacher with a comprehensive framework to design a series of learning-teaching episodes that would move away from traditional skills-and-drill methods towards a more flexible learning context that could provide his students with greater opportunities for successful engagement with the English language at school" (158).

Deliverables:

A presentation of a culmination of literacy events, demonstrated on a PowerPoint or Prezi that lets each student group identify separate literacy events they identified in their selected episodes.

Activity 3: Training for New Events

What remains important here is that students have a role in shaping the definition of their understanding of literacy rather than imposing definitions upon them because, like many lessons concerning definitions of complex ideas in higher education, students make the mistake of narrowing definitions to whatever the instructor has said rather than thinking critically or actively about how definitions shape their understandings. By establishing complex, malleable definitions of literacy, students can move into other perspectives of literacy (myths, sponsors, metaphors) because they identify elastic definitions of literacy as having the ability to incorporate more distinctive, nuanced aspects of literacy. In doing so, students stretch their own literacy abilities with a clear understanding of what they are doing; rather than literacy being a byproduct of learning, it becomes the main focus.

Suggested Readings and Quotes for Discussion:

> Gee, James Paul. "The New Literacy Studies." *The Routledge Handbook of Literacy Studies*, edited by Jennifer Rowsell and Kate Pahl, Routledge, 2015, pp. 35–48.

"The NLS argued that literacy was something people did in the world and in society, not just inside their heads, and should be studied as such. It saw literacy as primarily a sociocultural phenomenon, rather than a mental phenomenon. Literacy was a social and cultural achievement centered in social and cultural practices" (Gee 35).

> Ryan, Mary, and Tony Rossi. "The Transdisciplinary Potential of Multiliteracies: Bodily Performances and Meaning-Making in Health and Physical Education." *Multiliteracies and Diversity in Education: New Pedagogies for Expanding Landscapes*, edited by Annah Healy, Oxford University Press, 2008, pp. 30–57.

"The obsession with the body is not an especially new, but recent social globalized of the body (rather than the rational measurement of it) now links the body to consumer patterns, lifestyle politics, new economic conditions, fitness, the posts back of aging through fitness regimes, and ways to enhance or even augment the body" (45).

MULTIMODAL DELIVERABLES:

A webpage that shows one multiliterate activity that a superhero in *Arrow* (Sarah, Diggle, Helena) uses (detective work on multimodal platforms, tracking one's fitness abilities) and provides several steps on how a student could improve his or her own multiliterate activities to be closer to those used in *Arrow* or other superhero media.

◆ ◆ 3 ◆ ◆

Scientific Literacies as the Scientific Method in *The Flash*

> However one chooses to define scientific literacy, its main objective seems clear enough: society (and the individual) will somehow benefit if its members are sufficiently literate to participate intelligently in science-based societal issues [74].
> —Morris Shamos, *The Myth of Scientific Literacy*

This chapter highlights the scientific literacy methods that empower Barry Allen, Caitlin Snow, Cisco Ramon, and Harrison Wells to conduct experiments in S.T.A.R. Labs and combat villains who have been enhanced through hyper-sci-fi alterations. The four scientists share many of Oliver's multiliterate events and skillsets, but while Oliver follows a more-general literacy practice, the scientists adhere to the scientific method as a literacy practice, grounding their literacy events in the discovery and advancement of scientific breakthroughs. As opposed to the early seasons of *Arrow* that keep the superheroes and supervillains strictly human, *The Flash* is filled with scientifically-enhanced or -modified characters, aliens, and alternate-universe doppelgangers.[1] Because of the inclusion of enhanced human and other beings, specialized literacies in *The Flash* reflect the needs of its characters across various scientific fields: physics, medicine, chemistry, forensics, biogenics, and aerodynamics. *The Flash* begins in Central City, but the show expands to other universes, all revolving around digital literacies and multimodal media. Driven to find new scientific discoveries, Cisco and Caitlin work in S.T.A.R. Labs, a research facility that aims for the advancement of scientific breakthroughs and new research methodologies. The accident that turns Barry into the Flash results from an experiment conducted by the lab, led by the research of Eobard Thawne, disguised as

Harrison Wells.[2] The superheroic activities of *The Flash* demonstrate intersecting multiliteracies as the characters exist in an ecosphere infused with knowledge and multiple practices of digital information and learning in life, community, and discovery. By studying their scientific literacy events, we can better understand specific and specialized literacy activities that require content knowledge from established fields of empirical and experiment-driven research.

The four main scientists operate from mindsets and skillsets that employ not only advanced literacies but skilled and specialized literacies within the sciences, facilitating their work within avenues of multiple directions and aptitudes. In this TV show, the question never seems to be *can* the superheroes manage to learn new science skills but *how* will the superheroes learn and master new science skills. While scientific literacies occupy a prominent place for the characters, the point of established literacies does not in any way hinder characters from expanding and adding to their knowledge base. In fact, the whole point of the show is that the characters wrestle with, fight against, and eventually overcome escalating challenges that groom and sharpen their superheroic abilities through new knowledge gathered over multiple modes of data. The plot of individual episodes often remains secondary to the depth and abilities of the characters who are driven by research and discoveries across scientific fields. Although the technology and the metahuman skills make for cool effects throughout each episode, the heart of the story lies in the ambitions and drive of the central characters to make the world a better place. Unlike Oliver who seeks to wreak punishment on the guilty, the characters of *The Flash* seek to balance out injustice by first protecting the innocent who inadvertently get in the way of various villains and their nefarious plans. In *Arrow*, most of the crimes from people named in The List that Oliver carries have been already committed or are part of a long chain of continual malfeasance from the wealthy power-players of Starling City. For *The Flash*, crimes usually are being committed or about to occur in the actual moment of the episode, and therefore the team has to respond in the urgency of the moment, testing their theories in the field, sometimes minutes after the team initiates a scientific breakthrough.

Enhanced Scientific Literacies

> Science literacy is desirable not only for individuals, but also for the health and well-being of communities and society. More than just basic knowledge of science facts, contemporary definitions of science literacy have

expanded to include understandings of scientific processes and practices, familiarity with how science and scientists work, a capacity to weigh and evaluate the products of science [1].
—Catherine Snow and Kenne Dibner,
*Science Literacy: Concepts,
Contexts, and Consequences*

What Are Scientific Literacies?

In 1996, the National Academy of Sciences defined scientific literacy as "the knowledge and understanding of scientific concepts and processes required for personal decision making, participation in civic and cultural affairs, and engagement in economic productivity. It also includes specific types of abilities" (22). In later years, the term became plural: scientific literacies, an indication of the many fields categorized under science such as chemistry, biology, geology, physics, and aerodynamics. According to Kimberly Lawless and Scott Brown in a discussion of global-based scientific knowledge, "science literacies involve much more than just content knowledge, but also require an understanding of the representation and interpretation of scientific data, scientific explanations and projections, and the process of science" (269). While other general literacies show the reader having the ability to purview symbols and codes and turn them into some type of intrinsic meaning, scientific literacies emphasize the content of science and the language of science above the ability to construct meaning from codes. In other words, the content of the meaning is the most important thing for scientists. The ability to navigate knowledge through science fields, especially intersecting discipline, remains crucial to developing effective scientific literacies that, like most multimodal multiliteracies, expand and acquire more information to further knowledge in and through literacy practices. According to Williams and Zenger,

> Developments in digital technologies have focused the attention of scholars on the role of technology in literacy practices and ways that had not been as explicit in the long period dominated by print as a medium. New technologies make it all but impossible to discuss literacy practices without also confronting the complexity of interpreting and composing texts that have been created by new media and online technologies [2012, 5].

The scientific method, rooted deep within the pattern of hypothesis, experiment, observation, and final analysis, stays central to those literacies both in the practice of proving a hypothesis and afterward in the verification of the experiment.

Throughout *The Flash*, characters use the scientific method: the team at

S.T.A.R. Labs conducts an experiment, usually regarding Barry's super-speed abilities and often in the middle of a dire fight between Barry and a metahuman, and the team uses the results of that experiment to propose a new battle hypothesis so Barry redirect his strategy to defeat the villain. Because of the vast fields of science with many intersecting disciplines, the ability that the characters have to navigate between these extreme fields speaks to the sophistication of their advanced literate abilities within the science arena. All four characters working in S.T.A.R. Labs—Barry, Caitlin, Cisco, and Harrison Wells either as evil Thawne or Earth-2 Wells—are well-versed in the content of scientific fields and the ways that science and literacy events interact as they complement each other in pursuit of gathering new knowledge. According to Istvan Karsai and George Kampis in their research on the scientific method and literacy practices, "Scientific literacy doesn't necessarily call for deep understandings of difficult concepts [...] but it does require a general understanding of basic scientific notions and the nature of scientific inquiry" (633). For those practicing scientific literacies, the aim remains to expound upon one's knowledge of the physical (or in this case metaphysical) world towards better understanding and more-accurate knowledge base that humans can achieve through testing, retesting, and compiling data about the physical world. For students beginning college, the knowledge gained through scientific literacy is not as important as the act of engaging in scientific literacy events and practicing the fundamental of the scientific method, events that the four scientists from *The Flash* practice routinely.

The developments of technology help all four characters in their capacities to improve and understand scientific literacies; most scientific literacies are only possible with the tools of technology, advancing the capacity of human senses to places where the microscopic can be seen and the macroscopic can be researched. According to Brandt, "It also may help to pinpoint current gaps in literacy achievement as occurring not so much between human skills and an absolute standard but between literacy as a human achievement and literacy as a technological achievement" (2011, 172). For scientific literacy, the intent is not so much the end product, but the process of learning, researching, hypothesizing, and testing which all provide reliable research methods over and over again throughout the study of physical matter in the universe. Whether embellished through superhuman activities or far-reaching science that counteracts the laws of physics, the implementation of scientific literacy allows us as viewers to sense the grounding of these well-intentioned, but flawed characters in pursuit of knowledge. The show acts as a reflection of our culture, highlighting the ways we have arrived at perceptions of the world and advanced technologies through these tools of scientific literacy.

How Are Scientific Literacies Exaggerated in *The Flash*?

> We've established that we were all uber-nerds.
> —Barry Allen, *The Flash*, Ep. 1.6

With the basic understanding of scientific literacy, characters in *The Flash* are able to expand their literacy practices to include missions dealing with metahumans, sci-fi machinery, and doppelganger universes. *The Flash*'s unique set of literacies speaks to the complicated, intersecting knowledge formations rooted in and around science and digital technology. *Arrow* operates in spaces of digitally-infused literacy practices, but *The Flash* expands upon those practices by portraying its characters in their scientific fields of study. Barry, in particular, moves from one literacy event to another smoothly as his scientific background complements his work as a superhero and empowers the detective skills he needs to outsmart and outfight villains. However, even though he does not possess as intricate or deeply-knowledge-based literate skills in bio-chem as Caitlin or in robotics and digital inventions as Cisco, Barry can still comprehend the information they produce, and with the new data, he can establish a foundation of intersecting science literacies that enables the team to remain vigilant.

Also, Harrison Wells and Eobard Thawne in disguise as Wells (both played by the versatile Tom Kavanaugh) possess overlapping literacy skills that empower wide technical and digital uses as both men bring advanced technology from Earth-2 to our world. Their literacy skills assist in monitoring Central City and crafting plans to aid the team or suit their own selfish needs: Wells to save his daughter from Zoom; Thawne to return to his own time by stealing the Flash's speed. All of the characters' intersecting scientific literacies speak to the fundamental nature of science—a need to study and collect data to form a hypothesis and then enact a plan to test the hypothesis. When preliminary plans fail to stop villains due to unknown information or shoddy technology, the scientific method for the scientists remains the same: to move forward from a place of a failed experiment with new knowledge about how to change and influence the test towards a more favorable outcome.[3] The fact that their intent for the results of the experiment remains the same—save the innocent, defeat the villain, and have the hero survive—does not deflect from the fact that their methods remain scientific.

Observe the following display in Ep. 1.6, "The Flash Is Born" when learning that Barry needs to fight his old childhood nemesis, Tony, who is a metahuman who can turn his body into metal. In S.T.A.R. Labs, the four scientists discuss how Barry can fight him after their first skirmish ends with the Flash getting pummeled. The team realizes that the only way to defeat Tony is to hit him at a velocity hard enough to shatter metal:

> Cisco: Factoring in the metal's tensile strength, estimated dermal thickness, atmospheric pressures, air temp, you'd have to hit him at approximately.... Mach 1.1.
> Caitlin: You want Barry to hit something at 800 miles an hour?
> Cisco: 837, actually.
> Caitlin: That's faster than the speed of sound.
> Cisco: I know, he would create a sonic boom, which as I've said before, would be awesome.
> Barry: I've never gone that fast.
> Wells: Yet.
> Caitlin: I can't believe we're actually entertaining this idea. I mean, he'd need a straight shot from miles away.
> Cisco: Yeah, 5.3 miles, theoretically.
> Wells: Do it right, you'll take him down.
> Caitlin: Do it wrong, you'll shatter every bone in your body.

This exchange between the four main scientists demonstrates the knowledge that they need to accurately estimate the outcome of an experiment, grounding the show within the characters' scientific literacy abilities. The scientific experiment here, of course, is not possible at the moment as no human can run 837mph, but the show permits the characters to create a hypothesis from established science fields (primarily physics and biology) into the realm of the sci-fi and provides credibility by having the characters discuss their theories before implementing them. This interconnection of scientific disciplines demonstrates a key facet in the scientific method and the various approaches on science: because scientists rely on previous knowledge and research done in the fields, literacy sponsors of science are a significant contribution to empirical exploration.

Literacy Sponsors

A central staple in understanding scientific literacy is the importance of literacy sponsors, first as a general phenomenon and then more specifically in the fields of science. **Literacy sponsors** are individuals or groups of individuals in institutions that promote certain usages and perspectives of literacy and usually reap some benefit from their sponsorship. Different scientific fields have different means of sponsorship, but the main impetus of scientific literacy relies on the establishment of previous scholars and researchers to ground practical and theoretical knowledge within a specific study and to provide the basis of data and information for further research. In *Literacy in American Lives* (2000), Deborah Brandt defines a literacy sponsor as "any

3. Scientific Literacies as the Scientific Method in *The Flash* 73

agents, local or distant, concrete or abstract, who enable, support, teach, and model, as well as recruit, regulate, suppress, or withhold, literacy—and gain advantage by it in some way" (19). Her research upset more-traditional perspectives about the purity of literacy and education: because current cultural mores tend to promote literacy, criticism of literacy sponsors usually does not occur.[4] Later, in *Literacy and Learning* (2009), Brandt observes "a range of human relationships and ideological pressures that turn up at the scene of literacy learning—from benign sharing between adults and youths to euphemized coercions in schools and workplaces, to the most notorious imposition and deprivation by church or state" (287). Sponsorship in higher learning proves particularly resilient; most of us in academia had strong sponsors—teachers we admired, professors who enlightened us, scholars who challenged our academic perspectives. In response, we developed our educational selves so we could become teachers, and thus sponsors, for emerging students to whom we tried to pass on the same academic passion and similar methods of reading and comprehension that we learned. Criticism might fall on the sponsors if and when mainstream opinion believes that sponsors, notably teachers, of literacy are not having desired effects in their literacy instruction, and then national campaigns rise up to curb mass illiteracy.

Concepts of sponsorship are complicated and multilayered in their intricacies because sponsoring someone else's literacy events and subsequently inducing someone into larger social literacy practices require an amalgamation of cultural ideology and particular perspectives of literacy, usually resulting in specific types of literacy instruction. Sponsors of literacy, no matter how well-meaning, consistently promote and insist upon particular criteria for literacy that the student learns to develop. "In whatever form, sponsors deliver the ideological freight that must be borne for access to what they have" (Brandt, 2009, 27). Usually, the ideology behind literacy sponsorship leans towards more educational, traditional understandings of literacy, often centering on alphabetic texts with language that grows progressively more dense and abstract as the reader's skills improve. Teachers and parents urge young children to read alphabetic, print texts, and the parents' and teachers' criteria of reading activities and legitimacy limit texts to that of the literary canon or educational approval.[5] Yet, Brandt argues that even this definition of educational sponsors is too narrow because greater institutions of our current culture promote distinct literacy practices which influence not only how Americans read and comprehend texts and other media, but also influence the ways Americans conceive of literacy itself. This occurs mainly because history can "serve as both a sanctioning force and reserve of ideological and material support" (43). Academic institutions have their own specificities regarding literacy; the humanities make distinctions between popular and academic sources for support of student essays and research, consistently promoting academic, peer-reviewed sources above popular, widely-dispersed media.

Sponsors of scientific literacies endorse literacy practices that reflect the ideology, practices, and events of the scientific sponsor, and therefore their perspectives often are limited by the goals and values that the sponsor equates not only with her or his own literacy events and larger social practices but also with the goals and values which literacy acquisition should have for the one being sponsored. In "Seeking Sponsors, Accumulating Literacies," Michael Smith emphasizes, "We always need to think about how the literacy teaching we do today prepares students for the literacy of learning in which they will engage both in and out of our classrooms, literacy learning the nature of which we cannot predict" (163). Sponsors of scientific literacies carry particular biases for their disciplines: how they believe scientific literacies should be learned, expanded, performed, and changed usually reflects the how, when, and where they sponsor these literacies. In her work on Native Americans and literacy sponsors, Ellen Cushman argues, "At the perimeter marked by the acts of sponsorship, one finds the workings of power—the economic and political forces that allow and circumscribed its circulation between individuals and groups for gain" (15).

These forces create boundaries that Cushman states reveal "the ways in which those who sponsor are ultimately impacted for better or worse by their sponsorship efforts" (15). For those in the fields of science, sponsorship involves adherence to the scientific method along with an establishment of past research and study that outlines each of the intersecting fields through rigorous debate, experimentation, theoretical models, and collective investigation. Each of the four scientists in *The Flash* acts both as sponsor and sponsored, sometimes being their own literacy sponsor as they research and learn more in the field through persistence and diligence in a quest to find answers. The following sections explore the scientific literacies of the four scientists as well as their sponsorship of multiliterate, investigative events as participation in larger scientific literacy practices.

Barry Allen: Superhero, Forensics Scientist and Detective

When looking at *The Flash*'s range of scientific literacy as advanced multiliteracies, we see a range of literacies: genetic, medical, forensic, and aerodynamic. Barry starts the show as a forensic scientist who gathers information at crime scenes for the police of Central City. His job requires a literacy of investigation and data, looking at small bits and pieces of DNA, fingerprints, and other external signs at a crime scene; he then tests and compiles data into reports for the D.A. to be used as evidence in prosecuting criminals. His work also requires the ability to read a crime scene and to look for physical discrepancies that will lead to an explanation of who committed the crime and will support a prosecutor's need for evidence. From the very first episode of *The Flash*, we as the audience can see Barry's scientific literacy at work at the scene of a robbery/murder. He kneels down in the street to examine mud left from a tire wheel, and the screen shows the calculations of what he is seeing, most notably that the tire marks were made with a rear tire. As he gets up, he announces, "The getaway car's a Mustang Shelby GT500. Shelbys have a rear super-wide tire specific to that model, 12 inches with an asymmetrical tread." Through an exhaustive study of physics and forensics, he can survey crime scenes with confidence and connect pieces of evidence together to create a whole picture of past events that have already occurred yet still have significance for law enforcement.

From its very first episode, *The Flash* hosts heroes and villains that have extraordinary powers, physical morphing abilities, or other sci-fi elements. Because of their metahuman bodies, the resulting literacies are those beyond human capacity; for example, due to his super speed, Barry can read a 200-page book in a matter of seconds. His literacy, at the basic, alphabetic level, affords him faster and more-thorough comprehension than even a speed reader can achieve. Most readers read between 350–500 words a minute; when speed reading or scanning texts, some readers can push themselves to 650 words, but higher than that, they tend to no longer read actual words but only skim over sentences, catching random words in the swift activity. In comparison, Barry is reading around 480,000 words a minute. This superpower allows him to access and comprehend much more data than other human superheroes, but even in-taking information at an exponentially-faster rate does not make him superheroic alone. He still has to process the information he reads, arrange it into logical structures, and form a plan of action from the new data.

Barry's superpowers are considered metaphysical in nature, making him a metahuman, rather than being based on actual training of human abilities like Oliver's, but Barry's scientific literacy skills rival those of Oliver's. Barry can move within scientific spaces and discourse about theories of physics, biology, chemistry, genetics, and aerodynamics without hesitation, comfortable in the language and discourse of intersecting science disciplines. Here, a distinction lies in these two main characters of their respective shows and their access to literacy structures within privileged spaces. Oliver comes from wealth and privilege and has his advanced literacy skills beaten and tortured into him while on the island and throughout his various encounters with mercenaries; Barry, the adopted son of a police officer, has more of a middle-class upbringing and learns his primary literate skills through normal educational pathways such as going to college and specializing in the field of forensics precisely and science more generally. The reading skills that require advance literacies to identify and fight evil metahumans are extensions of the skills he had developed as a young man in his 20s, skills that enable him to work as a forensic investigator as his primary job and an amateur detective trying to solve his mother's murder on the side.

In the early scenes of the pilot episode, we see him standing in front of a bulletin board on which he has taped up pictures and articles of his mother's murder, linking together data in an attempt to form a conclusion that will point to his father's innocence and identify the actual killer. This requires a literacy of specific interrogation and knowledge gathering, the ability to sift through massive amounts of news, reports, medical evidence, and data collections. Once Barry receives his superhuman powers, his activities as the Flash also require new literacies to process information he finds while traveling at terrific speeds or engaging in physical fights with opponents. In the midst of peril, he has to read his immediate circumstances and report back to S.T.A.R. Labs where Cisco and Caitlin feed his information into their computers or respond with their knowledge base and provide constructive feedback for him to act next. Their instructions often become directives, ordering Barry to abandon the fight, to engage the opponent in a new way, or to experiment with some new type of scientific possibility to combat the metahumans who oppose the Flash. Barry has to balance out his super speed with his detective work, relying on each skill to empower his superheroic activities.

Caitlin Snow and Cisco Ramon

Barry Allen has metahuman powers that enable him to respond in physical moments of danger; Harrison Wells, both as Eobard Thawne and the Earth-2 version, possesses scientific and literacy skills belonging to another universe in which scientific advancements are greater than our own. For the beginning of Season 1, Caitlin Snow and Cisco Ramon enter the storyline as normal, completely-human scientists who have joined S.T.A.R. Labs in search of furthering scientific exploration through the particle accelerator. Though later Cisco becomes Vibe and Caitlin realizes that her Earth-2 counterpart is a supervillain (Killer Frost), both of them in the first season have sharp literacy skills of ordinary scientists, now dealing with far-science applications. Their entire approach to metahuman anomalies requires extensive knowledge about scientific data as a baseline and a very open mind to process the metahuman abilities of superpowered villains. When either Caitlin or Cisco faces a new challenge, their first step is to observe the signs of change and add that to already-established scientific information. They then come up with a hypothesis that usually involves a plan for the Flash to physically subdue a foe

3. Scientific Literacies as the Scientific Method in The Flash 77

and create a scenario in which the science would support the activity. Sometimes they operate from a dearth of information about the villains' powers or a miscalculation about Barry's own powers, but their scientific approach remains consistent as they read new information and assemble new data into existing structures of knowledge. Throughout the first two seasons, they observe and respond to information in the fields of genetics, molecular biology, cosmology, genealogy, chemistry, climatology, evolution, and physics, both experimental and theoretical. Though the science they deal with is beyond the possible in our reality, they practice the scientific method, and when a hypothesis falls through, they reassemble existing data, form a new plan of attack, and—to follow the old adage—try, try again.

Medical knowledge and bioengineering form the basis of Caitlin's scientific literacies as her concerns center on biological materials, usually the (meta-)human body, mostly Barry's. She is more cautious than Cisco, having lost her fiancé in the particle accelerator mishap, but she also wants to see scientific advancements, especially in her role of keeping Central City safe from metahuman villains. She finds meaning in the physicality of living and dead matter, reading patterns in DNA sequences and rebuilding from the core of genetic makeup as she works from a process of scientific discoveries that feeds into her literacy process. In Ep. 1.2, she grows a clone from a metahuman's DNA, and in Season 2, she creates different versions of the velocity serum for Jay to regenerate speed. Of the four scientists on Team Flash, she perhaps best realizes the Frankenstein tendencies that their lab has generated, most notably in the irony that the Flash has to battle against metahumans created by the particle accelerator accident of the machine that she helped create.[6] Despite the setbacks, Caitlin considers the results of scientific discoveries to be worth the consequence and possible negative results of testing with the scientific method. Learning more about the world and the universe—and multiple universes—lets the characters better understand themselves as participants inside the vast schemes of interlocking systems.

Although Cisco appears to be younger and much more energetic than Caitlin, he has the same intense literacy skills that allow him to hypothesize and solve many of their problems through scientific methods. While Caitlin concentrates on the body and other biological systems, Cisco's forte remains the creation and improvement of technological machines and digital systems. He creates the Flash's suits and infuses them with monitoring capacities so the team at S.T.A.R. Labs can monitor Barry's actions and vitals when he engages in physical combat with another metahuman. Cisco sees the relationship between technology and scientific literacy as the ability to comprehend information through a scientific lens and then filter that information through machines and bodies often simultaneously. Many of the Flash's missions are conducted in the field where Cisco is not present, but the monitoring systems he has created gives him and the rest of the team a remote eye to observe the action and physical circumstances that influence both the superhero's and supervillains' activities. Often this monitoring is done through multiple screens in S.T.A.R. Labs that detect and report on the condition of the Flash's suit as well as digital maps of the landscape on which they watch the tracker inside of the suit. Not only does Cisco create and read these systems, but he develops quick literacy skills in monitoring scientific data because, due to the Flash's extraordinary speed, comprehension and reaction become nearly instantaneous during fights with other super-powered metahumans.

Sometimes, Cisco makes machines just for the cool factor of creating a new device; when Barry goes blind temporarily, Cisco makes sunglasses that he can see through, allowing Barry to go on date with Cisco monitoring his activities. Throughout the first two seasons, Cisco designs and builds new technology that enables and furthers the superpowers of the Flash. Cisco even creates technology used by villains; in Ep. 1.4, Captain Cold steals the cold gun (a gun that emits a freezing blast) and Cisco builds a heat gun to counter the effects of the instant frost. With the emergence of each new metahuman, Cisco provides the names of the villains (The Mist, Girder, Plastique), a gimmick used for comedic purposes, but usually an accurate summation of the villains' powers and threats to stabilize culture. Perhaps this is what makes Cisco such an effective scientist: his ability to observe and then connect his observations to appropriate language that describes what he observed succinctly and efficiently. In the next step of reporting in the scientific method, Cisco must develop language so that his research can be relayed to others through standard writing or multimodal methods of summarizing: video, audio recording, still images, graphs, and combinations of these modes. Scientific literacy as access to the scientific methods broadens Cisco's understanding of the world, and he wants to participate in the expansion of scientific knowledge because of the effects of good it can have for the citizens of Central City and beyond.

The partnership that Cisco and Caitlin have developed works off their scientific literacies and language as they collaborate over ideas, information, hypotheses, and results, existing in a continual cycle of new information, testing that information, and then assembling the results into existing data over and over again. Therein lies a particular perspective of scientific literacy and literacies in general: "Literacy, for instance, is not only about rules and their correct application. It is about being faced with an unfamiliar kind of text and being able to search for clues about its meaning without immediately feeling alienated and excluded from it" (Kalantzis and Cope, 2008, 203). The unknown does not scare or intimidate those with scientific literacies; rather it allows those who seek answers to proceed forward working with partial or limited information to a place of clarity with the help of enhanced literacy events which speak to a need to learn more, understand more, and do more. Whether these literacies stem from a place of cool assemblage like Caitlin or excited exuberance like Cisco, the development of scientific literacy enables students to process forward in various fields and build upon previously-discovered knowledge to advance our understandings of our world and the way that physical matter constructs and limits our abilities. In this superhero world, scientific literacies let them step beyond these limitations and construct new, inventive ways to challenge barriers to their objectives and self-directed research methods.

Harrison Wells, the Real One from Earth-2

As an older wiser mentor, self-appointed to serve as the literacy sponsor to Team Flash on Earth-1, Harrison Wells from Earth-2 has all of the scientific literacies that his counterpart Eobard Thawne possesses as well as an understanding of the alien technology that relies on scientific literacies of both Earth 1 and Earth-2.[7] Early in season 2, Wells has a digital device that he wears like a watch which can identify metahumans, a device that he uses to read his environment and perceive danger to both himself and the rest of the team before it happens. When he goes back to Earth-2 with Barry to save his daughter and defeat Zoom, Wells appears as comfortable in the high digital universe as he is in Earth-1 low-tech affordances. On Earth-2, he creates his own particle accelerator in their version of Star Labs which also explodes and creates metahumans that plagued Earth-2. Rather than take responsibility for the botched experiment, Wells instead becomes part of a task force that hunts down metahumans and gains fame for his work. When confronted about his actions, Wells brushes them aside by claiming that all of his work has one singular goal in mind: to unveil the mysteries of the universe. This scientist-as-God trope—a commonality across many narratives in which the pursuit of knowledge leads to infamy and chaos—assimilates well into a show driven by the exploration and furthering of scientific literacy through multiple avenues of research and metahuman experimentation.

Early in Season 2, Wells travels to Earth-1 to create technology that will stop Zoom and save his daughter from Zoom's clutches. In his secret mission, he develops new machines and techniques for tracking Zoom's whereabouts in both universes, and Wells keeps building on the technology to enhance his machines and the Flash's abilities. For Wells, scientific advancements always require expansions of new knowledge throughout multiple literate processes. Determined, focused, and singularly-minded, Wells sees advancements in scientific breakthroughs as a way of achieving his goals, and he uses both his scientific literacies as well as the literacies of the other scientists to further his advancements of scientific discoveries. He does not hesitate with the implications or repercussions of his discoveries as Caitlin does, nor does he act amazed at the coolness of new tools or scientific advancements as Cisco does. Wells even rebuilds a new particle accelerator in the latter part of Season 2 that temporarily disintegrates Barry and sends him to a dimension of the speed force; although Wells regrets the outcome of his action, he implies that he would make the same choices to play God again if given the opportunity. For Wells, science is always a tool for advancement, a stepping stone to objectives rather than a procedure to discover more knowledge or further scientific literacy. He has fixated goals as his objectives, and whether he uses a glass board to write out physics equations or creates digital devices to detect metahumans, Wells relies on the data created from scientific experiments and theories to promote his goals towards singular or collective objectives.

Studying Wells' scientific literacies allows us to see how the skillsets of reading and experimentation in several fields across scientific domains enable the researcher to explore and open up new areas of knowledge. Cynthia Tomovic et al. explain that being more scientifically literate for a large community means "citizens would realize the strength of their individual decision making as it relates to their purchasing power and to their support of corporate social responsibility. When citizens lack scientific literacy, they do not understand the links between their actions and potential impacts" (179). Wells perhaps best demonstrates the danger of literacy sponsors that promote particular avenues of literacy development and acquisition without looking at the consequences of that acquisition or the implications it will have for those being sponsored. When scientific advancement becomes the most important criteria in one's determined work and becomes linked to scientific discoveries for superheroic actions, repercussions of those advancements rarely occur. Even if they did, Wells is a risk taker who believes that the goal of any endeavor outweighs any possible repercussions that one or one's community might suffer in reaching for that goal. His aims and his sponsorship are isolating and single-minded, and while he is not evil as Eobard Thawne in Season 1, the cold detachment of Well's singular focus often illustrates the danger that arises when scientists do not consider repercussions for their scientific endeavors.

Chapter Conclusion

This chapter explores the four scientists of *The Flash* and their specialized literacies. The first new term of literacy representations in this chapter is *sponsors of literacy*: those who teach or endorse their perspective and methods of reading. The second term, *scientific literacies*, demonstrates a type of specialized multiliteracies tied to a career objective, and even scientific literacies have further particularities when broken down in various scientific fields: aerodynamics, genetics, robotics, etc. Sponsorship of scientific literacies occurs in *The Flash* as the scientists employ the scientific method in their work—in the lab and out in the world fighting metahuman villains—and solicit feedback from each other as a vetting process for the validity of their research.

Class Activities

As opposed to the activities in the previous chapter which focused on multiliteracies with digital texts, these activities focus on scientific literacies as means of branching out and expanding literacy practices and personal literacy events beyond the humanities. Even though the science in *The Flash* is fictional, involving far-out and hypothetical science, students can mirror superheroic literacy practices in scientific expanses of their knowledge bases. Other researchers have used the advanced science of superhero media as a teaching tool; in "The 'Marvel'-ous Nature of Science," Daniel Bergman explains, "Teachers are wise to harness this enthusiasm [for superheroes] and direct it towards science learning. Specifically, we can use scenes and examples from MCU movies to explicitly address themes related to the nature of science" (22). Because multiliterate, scientific activities seek to expand on perspectives of literacy, students may consider that all science activities become multiliterate and begin to consider multiliteracies as skillsets to understand all aspects of human life.

Activity 1—Defining Scientific Literacies in *The Flash*

While definitions of multiliteracies have grown broader, more inclusive, and more diverse in their understandings of how humans engage and comprehend external and/or interlinking material, students should also recognize that the relationship between the individual and the outside material defines the understanding of multiliteracies. In other words, the individual must be acting or interacting with outside texts; therefore the understanding of scientific literacies demands perspectives focusing on how one interacts with those texts rather than how one interacts with all aspects of human life. Yet, students can see that Team Flash's multiliterate skills have improved, too, because of the research and learning they have done with physics, technology, chemistry, medicine, and the interlocking networks of information as a means of improving their scientific literacy skills.

Questions for Students to Answer:
- How are scientific literacies portrayed and enacted in superhero TV shows?
- How are they exaggerated and at what point do they have truth to them in the scientific method and previous knowledge to make accurate estimates and hypotheses?
- How do superheroes expand their scientific literacies?
- What types of activities could students perform to expand their own scientific literacies beyond taking science classes or just reading scientific research?

Suggested readings and quotes for discussion:

Wu, Siew Mei, et al. "Teaching Academic Literacy Using Popular Science Texts: A Case Study." *Teaching & Learning Inquiry*, vol. 6, no. 2, Jan. 2018, pp. 29–49.

"The embedding of academic literacy skills takes the form of student engagement with science related texts and topics. [...] The awareness of the use of metacognitive strategies, including the activation of schematic knowledge to construct new meaning and to connect prior and new knowledge, all contribute to the reading comprehension process. The teaching of writing competence would then entail the teaching of effective reading skills to construct relevant scientific knowledge" (Wu et al. 35).

McMillen, Cynthia M., et al. "Tackling Literacy: A Collaborative Approach to Developing Materials, for Assessing Science Literacy Skills in Content Classrooms through a STEM Perspective." *Language and Literacy Spectrum*, vol. 28, no. 1, June 2018, Article 2.

"Keeping the focus on the development of an informed citizen, it was important [in our study] to realize the difference between scientific literacy and literacy in science. [...] A student competent in literacy in science had the ability to transfer the skills mastered to multiple content areas, whereas scientific literacy focused on skills specifically related to the comprehension of scientific literature and content" (Article 2).

Deliverables or Writing Project:

A flow chart that establishes steps to identify and improve scientific literacies. Each step could function as a mini paragraph.

Activity 2—Scientific Literacies as Collaborative Ecologies

Students (and instructors) often want to have expansive, complex multiliterate skills and highly specialized literate skills without actually engaging the time, energy, and resources necessary to create those skillsets. According to Barton, "Rather than isolating literacy activities from everything else to understand them, an ecological approach [to literacy] aims to understand how literacy is embedded in other human activity, its embeddedness in social life and in thought, and its position in history, language, and learning" (1994, 32). In other words, we want to have advanced literacy practices without the work of engaging in literacy events and establishing strenuous multiliterate practices. This understanding of literacy is especially applicable to incoming freshmen at the beginning of their college careers when they desire to have high literacy skills and a fair range of multiliterate skills but often feel reluctant to wade through the language, texts, and knowledge bases of higher education to enhance those skills. To this end, this activity includes group participation as a means of exploring scientific literacies together, allowing for the discussion and exploration of learning about the literacies required for various scientific disciplines.

GROUP ACTIVITIES:

Groups create arguments for why students need to improve not only their understanding of scientific literacies through superhero narratives. They then provide discussion on how scientific literacies aid in other literate events and practices across disciplines and specific careers.

SUGGESTED READINGS AND QUOTES FOR DISCUSSION:
> Miller, Sue, Hilary Janks, and James Stiles. "Literacy with Mobiles in Print-Poor Communities." *The Routledge Handbook of Literacy Studies*, edited by Jennifer Rowsell and Kate Pahl, Routledge, 2015, pp. 634–48.

"To build upon the idea of a social practice of literacy, student pairs are assigned to a single device, forcing students to negotiate their practices on the device with their partners. This allows the researcher to monitor how devices are shared, allows the opportunity for knowledge to be transferred between pairs of students at different levels of literacy practice and create the opportunities that require students to negotiate the creation of shared texts" (Miller et al. 644).

> Young, Morris. "Writing the Life of Henry Obookiah: The Sponsorship of Literacy and Identity." *Literacy, Economy, and Power: Writing and Research After "Literacy in American Lives,"* edited by John Duffy et al., Southern Illinois University Press, 214, pp. 61–78.

"Understanding how we acquire and are able to access literacy—who sponsors our literacy—lets us situate literacy within a broader context of social and economic relationships that move beyond the 'literacy myths' that value individual acquisition and achievement" (63).

DELIVERABLES:

Group presentations where each group demonstrates how to link scientific literacies. Each participant could take a scientific field, and the group could demonstrate how knowledge builds through scientific literacies across various empirical disciplines.

Activity 3—Expanding Scientific Literacies

Once students identify scientific literacies, they can reflect on their scientific literacy events as part of larger social and progressive changes in the way we have come to understand literacy in this age of digital media and ever-accumulating information in scientific fields. Then students can understand the expansion of these multiliterate activities as part of a growing concern for human knowledge and access by the way in which we come to read the physical world and our studies of it. Through viewing shorts scenes of characters researching in the field, students can see them participate in scientific, multiliterate activities, creating greater and greater methods of accumulating knowledge and information. Mirroring the abilities of the four scientists, students begin to stretch their multiliterate practices towards that of specialized scientific literacies.

SUGGESTED READINGS AND QUOTES FOR DISCUSSION:
Newfield, Denise. "The Semiotic Mobility of Literacy: Four Analytical Approaches." *The Routledge Handbook of Literacy Studies*, edited by Jennifer Rowsell and Kate Pahl, Routledge, 2015, pp. 267–81.

"Understanding different ways of looking at transmodal chains is useful for teachers, students and researchers, since each way privileges different aspects of meaning-making and backgrounds others: comparing and contrasting the meeting and representational forms of differently modalised texts in sequence foregrounds the role of the mode in the shaping and reshaping of meaning and individual texts" (Newfield 278).

MULTIMODAL DELIVERABLES:

A webpage that hosts a clip of the scientists from *The Flash* performing in the lab. After the clip, the students detail the knowledge and information-gathering behind scientific literacies and their acquisition.

◆◆ 4 ◆◆

Gotham as a Place Mired in Print-Privileged Literacy

> Technology then becomes one of the central keys to Batman's success. Lacking superpowers, he must rely on technology to help him succeed against the odds [172].
> —Alex Romagnoli and Gian Pagnucci,
> *Enter the Superheroes*

This chapter surveys the characters of *Gotham* and their dependencies on written, alphabetic modes. *Arrow* and *The Flash* take place in digitally-enhanced, technology-heavy worlds where characters rely on multimodals to provide, track, and reinforce data; *Gotham* stands in stark contrasts with low digital usage, few technical devices, and near-nonexistent networking of information. Shot with a noir color palette, the world of *Gotham* exists in an America of blended time periods where characters have basic cellphones but no computers; TVs exist but not digital surveillance; civil right and feminism have led to equal opportunities for characters, but markers of American history are notably absent. Because of the severe lack of digital information, characters have advanced skills of traditional literacy, making print and written documents of the utmost importance. I choose this superhero TV show because of its unique position of timelessness: many of the stylistic choices reflect important decades of American history without specifics events. Some of the haircuts and clothing styles look like the 1950s, the desks and lamps in the police station have a 1960s vibe, the graffiti on buildings and the car models suggest the 1970s, the TVs and tape recordings resemble those used in the 1980s, and the cellphones are mostly flip phones from the late 1990s.

The culture of *Gotham* is confined to the actions and movements of the city without any larger reference to American pop culture across media. *Daredevil*, *Arrow*, *Jessica Jones*, and *Luke Cage* all reflect the time-period of the current day in which they are set, and most of the technology and scientific discoveries of other superhero TV shows point forward to the future. *Gotham* invokes the past, a conglomeration of America's aesthetics all crushed into one city. Unsurprisingly, the malleable city is overrun by criminals, gangs, maniacs, and desperate people trying to prove themselves as powerful players. Will Brooker stresses, "The importance of Batman's readership—the active fans, the wider, non-participatory group, and the millions who may rarely pick up a comic but still know the character intimately—in maintaining the Batman myth into the new millennium" (2001, 317). Because of the familiarity of these characters, retelling Batman's story from his early years lets viewers see his growth into the iconic character and the other characters and challenges that turn him into Batman.

Gotham acts as a prequel to Batman's later years and has a range of Batman characters (heroes, villains, minor characters) that interact with each other.[1] Though this show depicts the early years of the characters, it is not a direct sequel to any specific narrative such as a comic book arc or *Batman Begins*. The world of *Gotham* has characters featured in the iconic Batman canon and shares similarities with the *Arkham* games, *The Dark Knight* trilogy, and Batman comics of the 80s and 90s; yet, it does not reference one specific Batman text, making vague references to the whole of the multimodal canon. The show begins with the murder of Bruce's parents and a 30-something-year-old Jim Gordon investigates the murders, a decision which unravels the concealed corruption of the city as two feuding mob families struggle for dominance of the crime world.

The show narrates both Jim's story as the protagonist who attempts to work from within the law and Bruce who lives in the safety of Wayne Manor under the guardianship of Alfred. As Jim struggles to take down the mob, Bruce's determination to find his parents' killer leads him to research his father's company, befriend petty thief Selina Kyle, and begin physical training to strengthen his body, all early activities that lead to him becoming Batman. Literacy practices in *Gotham* allow us to see basic literacy events and practices using traditional, alphabetic texts. While more current superheroes tend to have an array of state-of the-art, cutting-edge technology, the characters of Gotham have to develop cognitive processes and reading activities around the data found in early mass media: newspapers, books, records, and police files, all with hardcopy, physical modalities. Literacy activities in *Gotham* involve printed text that one can hold, and any networking of information must take place in a character's head as a cognitive process, not onscreen as a digital interconnection.

Gotham: *Limited Texts, Limited Literacies*

Batman, then, is one example of the significance of pop culture. He's part of a mass culture (nearly everyone in

4. Gotham *as a Place Mired in Print-Privileged Literacy*

> America can tell you who Batman is); he is part of a text (the comic book itself in one sense, but also a cultural morality tale about good and evil; our way of life) produced by a group of people (the team who produce the comics, but also ourselves: we help produce Batman by continuing to support his existence) [6].
> —Megan O'Neill, *Popular Culture*

Because *Gotham* exists in a pre–Internet, pre-digitalized, pre-computer-information world, characters live and work in an era in which information is limited to hardcopy, handwritten, or a typewriter-written text. The knowledge rests in printed files, handwritten notes, or dense books so access to information occurs at a slow pace. Most of the clues to solving crimes that Jim Gordon and the other detectives find come through spoken conversations, usually in interviews with suspects, and as a result, the cases feel less complex and simpler than the criminal schemes that other superheroes track.[2] The noir aspect of *Gotham* does present a pre-digital world charm, but the episodic narrative of the show often feels limited as the characters would be able to accomplish more if they had the means of technological databases and multiliterate abilities to access information across platforms other than hardcopy, print text. The dichotomy between the world of *Arrow* and *The Flash* and the world of *Gotham* indicates perhaps most effectively our core beliefs about the ability to engage with multiliteracies involving digital and technical platforms: that we are somehow more than average, perhaps more than human when we enter into digital modalities that require us to broaden our perspectives from traditional literacy practices to something more complex and complicated.

Gotham feels mired in the past and rife with the suggestions of future possibilities (many of the cases Jim Gordon works on would be solved more quickly and efficiently with a criminal database on digital files instead of ceiling-high filing cabinets) while other superhero TV shows feel futuristic as they imagine a time when the limits of technology allow us the capacities to not only use multimodalities but also to create them better and more effective than before. The information found on the printed page is not only important; it exists as the only information available because the modalities of data are severely limited in this superheroic world. In his review of the rhetorical nature of literacy, John Duffy defines these traditional literacy events as reflective of "the conception of literacy that has for years dominated in the schools, where reading and writing have been understood and assessed in terms of individual ability, motivation, and effort" (2003, 8). The show implies that to be an effective superhero later and counteract the chaos of his city, Bruce will have to create advanced technology to gain knowledge and track criminals as the outdated methods that Jim and Harvey use impede and slow down their police work.

Two central characters in *Gotham*, young Bruce Wayne and Jim Gordon, both occupy literate spaces that speak to their particular events: the library at Wayne Manor where Bruce studies and Jim Gordon's desk at the police station. In Ep. 1.4, the scene opens in the manor and the camera pulls back to display the dark-toned library where bookshelves reach the ceiling, and cases of paper records and reports are stacked by the desk. In the background, Bruce has placed an enormous bulletin board where he pins up pictures of suspects, politicians, and police officers along with newspaper clippings and police reports, all related to his parents' murders and political activities in Gotham. Alfred, looking cynically at the array of texts, asks him, "What if all of this was a complete and bloody waste of time? [...] What if you never get revenge?" With his eyes centered on the board, Bruce answers, "I don't want revenge. I want to know how it all works."

His drive to improve his learning—and consequently his literacy skills—reflects Bruce's dedication to his self-imposed mission to be strong and heroic. Yet, the solitary confinement of the Wayne library contrasts sharply with the busy hustle of the police station where Jim works; there, the focus is not on written or print documents but on the people that move within the space. Compared to Bruce's text-cluttered workspace, Jim Gordon's desk remains mostly empty. Random files and police reports cross the desk throughout different episodes, but he and his partner, Harvey Bullock, glance over them intermittently, and they report on what they see or the important information they have discovered. Without the flashiness of screens and the high-tech channels of information, detective work in *Gotham* narrows to events of basic, alphabetic literacy and a cognitive process which must weave and connect information together to reach a state of certainty for the detectives.

Literacy Stewards, Protectors of Knowledge

Because of the limited information in *Gotham* and the constant threat of violence from the organized mobs, most institutions act as literacy stewards that guard information and other people's access to it. The instance of literacy sponsorship often relies on the superhero himself to become sponsored past basic literacy skills in multiliterate abilities. His self-sponsorship is certainly understandable in the light of the value that systems within America have placed on literacy, all tied to economic and power structures. According to Brandt,

> Literacy, like land, is a valued commodity in this economy, a key resource in gaining profit and edge [...] it also explains why the powerful work so persistently to

conscript and ration the powers of literacy. The competition to harness literacy, to manage, measure, teach, and exploit it, has intensified throughout the century [20].

Higher, more specialized literacy skills enable us not only to interact with literacy or more complex levels but also allows us to control and limit others' literacy acquisition and usage as well. The same way that institutions control the information shown and given reflects how we as instructors serve as stewards of literacy for our students as we bring limited—by time, space, and intent—information into the classroom and into our pedagogy and praxis as well. **Literacy stewards** are individuals or a group of individuals that withhold or suppress literacy learning and access. Literacy stewards have real-world gravitas outside of superhero TV shows as many of our institutions act to guard and restrict information: governmental bureaucracies, higher education, law, medicine, and even religious institution.

While the term "sponsors of literacy" has appeared frequently in recent scholarship (Graff 2007, Duffy et al. 2013, Jacobs 2013, Canagarajah 2013), "stewards of literacy" has been used more sparingly. The few times the phrase has been mentioned, it usually functions as an extension of literacy sponsorship. Alena Frost (2011) states, "This term, literacy steward, can be applied to any individual who demonstrates persistent dedication to the practice or promotion of a literacy considered traditionally important to his or her community" (56). In a short piece about the problems with the university's reading and digital texts, Mark Bauerlein (2008) expresses concern that academia should embrace online literacy, diminishing the chances where "teachers and professors so cavalierly violate their charge as stewards of literacy" (B11). More recently in "Stewards of Digital Literacies" (2012), Howard Rheingold explains, "Librarians have always been stewards of literacy as well as curators of knowledge" (53). He proceeds to emphasize that, since these librarians have specialized knowledge and skills, they should help to disperse and broaden their skillset, mainly because "today's literacies require knowledge of how to use information skills in effective collaboration with others" (53). Scholarship on literacy stewards tends to consider stewards as trusted guardians of literacy, deigning the steward's guardianship of literacy acquisition and textual access as a sacred, higher calling. For these scholars, recognizing stewards of literacy often serves as the first step in creating a more opportunistic democracy in which information can be accessed, shared, and reinforced throughout socioeconomic classes and geographies.

The way that I use the term "stewards of literary" is in the denotation of those within institutions or places of privilege that seek to limit access to literacy, restricting its acquisition, development, or continuance. Much like sponsors, stewards of literacy seek to control literacy from ideological assumptions of protection. In "Layered Literacies," Kelli Cook summarizes the problems that occur when access to literacy is controlled or limited by arguing, "Restricting literacy to such codified skills and forms, consequently, denied the significance of writers' choices for their specific audiences, discourse communities, and social contexts" (9). Most common is the event of literacy restriction and access to literacy education for political reasons; in medieval and Renaissance eras, literacy belonged mostly to those in power: political, religious, or monarchial (Jones 2003). Though literacy expanded in usage and instruction through the Age of Enlightenment, women still suffered from low or non-existent literacy levels as did poverty-stricken sections of almost all European and American cultures (Graff 1979, 1981, Mitch 1992). African Americans were denied literacy acquisition during slavery, but even once emancipated, they did not have access to education or improved literacy due to segregation, biased literacy tests for voting, and oppressive Jim Crow laws that marginalized any efforts towards better education (Royster 2000, Richardson and Johanningmeier 2003, Belt-Beyan 2004). Throughout historical, political, chauvinistic, or racial discriminations and the resulting restrictions of literacy access, literacy stewards had power or privilege to protect their authority by containing knowledge or impeding access to it.

The difference between literacy sponsors and literacy stewards has finer distinctions in mainstream American culture than it does in superhero media.[3] Within superhero narratives, because of the exaggerated narrative form, sponsors and stewards blend together, promoting particular ideological instructions of literacy by sponsoring others through ascertained beliefs and restricting literacy uses through stewardship that aims to protect and sensor information.[4] More often than not, the superhero himself is both the sponsor and the steward of literacy; throughout many narratives, the superhero passes on his literacy events and practices to a younger sidekick or worthy colleague to continue the superhero legacy. However, the superhero often restricts uses of literacy in an effort to maintain and even sequester information that would render the superhero less powerful and more egalitarian if others developed his levels of literacies. Through this lens, stewards not only discourage literacy and specialized literacy skills but also withhold information that developed literacy skills would eventually lead to, restricting knowledge and information flow for some ulterior motives. For both stewards and sponsors, there is vertical dissemination of knowledge in which the sponsor instructs and the steward represses information that flows down to the protégé, including developing literacy abilities.[5] Either way, the protégé is dependent on the sponsor or steward; Graff argues that, historically, literacy has stood "at the center of training that embraced social attitude and control, and civic morality, along with at least a rudimentary intellectual practice" (120). While sponsors of literacy tend to instruct from a place of widening the protégé's knowledge, even if that instruction is deeply entrenched in the sponsor's ideology, stewards focus on the control aspect of literacy, particularly in limiting its access and restricting its development. *Gotham* features two protagonists who have their literacy events curtailed by stewards and who must become their own literacy sponsors to fight against corruption from organized crime and social institutions.

Jim Gordon: A Weary Warrior

Restricted by the texts of his job and the culture of Gotham where the criminal justice and surveillance processes are limited by technology kept by alphabetic, printed texts, Jim Gordon often proves unsuccessful in achieving his goals. He becomes a lone man fighting in a system of low literacy and low intel, unable to overcome the impediments of the restricted system which prohibits the full range of data and information he needs to deliver justice to any needed effort. For the majority of the first season, Jim's abilities to execute actions of the law are impeded by the lack of information he discovers. All data and research in this world exist as written texts. Sometimes the officers have printed, still images that they use to connect cases and coerce suspects, but any moving images on a screen such as a TV camera or news program looks grainy and hard to read. Because Jim cannot rely on digital tools to gather information, all detective work he does must be executed deliberately and carefully. He must piece together information slowly through printed, alphabetic text, and this takes longer to complete then the fast research done in *Arrow* and *The Flash*.

For example, in Ep. 2.3, the officers of the Gotham Police Department are tracking missing Arkham escapees using phone calls, paper trails, and collected files. While the characters discuss different options in hunting down Jerome (a sociopathic maniac who serves as an early prototype of the Joker), the background hosts paper file boxes that are stacked and filled with files, showing the limitations of the detective work in this universe. Later on in the episode, Bruce and Alfred attend a ritzy gala in which a rogue attack occurs, led by Jerome, and Gordon must respond using the technology he has—a cell phone and the broadcast of live TV—which impedes his ability to have better surveillance of the situation. Jim cannot have a bird's eye view of the action like *Arrow* when Felicity hacks security or a digital map of the area that Team Flash has. Jim has only meager tools at his disposal, and often he feels as trapped and helpless by his lack of resources as he does by the bureaucracies and political factions of his city that teeters on the brink of chaos. Students and literacy scholars can observe the limitations of low multiliterate abilities as Jim is frustrated and handicapped by the lack of digital tools to implement change on a superheroic level as Batman later will.

In the fallout of the gala and the taking hostages, new management arrives in the police precinct led by the new chief, Nathaniel Barnes (Ep. 2.4). All the officers stand at attention to watch Barnes who pulls out paper files with the GPD emblem on the front. Marching up and down in the low light of police station, he snarls about the lack of transparency and the abundance of corruption in the department: "I've got your files here. I've read them all." He calls out various names, and once those officers step forward, he then throws the files at each officer, shouting out various accusations for each officer: "Bribery, drug abuse, extortion, racketeering. Sons of bitches. You're all fired!" Though we do not see the actual written accusations, we know the files contain damning evidence, and Barnes' threats—arrest of the indicted officers if they do not leave voluntarily—carry weight because of the textual information inside the closed folders. A few seconds later, Jim is called into the chief's office and gets promoted because of the information that the chief has read about him in his file. Whether promoting or condemning the officers, the files have social weight to them, similar to The List that Oliver uses. In their criticism of textual evidence and literacy events in film, Williams and Zenger note the importance of information in files: "What is actually written in the file almost becomes less important than its talisman-like presence as the container of 'truth'" (2007, 4). This concept of the file as a container to hold information of truth brings an externalized significance to an object of a literacy event that belongs to a particular literacy practice: a significance of criminal justice law and institutional performance reviews.

Part of the information that exists in this world makes finding evidence harder because it relies on printed, traditional forms of textual information. In Ep. 2.8, Jim goes into the chief's office and shows him pictures of crimes, pointing out that the politician Theo Galavan is responsible for a string of criminal activity throughout the city. However, Jim lacks concrete evidence with which the police need to arrest Galavan who has recently been elected mayor of Gotham and has considerable sway over powerful figures in the city. Barnes shakes his head and says, "You want to arrest Galavan? You do the police work and you bring me back some real proof." The show does not clarify what that real proof would look like or what constitutes real proof versus the pictures that Jim has found, but the chief infers that the evidence will exist in some type of hardcopy, printed format. Throughout the show, whenever they work on cases, all the police officers take folders with them throughout the police station. These folders are opened, read, given to another person, added to, and destroyed, depending on the action of the narrative. The information flow becomes static, impeded, forever slowing down the GPD and their effectiveness in curbing crime. The reliance on written texts and the limitations of written texts keep Jim from making the progress he wants in cleaning up organized crime syndicates in Gotham, and we witness his struggles as a multitude of mob bosses, supervillains, and corrupt politicians take advantage of a world with little technology to monitor it.

Bruce Wayne: A Rising Hero

> Although Batman possesses no superhuman powers, he is one of the world's smartest men and greatest fighters (as perceived by the audience, a construct seen in the comics). His physical prowess and technical ingenuity make him an incredibly dangerous opponent [37].
> —Jonita Aro M., "Constructing Masculinity: Depiction of the Superheroes Superman and Batman"

Jim spends most of his time restricted by the low-level literacies of the police department, but Bruce exists on the margins of the established social order of Gotham, both financially and geographically. A preteen from a wealthy, privileged family, cloistered in his family estate, Bruce has opportunities to grow his literacy skills and to create multimodal tools to become Batman in the future. Literacy development, for Bruce, leads him to progress past the numbing grief of his parents' deaths and to set himself objectives in learning and training that provide incentives and directions. Reeling from his parents' deaths, he feels he has to do something, work towards something, and the idea of improving his literacy and comprehension complement his early activities of testing himself (seeing how long he could hold his hand over a burning flame). The externalization of the literacy activities allows him to separate himself from grief to concentrate on a singular activity of detached logic, helping him to narrow his attention to the cold event of reading. Throughout the first season of *Gotham*, Bruce's inadequacy in dealing with his parents' deaths initiates his training as a superhero which involves long hours of reading, studying, and mapping out written connections on a bulletin board that hangs over his study area. For Bruce, literacy and learning facilitate healing from the ramifications of his parents' deaths as he trains to become stronger and more resilient; for Selina Kyle who lives on the streets and commits petty crimes to survive, school learning is entrapment into a system where she is helpless as a young teenage girl with low traditional literacy skills. Both of them do not have formal educational practices yet, but the metaphors for literacy (literacy as survival, literacy as ingratiation into a social system) still heavily influence them.

Though several of the adult characters in *Gotham*, namely Alfred and Jim, try to protect Bruce in the first season and could theoretically be literacy stewards by the methods of which they try to protect him, the most formidable stewards of literacy are the board members of Wayne Enterprises. In Ep. 1.16, Bruce goes before the board of Wayne Enterprises to ask them questions about the company and accuse them of bribery, racketeering, and corruption. Yet, they dismiss his concerns because he has no documented proof; he brings with him a composition book in which he has scribbled down ideas about what he thinks is taking place inside his father's company and the board dismisses his concerns. Because the narration of *Gotham* has emphasized Bruce's capabilities (and because we as the audience know that he becomes Batman), we expect to see him overcome his obstacles through sheer force of will and continue to learn and develop his skills

The members of the board initially treat Bruce's determination to hunt out corruption in the company as a childish endeavor without much of a threat. Later, they hire a rogue agent to scout out what Bruce has discovered thus far, but their interactions with Bruce are ones rife with repressed information because they do not want him to uncover evidence of fraud or extortion. As stewards of literacy, the board deliberately keeps Bruce from information about Wayne Industries, information that would motivate Bruce to act out of moral compulsion and a desire to protect the integrity of his family name. The closest anyone comes to admitting guilt is the chair of the board, Blunderslaw, who informs Bruce that his father knew about the corruption inside the company and did nothing. Rather than give Bruce evidence of Thomas Wayne's guilt or show him any additional information, Blunderslaw keeps whatever textual evidence he has to himself. The confrontation takes place in Blunderslaw's office lined with books and with various files on an immaculate desk, suggesting that there is probably proof of misdeeds inside the office, but Bruce does not have access to them and even if he did, he would struggle to understand the implications that Blunderslaw discusses.[6]

As Bruce is dismissed from the office, the narration implies that any information he finds about the company will be through his literacy development and investigation; he will not find sponsors at his father's company but only stewards who aim to guard, protect, and censor any textual evidence that might reveal the true implications of Wayne Enterprises over the previous years. Similar types of stewards appear throughout the Batman canon, leading to Bruce/Batman acting on his own part to educate himself and not relying on others to train him. In their research about superheroic gifts, Robin Rosenberg and Ellen Winner argue, "Some 'fully human' superheroes, such as Batman and Iron Man are gifted with significantly above average intelligence, but they honed their abilities through intensive and persistent practice" (121). Batman does this, they note, by "systematically learning what he needed to learn and then practicing it until he fully mastered the body of knowledge—whether it was chemical reactions or flying sidekicks" (121). This continual practice is reflected in *Gotham* by the seriousness that the narrative and Bruce show towards the act of learning, of knowledge gathering, of practicing skills repeatedly. Literacy skills are those that require frequent use for mastery, a trait that students can understand from their extensive learning processes in secondary and higher education.

The control and imposed limitations that literacy stewards place on those they want to restrict and subdue often have the opposite effect: realizing their literacy access had been limited, those under stewards may use to the knowledge of the imposition to fuel their literacy events. They feel a need to rebel, fight back, and resist the limitations of the stewards' control. The most striking examples of this appear towards the end of the first season where Bruce, realizing that his parents' company has become infected and corrupt, pushes himself to read, comprehend, and then sort through reports of Wayne Enterprises in order that he may go and accuse them of corruption with the correct evidence. Sometimes exemplifications of the myth for the superhero and its failure to deliver the American Dream for the average American are the main drive behind the superhero's learning process. Like the range of events and practices observed in traditional literacy usage, the reading and building of machines differ from superhero to superhero depending on his or her particular needs.

Early in Season 2, Bruce encounters a locked vault that his father left for him to open. The vault is protected by an encrypted keypad, and after a series of failed attempts to open it, Bruce attacks it in a fit of preteen rage. When that proves futile, he along with Alfred devises a homemade bomb to blow open the door. Inside, a computer with two monitors covered with dust lies on the table (the first computer ever appearing on the show), the implication being that Bruce will have to create other machines to supplement the superhero endeavors and to monitor the city. This small acknowledgment of the literacy that Bruce will have to learn clashes sharply against the overabundance of technical devices that other heroes have. However, Bruce's reaction to the locked door (if you can't get it to work, blow it up) feels slightly out of character for Batman who, in other incarnations of his character, does not resort to destructive tactics but has an array of devices to hack through securities, many of those devices being ones he built himself. This action demonstrates the maturity that he will need to develop later as a superhero; adult Batman cannot react the way pre-teen Bruce does with average capabilities for handling problems. Yet, we as an audience often become so accustomed to seeing a superhero handle a situation that would prove impossible for the average person, and *Gotham* illustrates the distinction between the average person's understanding of machines and the complex multiliteracies of machines that superheroes have developed.

Literacy, multiliterate development, and access to information are all tied to social structures and political power with the city of Gotham. The ideology of the American Dream is a reflection of the ideology of the power of literacy, primarily in its promise to pull individuals out of repression and poverty and into greater social and cultural prosperity, as well as make them important members in their own groups/cultures. It is not surprising that notions of the literacy myth appear throughout superhero media because the myth speaks to our beliefs about the American achievement as well as individualism, a paradoxical state of both belonging to the dominant culture (and submitting to it) while at the same time changing the dominant culture (and overruling it). However, because the narration of *Gotham* has emphasized Bruce's capabilities (and because we as the audience know that he becomes Batman), we expect to see him overcome his obstacles through sheer force of will and continue to learn and develop his skills as he grows in maturity towards the iconic detective and gothic superhero we know him to be.

Chapter Conclusion

This chapter examines *Gotham* as a place of low-technology and mainly alphabetic, print text with traditional literacy events that impede the heroes in their detective work. The term *literacy stewards* refers to those who seek to limit, prohibit, or sanction literacy events for others out of a need to remain in power or maintain the status quo. The two characters examined—Jim and Bruce—participate in different literacy events as Jim works as a police officer within a (corrupt) hierarchical institution and Bruce is training himself independently to become a superhero. The lack of technical software, digital systems, and networked databases defines Gotham as neo-noir and confined by a setting that breeds criminals and obstructs the democratic process of disseminating knowledge and information.

Class Activities

In "Expanding Student Capacities: Learning by Design Pedagogy," Annah Healy clarifies, "Texts are no longer restricted to print technology as multimodality stretches its wings; they rather morph themselves in ways that neither have a standard format nor are bound to genre as we have thought of it in the past" (5). These class activities on *Gotham* allow students the opportunity to research a superhero TV show set in a non-digital, low-tech environment where characters use primarily print, alphabetic text to gather information and collect knowledge. Both Jim's and Bruce's literacy growth translates into greater knowledge capacity, more analytical reasoning, and large processing cognition that continues to expand with each new challenging text, machine, databases, or information system they discover.

Activity 1: How Gotham Limits Literacy Access

Students can see that Jim starts his detective activities in a world limited without technical tools and Bruce immediately starts developing new literacies through his designing of new technologies. By seeing the superhero in training and his early literacy and multiliterate acquisitions, students can compare how literacy perspectives become limited through the construction of divides. Students can understand a culture's role in expanding or limiting literacy activities and how those roles often impose binaries of literacy on its citizens: literate and illiterate, educated and indigent, scholarly and mainstream.

QUESTIONS FOR STUDENTS TO ANSWER:
- How does one's limitations of literacy make one dependent on existing systems?
- How do we need traditional understanding and uses of literacy and how do we expand our own literacies through alphabetic, print modes?
- What would research and communication look like inside communities of *Gotham*?

SUGGESTED READINGS AND QUOTES FOR DISCUSSION:
Brandt, Deborah, and Katie Clinton. "Limits of the Local: Expanding Perspectives on Literacy as a Social Practice." *Journal of Literacy Research*, vol. 34, no. 3, 2002, pp. 337–56.

"In the autonomous model of literacy, the decontextualized text is all important, representing not only the capacity of written language to break free of the limits of time and place but also the capacity of print to reorient sense-making away from the interactive settings of speech and toward literal words on their own. The decontextualizing powers of text were central to the claims that literacy induces changes in thinking and social organization" (Brandt and Clinton 340).

DELIVERABLES OR WRITING PROJECT:
Two paragraphs that clarify how the characters of *Gotham* go about gathering information through written, hardcopy sources and how that compares to how students and other professions now use digital databases and online platforms to gather information.

Activity 2: Researching Literacy Divides

Students can observe the difference between an environment with high, complex multiliterate skills, events, and practices and an environment limited to alphabetic literacy skill. These observations emphasize the split between the usage and effects of not only digital and technology tools available to an advanced culture but also characters who depend on or are made less efficient by the presence or lack thereof of the knowledge and control from digital and technological tools. Henry Jenkins in *Convergence Culture* notes, "If the digital revolution paradigm presents that new media would displace old media, the emerging convergence paradigm assumes that old and new media will interact and ever more complex ways" (6). Both *Arrow* and *Gotham* are based in America (Starling City and Gotham are both fictional urban cities), but their settings differ from the current state of America. By noting the difference between the world of *Arrow* to ours, students can examine superhero multiliteracies that have developed beyond our capacities at the present time. In the same way, students can look at a setting less technologically advanced than our culture and can explore the ways that our literacy and multiliterate activities have contributed to our multicultural identities here in the 21st century.

GROUP ACTIVITIES:

Students discuss the following questions:

- How do *Arrow* and *Gotham* show differences between characters' activities, acquisition, and attitudes regarding literacy, highlighting the role of literacy and multiliteracies?
- How does *Gotham* allow students to look back at past decades of literacy use and see how it shaped access and understandings of human knowledge?
- How does *Arrow* allow students to theorize on literacy uses in the future, a place where human knowledge, communication, and accessibility have reached further advanced states of potential?

SUGGESTED READINGS AND QUOTES FOR DISCUSSION:

Bezemer, Jeff, and Gunther Kress. *Multimodality, Learning, and Communication: A Social Semitic Frame*. Routledge, 2016.

"The affordances of modes enable designers to do finely tuned semiotic work in relation to their interests, shaping their rhetorical intentions and adaption to their sense of the needs of the audience" (Bezemer and Kress 64).

Graff, Harvey. "Epilogue." *Literacy, Economy, and Power: Writing and Research After "Literacy in American Lives,"* edited by John Duffy et al., Southern Illinois University Press, 2014, pp. 203–32.

"Interdisciplinary literacy studies continues to struggle with foundational dichotomies—the making of myths—between oral and literate, writing and print, print and electronic, and literacy as transformative—that continue to guide and divide opinion and orient studies" (Graff 215).

DELIVERABLES:

A presentation that compares and contrasts literacy events and practices in *Gotham* to that of *Arrow*. Other groups might take on a different multimodal, multiliterate world in another TV show or may want to expand to superhero media such as films or comic books to demonstrate a deeper, broader perspective of literacy practices in low- and high-digitally-infused spaces.

Activity 3: Creating New Literacies for Individual, Personal Use

This last activity allows students to use a webpage or portal to explore some of their traditional, print-privilege literacy events. So much of college work still involves deep immersion into traditional texts and learning materials. Being able to concentrate on the written language and deriving meaning and context from it remain valuable skills in college work as well as most careers. While *Gotham* does feel regressive in its lack of digital text, it shows characters working deliberately and diligently towards gathering meaning from these places of limited information.

SUGGESTED READINGS AND QUOTES FOR DISCUSSION:

> Henderson, Robyn. "Mobilizing Multiliteracies: Pedagogy for Mobile Students." *Multiliteracies and Diversity in Education: New Pedagogies for Expanding Landscapes*, edited by Annah Healy, Oxford University Press, 2008, pp. 168–200.

"Knowledge of students and their strengths and weaknesses in literacy learning is an essential component of designing effective literacy pedagogy" (Henderson 184).

> Rice, Jeff. *The Rhetoric of Cool: Composition Studies and New Media*. Southern Illinois University Press, 2007.

"To apply this cool method of writing, students are asked to identify specific cultural influences from their lives. These influences may come from background, school, history, politics, music, objects they've owned, anecdotes, and a variety of other sources" (Rice 71).

MULTIMODAL DELIVERABLES:

A webpage that lets students explore their traditional literacy events through multimodal images, clips, and links.

♦♦ 5 ♦♦

Literacy as Agency and Equality in *Jessica Jones*

> It is important that we continue to expand and critique the ways in which feminist rhetoric and empirical research inform one another and writing studies in our ongoing efforts to realize what we can know, how we can know, who can know, and who can speak of what we know [136].
> —Joanne Addison, "Researching Literacy as a Lived Experience"

This chapter focuses on the three main women of the TV show *Jessica Jones*: Jessica Jones, Trish Walker, and Jeri Hogarth. Each woman has a specific job that demands specialized literacy skills and immersion into specialized texts, both print and digital, that influence her career, requiring her to immerse herself into the language of the career and the knowledge that forms and propels that career. Literacy acquisition has often served as the catalyst in advancing social conditions towards a more-diverse, opportunistic society, and literacy promotion as national and local concerns proved instrumental in assisting women forward in democratic institutions. The many needs for literacy development in careers often reflect Valerie Kinloch's perspective of literacy acquisition: "because literacies occur in multiple contacts, literacy practices cannot exist separate from social institutions" (142). Jessica, Trish, and Jeri's jobs seem relatively gender-neutral, although careers as a private detective and a lawyer often are thought of as men's jobs in spaces dominated by self-promotion and long work hours; how these three women read and improve their literacies speak to their understandings of the importance in which reading, comprehension, and rhetoric have improved the lives of women over the last two centuries. No longer restricted to the option of mother and housewife, women's roles in corporate and consumerism America in the last fifty years reflect educational and technological advances that allowed women to excel and become competitive with men in the workplace.

Women's Work, Education and Literacy Acquisition as Historical Context

Literacy events have facilitated and promoted educational advances throughout changing cultures, technologies, and communities, both macro- and micro-focused. Because of these strides towards equal opportunity in career-choices and education, I make special note here of the technological growth that has encouraged women to pursue jobs outside of the home; the same growth that facilitates Jessica to be a private eye, Trish to work in mass media, and Jeri to do research as a lawyer also creates a world in which survival (food, shelter, clothing) becomes a secondary concern to social and financial success. In his article "A Theory of Motivation," Maslow notes the change a developed nation has on its members:

> The peaceful, smoothly running, "good" society ordinarily makes its members feel safe enough from wild animals, extremes of temperature, criminals, assault and murder, tyranny, etc. [...] If we wish to see these needs directly and clearly we must turn to neurotic or near-neurotic individuals, and to the economic and social underdogs. In between these extremes, we can perceive the expressions of safety needs only in such phenomena as, for instance, the common preference for a job with tenure and protection, the desire for a savings account, and for insurance of various kinds (medical, dental, unemployment, disability, old age) [378-9].

Maslow's article was published in 1943, and in the decades following, the comforts and amenities of America as a first-world country multiplied, often at an exponential rate, with the emergence of complex technology that became available and affordable for the average citizen. For example, the feeding of people in a household had existed as a primary concern for centuries of recorded history, and often women's work that included canning, salting, and preserving food and drink stood as the main catalyst between starvation and survival for many cultures (Thistle 2006). In 1943 at the time of Maslow's writing, many homes had small refrigerators but not freezers so the feeding of the family was still a weekly, if not daily, concern.[1] Today, many Americans in cities and suburbs can order food online via Amazon Fresh and have it delivered within 24 hours. As modern-day life became more convenient, traditional gender roles of the nineteenth and early 20th century underwent massive changes, especially as the technically-enhanced world grew steadily more expensive. As these two changes reconfigured the cultural landscape, educational expansions also were restructured to include large numbers of women who were destined (by choice or circumstance) to join the workforce (Damaske 2011, Greenwood et al. 2012, Strassel et al. 2006).

Stuart Selber in *Multiliteracies for a Digital Age* argues for broader perspectives of literacy as a tool to aid in a workplace of equality, noting that we should "condemn perspectives that understand literacy as a set of value-free skills that can be defined, learned, and measured in absolute terms and whose main purpose is to serve economic development. Such perspectives ignore the integral ties among literacy, power, culture, and context" (27). The role of education in shaping women's literacy practices reflected expansive technological growth; machines replaced workers, and a myriad of new jobs arose to create these machines, oversee these machines, and design more complex machinery (Cortés 2018, Blau and Winkler 2018). The development of the computer as an administrative tool, networking across businesses, and engineering and IT fields all demanded new multiliterate skills. Whereas past literacy campaigns of previous centuries sought to spread mass literacy for religious reasons (Arnove and Graff's *National Literacy Campaigns and Movements*, 1987), literacy campaigns of the last few decades have sought to shape mass literacy for economic prosperity and success. According to F. Niyi Akinnaso in researching literacy as a social consequence, "the forms and functions of literacy itself are a reflection of the variation in cultural history, social structure, and the socioeconomic environment" (109). As American culture has become more egalitarian, the role of literacy has played into reflective understandings of gender and identity through autonomous models of literacy. To keep from falling in the trap of defining feminism through literacy as too autonomous and marginalized, I look at literacy practices of women in superheroes TV shows that become catalysts for their own agency and growth. Literacy development alone is not responsible in creating social change as a feminist movement, but literacy can serve as a tool in equipping women at the margins of the social order to gain voices and individual agency, strengthening the drive to shape communal messages, work, and texts that affect both genders in the workplace.

Jessica Jones, the Private Eye

> I track people for a living. You know how strong I am. So let me get to work in finding her.
> —Jessica Jones, *Jessica Jones*, Ep. 2.2

Jessica Jones in particular demonstrates a need for women to have agency over their own minds, own bodies, and own choices in determining life decisions. As a child with super strength, she spent her turbulent teenage years with a foster family, the Walkers, before working small jobs in early adulthood only to be derailed by Kilgrave whose mind-control kept her as a submissive, brainwashed sex slave for months. Once free from his influence, Jessica's PTSD and trauma often mirror that of Oliver Queen's as both

5. Literacy as Agency and Equality in *Jessica Jones*

heroes have past tribulations and sufferings that made them into formidable superheroes who have trained their bodies and their minds to withstand manipulation and torture. However, whereas Oliver suffers physically from his tormentors such as Slade and the slew of villains he fights, Jessica's psychological trauma (the results of prolonged rape, domestic abuse, and sexual brutalization at the hand of Kilgrave) influence her detective work, her friendships, and her sense of identity. For Jessica, the control of her body is not as devastating as the control of her mind, and the markers of her abuse, unlike Oliver's physical scars and tattoos, are more deeply ingrained in her psyche and mental state and often affect the ways that she acts and interacts with others. As opposed to other TV superhero shows featuring a female hero, Jeffrey Brown argues, "*Jessica Jones* is a modern-day neo-noir series far darker in tone and deals with the trauma of a woman who survived horrendous sexual and psychological abuse at the hands of a supervillain" (2017, 58). Because of this mental abuse, she distances herself from others, particularly her adopted sister Trish, in an attempt to control her surroundings and her interactions with others. Given her self-imposed solitude, her literacy abilities—especially those relying on keen insight and sharp observation—grow stronger the longer she works at her given job, enabling her with the ability to navigate mass media reports, online evidence, and legal documents.

While other superheroes engage in detective work as a way of filtering information to identify villains, Jessica actually works as a private eye with her own detective company: Alias Investigations.[2] The show opens with a demonstration of Jessica's detective skills: as the screenshot approaches the closed door of her office where "Alias Investigations" is printed on a glass window, we as the audience hear an escalating argument between Jessica and the client. When the argument becomes physical, Jessica flings the man through the window, breaking the glass. As he slumps over the broken door, photos flutter to the floor below, evidence of the client's cheating wife. This type of detection feels seedy and below a superhero's usual task, but this type of investigation occupies Jessica's normal work and pays her bills until she gets thrust into a deadly battle of wits with Kilgrave. Jessica tracks patterns of human behavior and activity, predicting other's movements by compiling long lists of data on her targets: where they go, what they do, what crimes they commit or are about to commit, and how best to present damning evidence on their illegal activities.

Throughout the first season, in her cat-and-mouse game with Kilgrave, Jessica's detective skills run a full gamut of information-gathering. She collects clues to track down Kilgrave's movements, visits survivors of his attacks, and works through networks of people that he has used and abused, and she gathers enough data to successfully mount a plan of attack against him. Her literacy skills are always keen towards information gathering, noticing little details that become evidence in her quest to stop her greatest foe. While Luke Cage, her equal in combative strength and superhero fortitude, does his best to stay below the public's radar and hide in plain sight as a mild-mannered bartender, Jessica remains in the center of the action. She does not try to hide her superhero persona like Daredevil but rather lets her physical strength speak for itself. Her physical body, shorter than most of her male counterparts, hides her superhero strength, and she often allows her femininity to assist her in her detective work by pretending to be a nurse or disguising her voice as high-pitched and girly to get information out of other people. In every action, whether in pursuing Kilgrave in Season 1 or Alisa in Season 2, Jessica's greatest powers remain her intellect and quick thinking, both rooted in her multiliterate abilities that she develops from studying human behavior and collecting textual evidence.

Jessica's personality and PTSD become barriers to distance herself from others, and she is abrasive and guarded as a defense mechanism. Despite having an observant eye for idiosyncrasies in human behavior Jessica prefers to work alone with texts, rather than with people, because the texts—legal briefs, news reports, photos, bank statements—do not lie or hide truths from her. Unlike humans who lie out of social niceties or criminal intent, textual evidence has a simplistic honesty to it that Jessica prefers. In the first episode of Season 1, Jessica goes to Jeri to ask for another job, and even though Jeri is reluctant to hire her because Jessica refuses to work full time for the law firm, Jeri finally relents and gives her a court summons to deliver to Spheeris, the criminal owner of a strip club. After tracking down the mobster through a variety of modes—emails, phone calls, credit receipts—Jessica finds the man in a car on a dark street. When he tries to get away, she lifts up the back of his car and slams it down. When approaching him to give him the summons, he threatens to reveal her identity to the world. Scoffing that no one will care, she hands him the papers and takes a picture from her cell phone, documenting the proof that the serving of the summons was completed.[3]

Jessica often acts like an antihero more than a superhero, and her abrasive attitude and sarcastic quips help to alienate her further from others, but despite her attempts to remove herself from social situations, her job as a detective requires a sharp understanding of human behavior and patterns. Other TV shows have embraced the antisocial detective, most notably *Sherlock* and *House* where the titular character's brilliance and sharp intellect permit him to act with impunity and a callous demeanor that supporting characters excuse because he can do what others cannot: solve problems. Jessica's careful reading of others allows her to stay both in the system and out of it, belonging to her world while trying to distance herself from the people inside it. The detective's work aims for two directives: to clarify confusion and

5. Literacy as Agency and Equality in *Jessica Jones*   105

chaos into order and to gather external evidence to provide data for others to follow or use as evidence. Jessica works for Jeri in that capacity—finding and documenting proof of crimes that Jeri can use in court—and continues her detective work in deconstructing mysteries that have personal stakes in her own life.

Her value for human life and the safety of others keeps from killing her enemy even once she realizes she personally is no longer under Kilgrave's thrall. Yet, because he has endangered other people to make her subservient to him, she cannot attack him directly. Once she realizes she has become immune to his thrall, she goes to her old childhood home where he has set up shop and wants her to join him in some type of lovers' utopia of domestic bliss under his control.[4] Jessica goes to the house to collect evidence, preferably through video or audio recording, that Kilgrave had controlled Hope, a former client who murdered her parents after Kilgrave instructed her to. Jessica's instincts as a detective keep her wary and watchful, and she constantly reads and observes the situations in which she finds herself to aim for the best possible outcome. A reluctant superhero, she acts to protect those in danger because she understands what it means to be a victim, to be used and abused without access to agency or autonomy. Jeri and Trish both sympathize with Jessica's need to help the helpless, but Jessica's mission is a reflection of her core drive to protect and avenge, using all of her resources and skills to deliver justice and stop abuse. Her missions, rooted deep in uncovering truths about those around her, require sharp literacy skills that allow for her to interconnect the networks of the information she discovers in individual literacy events of reading and reviewing evidence.

The screen angle of the TV show often focuses on Jessica's eye-line as her main agency to information: her face stays drawn as she reads her surroundings deliberately and carefully. Because TV acts as a visual medium, we as viewers have the same visuals as she does, but we lack clarity of the importance of what we see until Jessica vocalizes what she has noticed. In Season 2 when researching her mother's movements, she lays out a bulletin board of important information and uses the detective trope of connecting separate ideas together with strings, physically connecting information together for clarity. The assimilation of clues into a larger pattern of data remains part of Jessica's strengths as even as a child she noticed Trish's injuries and began at an early age to comply data that would serve her purposes in delivering justice.[5] Her super strength is almost a secondary skillset as her dominant skill— her careful reading of people, documents, pictures, and situations—makes her a daunting foe. She may suffer from relentless depression, PTSD, and a near-nihilistic view of life, but her ability to focus on her job with persistent clarity and determination makes her an effective detective and a formidable superhero.

Trish Walker, the On-Air Host

> You have money, looks, a radio show, creepy if not adoring fans, and you're a freaking household name. What more do you want?
>
> To save the world, of course.
>
> —Jessica Jones and Trish Walker,
> *Jessica Jones*, Ep. 1.5

Bold, beautiful, and polished, Trish is the prototype of a successful woman in the series: a media figure who has embraced the limelight of recognition and social impact. As a child actor with her own show, she now has reached fame and success as a radio host, popular to the point that her face appears on billboards throughout the city. Her literacy abilities speak more to an appropriation of pop culture and trending news than Jessica's or Jeri's. Trish has a handle on mass media and understands what the culture wants to hear, and her femininity and beauty add to her worth as a media commodity for news-hungry America. She has confidence in her abilities and intelligence the same way that Jeri does, but Tricia's nice-girl persona mixes well with her smart, logical assessment of cultural trends and news. Throughout the first season, she feels out of depth in a world of superhero powers and villainy, a place where her appeal and popularity have little sway. Her success as a radio star provides her the wealth to buy accommodations to make herself tough and in control in a world marked by chaos and terrorism; her panic room outfitted with heavy insulation and technological monitoring proves fairly compatible against Kilgrave's vocal persuasion.

A media name and a former child star, Trish's situation highlights the problems with women living in the limelight: they become social commodities to be used and exploited. Paparazzi follow her and document her relationships, and she reveals that a former director sexually abused her when she was sixteen. The only daughter of a media-obsessed mother, Trish fights against not only cultural stigmatization of beautiful women but also her growing helplessness in a world overrun by superheroes and supervillains.[6] When she enters into mass media spaces—the radio studio which hosts her show, the film lot where her former director works—Trish immediately employs her multiliterate skills to gather information and verify data. Trish is highly educated and has both savvy street smarts and media astuteness, but her abilities to thrive in a superhero world depend on improving her body and physique, not her intelligence or multiliteracies.

Part of Trish's frustration stems from the gender prescriptions that have been placed upon her, an expectation that she will remain passive and polite despite whatever calamities fall upon her. As a teen icon, she constantly had to monitor her physical appearance and size, kowtowing to her mother's insistence that she always look and act perfect. In Ep. 2.1, she accuses a former movie director of sexually molesting her as a teenager, and the director snarls at her that she is just "utterly goddamn ordinary." This observation about her acting skills seems to affect her more than his earlier manipulation and harassment; she fears being ordinary and useless in a superhero world. Even after working with a trainer to learn Krav Maga, Trish realizes that these physical training sessions are not enough to make her superheroic when faced against supervillain plots, and she is helpless to fight off the police officer Stenson after Kilgore affects him and sends her to her apartment to kill her. Gender conformity tells women to trust police-officers and remain polite, and she follows those proscriptions enough though her common sense makes her hesitate before opening the door. Cultural prescriptions for women put pressure on them to act and react within the dictates of their larger social practices; Trish feels a need to follow these gendered rules of the social contract (women smile, women are polite, women do whatever a police officer at the door tells them) while Jessica shows contempt for social niceties.

Trish's training in the first season is about improving her stamina and reaction time, but when faced with Kilgore's thrall and Simpson's attacks, she realizes that she must alter her body into that of superheroic status to counteract the challenges she faces. Her quest for super-strength in the second season leads her to take the IGH drug which heightens her reaction time and improves her strength, rivaling her abilities with those of Jessica. Her literacy abilities and her multimedia multitasking become less and less important the further she delves into the gritty, hand-to-hand combat of the superheroes' world. Were she to join a team like that of *Arrow* or *The Flash* or even later become part of the Defenders, she would have valuable abilities to act as a sidekick or a supporting member of the team. Yet, Trish wants more than just to support superheroes; she wants to become one herself. In many ways, she is the mirror opposite of Jessica: Jessica is stand-offish, removed, and self-isolated while Trish is approachable, warm, and supportive. Jessica wants to exist and escape all relationships; Trish wants to matter to the world and prove herself important in all her relationships with family, friends, and love interests. Jessica has developed specialized literacy events that enable her detective work; Trish has groomed her behavior to help her rise to social prominence and recognition.

Her desire for power and control over her autonomy as well as a means of securing her future becomes her greatest motivation and also Achilles' heel as she risks the safety of herself and others to become superpowered. Even though she acts as a voice of the people with Trish Talk, she believes that she needs to be in the fight, not merely observe it. Her sisterhood with Jessica motivated her into stepping from her drug addict days to becoming a powerful voice of the media, but Trish has always had nobler and grander aspirations than Jessica. Jessica desires a place of quiet anonymity, but Trish does not mind the limelight and always wants to be and do more than she can as a mere human being. While other average citizens in their world would be thrilled to have Trish's popularity, good looks, and easy rapport with the media, Trish desires more than public praise and social recognition, two attributes of public adoration that now bores her. She wants to be a superhero for the public and she will use whatever tools at her disposal to accomplish that goal. Part of Trisha's tenacity stems from the fact that as a media figure, she has multiliteracy skills that have allowed her access to the news and to social, local, global, and political movements before other ordinary citizens have learned them. In the first season, she even attempts to take on Kilgore by denouncing him through her radio show, and when that backfires and Kilgore threatens to send a minion after her, she has to recant her position to save not only herself but the lives of others. It is in this hopelessness and power jockeying that Trish constantly lives as she has more notoriety and community recognition then either Jeri or Jessica, but Trish's popularity will never satisfy the need she has to control both her own destiny and the lives of others. Agency and autonomy for Trish in the ordinary human world is not enough; she wants recognition in the superhero world, but she does not have the multiliterate skillsets to let her function as a detective who can gather data to rescue others.

Jeri Hogarth, the Lawyer

> Pretty good for a girl. Then I became a successful female attorney. Read—pretty good for a girl.
> —Jeri Hogarth, *Jessica Jones*, Ep. 2.1

Jessica finds self-fulfillment working alone with texts, and Trish, as a media personality, works best within a culture of people: producers, assistants, managers, etc. Jeri's work as a lawyer has her working equally with texts and people: legal documentation on pages and screens and verbal arguments to move juries, opposing parties, and judges. As a lawyer living in Hell's Kitchen, Jeri's influence and power come from her elevated state of language and literacy. Smart and confident with a keen eye towards the affordances of logistics and legality, she climbs to a position of power in a firm by her sharp intellect, calm demeanor, and ruthless exploitation of the legal system; unfortunately, this legal system that attempts to control the world with ordered, first-world regulations to establish social imperatives operates in a world run amok by supervillains, mob bosses, extortionists, and low-level criminals. "The fact that the existence of superheroes points to shortcomings in the legal system is another reason why it is fruitful to read them vis-à-vis their context of production and the socio-political situation they react to" (Maruo-Schroder 5).

For Jeri, the struggle of an intellectual battle against the physical chaos of a superhero world highlights the difference between spaces of literate activities and spaces that have fallen prey to superhuman force or destruction. In Season 1, she attempts to help Kilgrave as his lawyer, believing herself to be his equal in terms of intellect and power. Annoyed with Jeri's presumptions, Kilgrave commands her ex-wife to kill her in the infamous "A Thousand Cuts" scene, and Wendy obeys by slashing at Jeri with a knife as she counts each cut. Here, we can see the striking difference between Jeri's role as a lawyer at the firm and her inability to withstand brute physical attacks. Literacy in places of established order fall away underneath physical mass assaults because the first is based on the system of social order and the second is based on a system of chaos where the physically powerful and, in superhero terms, those gifted with abilities prey on the weak and the helpless.

Jeri remains powerful in her space of literacy only when she is dealing with those who want something from the social order and its well-regulated system and those who need her to represent them in the eyes of the public because she can manipulate the legal system to afford them more positive, advantageous outcomes than they could get without her legal counsel. Jeri thrives in a space of equality in which men and women—regardless of physical strength, superhero abilities, or access to destructive weapons—can act and interact with impunity, confident within a place of complex ideas and quick wits to manipulate language and texts. As a mediator between acts of blunt force and spaces for higher learning and literacy, the law provides a chance for equality, not only for gender but also for imbalances of age, race, sexual orientation, and geography, promoting ideological altruism for a democratic citizenship. Alison Lee argues, "Situating a study of literacy at the intersection of curriculum, linguistic and feminist theory and analysis allows the possibility of engaging the complex politics of literate practices in specific locations" (8). Within the work of legal concerns, the ability to understand complex language in both written and spoken form relies on the lawyer's skillsets to respond with written and spoken refutations, explanations, and new information. Complex politics of literacy practices require Jeri to devote years to improving her literacy skills, primarily those regarding alphabetic texts and secondarily expanding to multimodal evidence that provides external weight to her literacy and writing events.

Literacy can serve as an equalizer in communities of established order and places where technology and machines provide physical labor such as growing crops, building houses, running hospitals, cleaning up debris, and repairing infrastructure. Once human beings reach a place where the lower levels of Maslow's hierarchy of needs become secondary because they are no longer worried about starving, freezing, or being run over by hordes of neighboring kingdoms, the concern then turns to capitalistic demands where literacy has a more established place. When under attack from her ex-wife or when succumbing to symptoms of her terminal disease, Jeri's literacy abilities are not enough to save her. All the assertive boardroom talk, the calm assertion of power, and the privilege that money and experience can bring her become useless in the onslaught of physical destruction or deteriorating muscular cells. Literacy practices, therefore, belong to the highest order in Maslow's hierarchy of needs, a place where existentialist perspectives of existence allow for one to find meaning, understanding, and knowledge about the way the world operates through textual representations rather than being brutalized by physical forces.

At the end of the second season, Jeri realizes the limits of her potential as she realizes that the body overrules the mind, a metaphorical analogy of the way physical destruction overcomes places of social equality where acts of literacy have importance and an established place in the social order. Jeri has less control over her life and her future opportunities though, on the scale of advanced and specialized literacies, she absolutely dominates Jessica and even has more specialized skills than Trisha. Jeri becomes a casualty of this world, despite playing such a powerhouse in *Jessica Jones*, *Iron Fist*, and even *Daredevil*, because she cannot overcome physical oppression with her specialized skills. When her disease becomes evident, her law partners try to buy her out, citing a medical disclosure clause in her partnership agreement. Jeri goes to Jessica for help, needing Jessica to investigate her two name partners to dig up dirt that she can use for blackmail. In a healthy world, money and power would enable Jeri to remain a mighty player with considerable sway, but all her education, all her training, all her language and literacy events cannot save her from an incurable disease. In the last episode of Season 2, she faces off with her new partners at her law firm, declaring, "Facing death has made me reexamine my priorities." Threatening her partners with exposure of a video of them admitting to money laundering, Jeri gets them to double her severance. Her work—legal and multimodal—facilitate her in having agency at the end, even as the disease robs her of bodily autonomy.

She leaves the old law firm with her clients and starts her own law firm, relying on her carefully-honed skills and specialized literacies, but knowing the end will still come for her. The final scene of Jeri is in her apartment with important papers in front of her: legal briefs, office floor plans, and law books. In between taking pills to dampen her ALS and interviewing new associates, she surveys the beginnings of her new legal, sometimes illegal, empire with evidence of her significance as a powerful player, surrounded by folders and printed documents that she will use for leverage and influence to accumulate more wealth and power. Death may be soon approaching, but Jeri will remain a fighter until the bitter end. In Ep. 2.3, she muses, "It's ironic, isn't it? I've spent my whole life amassing this power and control, thinking somehow it would protect me." Jeri's experience humanizes the story of a woman aggressively using education and literacy skills to rise through socioeconomic hierarchies, but her physical condition also plays a role in determining her fate.

Literacy Events as Opportunities for Equality

> They say everyone's born a hero. But if you let it, life will push you over the line until you're the villain. Problem is, you don't always know that you've crossed that line. Maybe it's enough that the world thinks I'm a hero. Maybe if I work long and hard, maybe I can fool myself.
> —Jessica Jones, *Jessica Jones*, Ep. 1.13

The first season of *Jessica Jones* highlights two tropes used in feminist narratives that have grown repetitive and overused in the last few decades: women traumatized and toxic masculinity. This is not to suggest that these tropes have lost significance; the #MeToo movement stressed the importance of recognizing how women are made objects and tools of men even in our digital, technology-heavy era that ushered in more opportunities for equality. In the second season, we see these three women in search of power and agency over their lives. Literacy acquisition serves as a resource to empower and enforce equality as the main characters move past the arc of the first season—defeating Kilgrave—into pursuing their individual paths. Jessica moves from her trauma as a rape survivor and an isolated superhero into an established detective on the search for her mother. Jeri faces off against the partners in her law firm and uses all her intellect, multiliterate skills, and manipulation to outsmart them. Trish reverts back to her addict days, but this time she chases an enhancement drug which lets her gain superhero powers. The historically male-dominated spaces of superhero narratives sometimes make female superheroes an afterthought, but the literacy practices of female superheroes often become catalysts for their agency and autonomy.

According to Joseph Bianco, living in diverse cultures means we "must be able to adopt a wider vision and envisage a linguistically plural society and future" (100). Jessica and later Trish (through the IGH drug) have superhuman bodies that allow them to combat outside threats, but their jobs depend on analysis and observation of multiple modes of data; the literacy practices of both women involve multimodalities and extensive networking of written and visual systems intended for public consumption. Throughout mass literacy campaigns of western history, the common theme of literacy has a great equalizer has been promoted vehemently by proponents of education; according to Graff, "Literacy was unreflectingly incorporated into the principal narratives of the rise of the West and the triumph of democracy, modernization, and progress" (2014, 206). American culture tends to see literacy acquisition and improvement as the great unifiers and weapons against inequality in matters of class, gender, race, and socioeconomics.

The tentative role of literacy and the way it enables people to succeed or elevate themselves from positions of helplessness to positions of control are evident in *Jessica Jones* because this TV show examines agency through the lens of brainwashing and conformity, first with those under Kilgrave's control and then with the larger social dictations which gender modern-day life, work, and relations. In their research on culture and literacy trends, Cheng-Wen Huang and Arlene Archer note, "Text and literacy practices are socially situated and as students read cultures they come to develop new notions of literacy" (45). Literacy along with specialized education may promote individuals to positions of power and prestige, but they become secondary and of lesser concern in the world fraught by havoc and chaos that threatens the established order. According to Chizu Sato, "many development institutions continue to implement programs that are apparently premised on the myth that achievement of some text-oriented literacy skill by women somehow causes women's empowerment and community and national development" (75). For those existing outside of middle-class securities such as the homeless or those disenfranchised by high poverty areas, the cry usually is for better education and a hand up to elevate people out of their socioeconomic disparity, while ignoring the situations and structure of American institutions that thrive off disparity.

Despite the emphasis that superhero TV shows put on physical activities, literacy skills do not become entirely useless in the face of brute power or mind control. As demonstrated in both seasons of *Jessica Jones*, the technology developed to fight against supervillains and their powers stems from advanced literacy skills that create technologies and tools to counteract evil powers and human brutality. These technologies which allow for gender equality and opportunities in the first place also support superheroic endeavors as far as technology and tools are concerned. Jessica endures as superhero not only because of her physical strength but also because of her detective work, and she would not be able to be as effective in hunting down and fighting the villains of New York without information from both Jeri and Trish. These networked abilities are most effective when in tandem with superheroic efforts to help the general public and to keep others from harm. Although it may seem that sheer strength usually prevails against literacy skills, the advances made through literacies, both ordinary and specialized, simple and advanced, instruct and empower the fight against evil regardless of gender or class.

Chapter Conclusion

This chapter observes literacy as a function of feminism as a historical progression and as a means of creating equality in the workplace. This chapter covers some the literacy events of the three main female characters and their livelihood: Jessica as a private detective who moves from seclusion into community outreach, Trish as a media personality who wants to be a superhero, and Jeri as a lawyer whose physical ailments change her life objectives and decisions. Characters' literacy activities are often changed after traumatic events; characters read, comprehend, seek out, and present information differently after the trauma: to revenge past wrongs, to show self-reliance, to prove sustainability, or to reclaim autonomy. Literacy events as feminism practices work against traditional perspectives of women's abilities and roles in western culture.

Class Activities

Rather than an attempt to divide up literacy events as traditionally masculine or feminine, these activities instead open up discussions about how literacy practices and multimodal multiliteracies have promoted equality in and out of the college classroom.[7] In 1989, Pam Gilbert defined the problems with moving towards a space of feminist literacy:

> a critical consideration of the assumptions upon which language and literacy education is based has not often been a research focus in a consideration of schooling practices disadvantaging young women. Instead, the rather revolutionary shift in language education practices over the past 30 years has been regarded as somewhat of an emancipatory and progressive move, apparently offering equal access to all students, regardless of sex, class or race [257–8].

The intention of these activities is to explore the means by which all people, regardless of gender, can move forward with their literacy practices and achieve new goals in reading, learning, working, and advancing themselves in all spaces of human activity.

Activity 1: Literacy Shaping Discourse Around Gender Equality?

This activity encourages students to look at literacy events and practices correlation with gender and how gender has been used to facilitate social, political, educational, and global ideology. Many superhero TV shows have explored garner disparities, and *Jessica Jones* in particular looks at the coded language which belittles and taunts women: woman as weak, selfish, frivolous, silly, helpless, and/or pathetic. Students can reflect how literacy acquisition and literacy events have participated in reshaping perspectives about gender, and students can observe these perspectives as indicators of the mental processes and logical cognition necessary for literacy activities.

Questions for Students to Answer:
- What current-day technology and resulting literacy practices have helped redefine "work"?
- How do individual literacy events provide opportunities for women to advance their circumstances in capital gain and investment?
- How much do literacy events include activities suited towards the momentum of both genders reaching goals and expanding knowledge?
- How do people—male, female, non-binary—express themselves beyond gender limitations with and through technological improvements?

Suggested Readings and Quotes for Discussion:
Mirabelli, Tony. "Learning to Serve." *What They Don't Learn in School: Literacy in the Lives of Urban Youth*, edited by Jabari Mahiri, P. Lang, 2004, pp. 143–63.

"The concept of multiliteracies supplements traditional literacy pedagogy by addressing the multiplicity of communications channels and increasing saliency of cultural and linguistic diversity in the world today" (Mirabelli 146).

Deliverables or Writing Project:
Students write a short paragraph about how literacy practices have affected, shaped, and changed our understanding of equality. They can use a literacy event from *Jessica Jones* as evidence to support their ideas.

Activity 2: What Other Multiliteracies Do These Three Characters Use?

Jessica Jones does not feature any advanced technology even though it belongs to the MCU which has hyper-realistic technology (Iron Man's suit, S.H.I.E.L.D.'s quinjets, Hydra's surveillance networks). Despite the lack of advanced technology, *Jessica Jones* features multiliterate events when characters engage with texts past those of alphabetic print. Students are able to recognize variations of multiliterate activities when compiling them together as a comprehensive list and marking differences or details about literacy events. Such activities on-screen could include photos, phone messages, medical files, chemistry formulas, etc.

5. Literacy as Agency and Equality in Jessica Jones

GROUP ACTIVITIES:

This group discussion lets a small group tease out individual literacy events for the three main female characters of *Jessica Jones*. The objective here is to divide up episodes or characters so each person in the group can share a part of the research task.

SUGGESTED READINGS AND QUOTES FOR DISCUSSION:

> Royster, Jacqueline, and Gesa Kirsch. "Our Own Stories of Professional Identity." *Rhetorical Voices: New Horizon for Rhetoric, Composition, and Literacy Studies.* Southern Illinois University Press, 2012, pp. 3–12.

"I have had a long-standing interest in and concern for including women's voices, visions, and experience in our work, for allowing them to speak—and be heard—in their manifold expressions, well beyond the 'museum pieces' they so easily become when we impose our values, views, and judgments upon them, speaking for or about them, not with them" (Royster and Kirsch 4).

DELIVERABLES:

Groups present for 6–12 minutes, highlighting how each of the three characters utilizes her own literacy skills to reach objectives and defeat enemies and/or personal demons.

Activity 3: How Female Superheroes Utilize Literacy

This multimodal activity gives students a chance to research primary superhero texts beyond *Jessica Jones*. This could include female superheroes in other narrative modes: Black Widow from *Avengers*, Supergirl from the 1990s comics, or Wonder Woman from the videogame *Injustice: Gods among Us*. Students can explain the connections between the superhero's human job/persona and their superhero work.

SUGGESTED READINGS AND QUOTES FOR DISCUSSION:

> Stuller, Jennifer. "What Is a Female Superhero?" *What Is a Superhero?*, edited by Robin Rosenberg and Peter Coogan, Oxford University Press, 2013, pp. 19–24.

"Thematically, the female experience of superheroism appears to differ most from that of men in it focuses on collaboration, love, and mentorship, which prompts questions about whether the ways in which these ideas play out in the lives of superwomen express or are representative of something distinctly female or are indicative of limited ideas about femininity" (Stuller 20).

> Vie, Stephanie, and Brandy Dieterle. "Minding the Gap: Comics as Scaffolding for Critical Literacy Skills in the Classroom." *Composition Forum*, vol. 33, 2016, n. pg.

"Thus, using critical literacy as a framework, students were guided to consider the ideologies (whether overt or subtle) at work in the comics they read and to research how these ideologies might be translated, represented differently, or repudiated in media coverage. In other words, students had the opportunity to explore feminism critically by looking at multiple perspectives of feminism" (Vie and Dieterle, "Minding the Gap").

MULTIMODAL DELIVERABLES:

A webpage comparing three female superheroes and their particular literacy events. Students could use a blend of images, embedded clips, and written paragraphs to convey meaning and illustration of literacy events.

♦♦ 6 ♦♦

How Ethnicities and Local Communities Shape Literacy in *Luke Cage*

> At first glance, you might think the new Netflix series *Luke Cage* is just another platitudinous superhero drama from Marvel Comics. But, there is something quite different about this hero: the hero is a dark-skinned black man dressed in a black hoodie [12].
> —J. Corey Williams, "*Luke Cage* and Police Brutality"

This chapter looks at the Netflix series *Luke Cage* and the different literacy practices that belong to urban settings and minority populations. Just as the imbalance of gender plagues superhero narratives, most superhero narratives also are saturated in white, middle-class culture.[1] Against this marginalization, the characters Luke Cage and Misty Knight illustrate assumptions about superheroes and their cultural identities that have long defined pop culture and its portrayal of literacy practices. The markers of ethnicity in the literacy practices of superheroes often are the result of racial and social bias, rooting connections between privilege and access to developing multimodal multiliteracies. This chapter explores these two main characters of *Luke Cage* before examining myths about literacy and the larger education system which exist for black superheroes that do not exist for white superheroes. By studying cultural spaces of literacy as communal influences on minority groups as developing local language usages, we can understand better the ethnographies of tight communities that face opposition from dominant cultural forces.

While other superhero media take place in expansive spaces across large cities, *Luke Cage* is grounded in the community of Harlem as a subset of the New York City and the lives of the people that live there, fight there, and die there.[2] In the MCU, the character Luke Cage first appeared on the first season of *Jessica Jones* as a romantic interest of Jessica's who works at a nearby bar and is impervious to harm. As the show advances, the narration reveals that Jessica had inadvertently killed Luke's wife, Reva, while under Kilgrave's thrall, and at the end of the first season, Luke is also affected by Kilgrave and tries to murder Jessica. However, the beginning of *Luke Cage* sees Luke back in Harlem, acting as a reformed criminal and normal everyman who seems content to remain low-key and act as an ordinary member of his community. When criminal enterprises threaten the safety of those in Harlem, Luke decides to out himself as a superhero and in doing so reveals that he, like Jessica, can perform extensive detective work alongside the work of a recognizable superhero to protect those vulnerable and marginalized.

Luke and Jessica also have roles in *The Defenders* (2017), but his presence in the first two seasons of *Luke Cage* demonstrates both his quiet intellect and ingrained literacy skills as a reflection of the community that he serves. As the first TV show to feature a titular African American superhero and mostly minority cast, the ways that his literacy events affect both his superhero and human personas speak to an understanding of literacy practices and events from minority communities. With the examination of Luke Cage, the presence of literacy myths, first introduced by Harvey Graff in *The Literacy Myth* (1979), direct the theoretic approach in this chapter. I also make connections between the literacy myth and the implication that literacy and knowledge can have in gaining power and sustaining it. Research on the literacy myth has explored beliefs about literacy acquisition on large, national scales (Arnove and Graff), but I emphasize in this chapter the importance of understanding implications of the myth in the marginalized characters of *Luke Cage*.

Urban Literacies for a Struggling Community

> We suggest that literacy sponsorship needs to be evaluated within the context of the multiple identities that race, gender, class, and ethnicity, among other identity markers, require us to negotiate [153].
> —Beverly Moss and Robyn Lyons-Robinson, "Making Literacy Work"

Early work on literacy studies sometimes spoke too broadly about the functionality of literacy through events and practices, but any literacy activity must take place in local settings that depend on the reader's task at hand. These activities reflect the ethnographic circumstances of the reader. The opening episode of *Luke Cage* begins in a local neighborhood barbershop in which Luke works for an elderly man named Pops. As the episode progresses, we learn that Pops was a former gang member who, after going to prison, reformed from being an important player of a local drug cartel to a respected member of his community. Acting as Luke's mentor, Pops stresses the importance of young people, especially boys, having a place and communal support to develop themselves as they grow into young men. This barbershop acts as a local hangout where various members of the neighborhood, both the lawful citizen and the gang member, come to hang out and discuss their lives, including their ideologies about the political stability of the neighborhood.

In researching the connection between local spaces and literacy activities, David Cole and Darren Pullen insist that "multiliteracies are concerned with the establishment of civil and prolific society, and this will happening through strengthening the educational mores" (3). Pops' barbershop serves as a space in which multiliterate activities of a predominantly ethnic community can shape language and prosperity of those inside the community. In the second episode, Luke and Pops discuss different black poets and writers as influential voices of Harlem, grounding the space and its historical circumstance in the important role that Harlem played in the shaping of the people that live there. In examining *Luke Cage*'s Harlem as a place of reinvention, Lea Garrido notes,

> It is striking that Harlem's urban space serves as the starting point for a discussion about racism in the United States that exceeds the discussion in dominant U.S. media outlets today. […] The doubtlessly specific and singular experience of Black Americans in the United States, however, also points to a larger tradition of Western historiography that continuously peripheralizes and erases experiences of those who are marginalized—and, given police brutality and vigilantism, are often literally erased—in society as well [11].

Likewise, Mariah's insistence on revitalizing the community focuses on the Crispus Attucks Complex, a building named for the first black man to take up arms against the British in the fight for independence centuries before.

As *Luke Cage* demonstrates, minority communities frequently rise up as a part of their own individual and idealistic cohesion, separating themselves away from more dominant national communities that have long oppressed and rigorously controlled minority people's actions, language, and access to literacy instruction. In comparison to *Daredevil* and *Jessica Jones* which occupy other sections of New York, Harlem feels isolated and removed from the large hustle and bustle of New York life and culture. The buildings are shorter, the streets reflect urban decay from the massive amounts of people cramped into small apartments, and the streets are narrow and riddled with graffiti. According to Rhea Lathan in her work on local literacies, "To the extent that any African American literacy theory embraces a broad spectrum of the African American Community, it must also consider the institutions, spiritual ideologies, and consciousness—thinking and souls—that connect the community individually to larger social systems" (43). The literacies that emerge from these community-infused spaces speak to the lives that have enacted themselves through daily and elongated choices.

In *Luke Cage*, Harlem houses many ethnicities from multiple walks of life: Mariah the corrupt congresswoman, Pops the barber and reformed criminal, Cottonmouth the drug kingpin, Misty the police detective, Scarfe the crooked cop, as well as smaller characters like the dancers at the nightclub, a lawyer whose son visits the barbershop, and gang members that attack Luke. These different walks of life each require different literacies, different aspects of a community that work within urban literacies. Valerie Kinloch explains her unique understanding of urban literacies: "I rely on the framings of literacy as an ideological and as a social practice as I move towards an understanding of urban literacies that are grounded in the history of Black cultural ways of being and its attention to identities, power, and living conditions and urban contexts" (141). From these multiple and diverse literacies fused from historical contexts, we can see the development of communities struck by poverty and lack of opportunity that limit the choices of those living within the communities. Their local literacies address immediate needs of marginalized communities who face additional repression and exploitation from other dominate communities who regularly decry urban groups as an Other.

Much of the growth of literacy in minority populations stems from racial oppression and lack of resources which rose to a crescendo in the mid-1900s. Kinloch insists, "The history of struggle that Black people have endured lends itself to investigating the movement of Black people into urban centers and the subsequent literacy practices they employed that forged pathways into economic, educational, political, and social justice" (143). As a cry for equality, for an America that welcomes diversity and creates opportunity across all communities, literacy campaigns have attracted scholars across broad educational disciplines, but much of the literacy outreach in schools was not to improve the social order but to maintain it and reinforce the hierarchy of the status quo, especially during the segregation years. Harvey Graff in *The Labyrinths of Literacy* explains that historically "schooling in literacy, thus, was useful to the efficient training of the population to the social order. [...] Literacy was hardly a goal, for isolated from its moral basis, literacy was feared as potentially dangerous" (39). Literacy thus occupies a double-edged sword in most social and political arenas: it offers liberation from poverty and oppression; at the same time, learning better, more advanced literacies solidifies individuals into the social order.

In researching local literacies that emerge in urban settings, Kinloch notes, "The literacy practices we employed (e.g., reading/writing in the world, documenting community conditions, critiquing community changes, using African American Language, engaging in cultural practices) stemmed from actions we experienced in the community" (142). In *Luke Cage*, these literacy practices stem from daily events in which survival habitually becomes a primary focus. The show features small businesses and small business owners who are trying to scrape together a living in a place that seems left behind by the rest of the 21st century in technological advances and superhero endeavors. The greatest tool at anyone's disposal seems to be the handgun which causes the death of so many characters and random citizens in the show, and the fight for survival trumps any literacy learning as an attempt to get out of poverty. The concern of the violence and nihilism of the gangs remains an important part of the average citizen's life, limiting opportunities or upwards movement of economic prosperity for citizens trapped in poverty. Most of the young teenagers seeing hanging out at Pops and admiring Luke's powers are told to go home and do their homework or are encouraged to hang out in the barbershop and play video games rather than getting caught up in the local drug trade. The concerns of communities in Harlem belong to the lower stratosphere of Maslow's hierarchy: safety needs for the individual that lead to security, employment, and resources. Because basic literacy is higher on the scale (love and belonging/esteem) and multiliterate skillsets are near the top (self-actualization), educational needs cannot be acted upon until safety and security are delivered.

However, like most literacy sponsors, those worried about the future of their children have bought into the myths of literacy and education that control their lives. In her observation of literacy narratives as reflections of community standards, Mary Hamilton notes, "Literacy studies can draw valuable insights from analysing the ways in which these narratives of everyday experience are constructed, sponsored and received: how they move within public discourse and make claims to the authenticity of first-hand knowledge" (504). Because politics and criminal activities are closely intertwined with Mariah and Cottonmouth's criminal enterprises, characters lack opportunities to escape criminal and violent threats, and even if escape through learning and self-improvement were feasible, the community center in Harlem is funded by Mariah's money through Cottonmouth's gun trading and drug distribution. Cottonmouth's thugs shake down some of the local businesses to extort money to pay for favors and protection from the violence of rival gangs, especially Diamondback who leads a Latino gang but also controls weapons and drugs. In "Multimodality and Sensory Ethnographies," Abigail Hackett insists, "Multimodality and ethnographies of literacy practices have for a number of years been concerned with multiplicity (of communicative modes, of meaning making, of literacies) and particularly with the non-linguistic aspects of how people communicate" (304). However, when that multiplicity of meaning consistently reaffirms the instability of a tenuous system run by leaders desperate to remain in wealth and power, complexities of language and therefore literacy often fall away as a physical language emerges: that of deadly violence and brute force which silences communities into submission.

Access to literacy and the affordances it can bring can play a dangerous role in upsetting the hierarchy of the local criminal organizations. In Ep. 1.4, after Luke attacks the community center where all the illegal drug money is stored, Cottonmouth instructs his men to retaliate against Harlem by extorting all small businesses for more cash and blaming the crimes on Luke Cage.[3] One of Cottonmouth's men is reading a book about the history of Harlem and the different ways its leaders acted and reacted in political movements of past decades. When this member speaks up about the possibility of passive resistance as a way to deal with threats to the drug empire, Cottonmouth responds by shooting him in the head. The other gang members are immediately scared into silence and instant obedience, and the scene shows the importance of literacy stewards in the world of organized crime in which fidelity to the leader takes precedence over any personal or educational advances.[4] In her research on literacy myths, Carol Mattingly argues, "Recent literacy studies affirm the complex circumstances that influence literacy acquisition and the difficulty in achieving literacy for groups who have been historically regular gated to illiteracy and oppressed in other ways" (49). This oppression comes from multiple angles including leaders within the community of Harlem who use historical oppression of minorities to their own advantage, restricting both language and literacy that might threaten their power. Through observing the literacy inside urban communities and the barriers to education, students can identify markers of oppression and repression that plague those trying to reach higher levels of self-actualization and security.

Luke Cage

> I'm Luke Cage. You can't burn me, you can't blast me, and you definitely can't break me. You wanna test me? Step up. I'm right here. I ain't going nowhere. You know where to find me. I am Harlem, and Harlem is me.
> —Luke Cage, *Luke Cage*, Ep. 2.1

Luke Cage as a superhero is unique in his creation and his response to his powers. He becomes superhuman by undergoing an experimental process while in prison and receives his superhuman strength and regeneration from a freak accident. After breaking out of the prison and marrying Riva, the psychologist who counseled him while in prison, Luke ignores his superhuman abilities and instead focuses on trying to remain underground and hidden. Even once his wife is killed, Luke does not go after her killer or try to hunt down her assailant, preferring to grieve in private while working at a bar

6. *Literacy in* Luke Cage

near Jessica Jones' apartment. At the beginning of *Luke Cage*, he works at a barbershop and keeps a low profile that speaks more to his reluctance to test and prove his own powers than it does his desire to avoid the limelight. Much of his superhero status conflicts with his desire to keep cool and calm as he fears a lack of control or loss of self-possession will result in mass destruction. His fear is not entirely unfounded as, when Luke does face off against assailants, he proves almost indestructible to hand-to-hand combat, bullets, explosives, and other types of assault, and he could easily annihilate his foes by tearing them apart. In his research on Luke Cage, Ramzi Fawaz defines his inner strength and character: "Though marginalized at the level of race and class, he is depicted as the paragon of black masculinity. His embodiment of ideal manhood (especially in the visual depiction of his hypermasculine black body) compensates for these forms of marginalization" (192). Luke's brute force conflicts with the quiet moments when he reads from leaders of the Harlem Renaissance and the Civil Rights, and he appears as a man continually torn between opposing binaries: help Harlem citizens vs. abandon them for mistreating him, resist the plays for power in his community vs. succumb to the lure of power, endorse passivity and education vs. physically pummel opponents into broken submission.

In their comparison of Luke in the Netflix series to his origins in comic books, Ken Derry et al. note that Netflix Luke is "much quieter, a more thoughtful and reserved; instead of shouting bombastically and punching supervillain, he reads books and eschews violence" (127). At the opening of the show, we see him working as a janitor cleaning up at a barbershop and a dishwasher in a nightclub to make ends meet. He keeps a low profile to avoid detection, but he has sharp intelligence and detective skills that enable him to notice and make connections that others do not see. When he does step into detective work, he participates in the normal activities of tracking down people that Oliver, Barry, Jim, and Jessica all utilize. In Season 1, when tracking down Diaz all through Harlem when he is worried that Cottonmouth's men will kill Diaz next, Luke collects evidence to supply himself with enough information to track down the scared gang member.[5] As Luke uncovers more information, he realizes that his family connection has contributed to the decay of Harem. Diamondback is his brother, and they were both raised under the guidance of a father who was ultimately disappointed in both of them.

When talking with Claire about his prison stay, Luke remarks that he feels that going to prison even though he was innocent was something that grieved his father, and this disappointment pushes Luke to judge himself and his own choices as well as lack of opportunities much more harshly than any character that he encounters. While Matt Murdock enjoys his actions as a superhero and serves his people as the guardian of Hell's Kitchen, Luke seems much more reluctant to take on the mantle of a superhero and even when acting under superheroic circumstances, he seems more disappointed by criminal activities rather than angry at them. Lea Garrido notes, "As a result of experiments conducted on him while he was falsely imprisoned, Luke's bulletproof body constitutes a symbolic space in which the perpetuation of state violence against racialized bodies in the United States is negotiated" (2–3). Luke's education and literacy skills have enlightened him, prompting him to act as a beacon of inspiration to his community, a means to escape the circle of poverty and the inevitability of illegal activities that desecrate Harlem.

Some of this disappointment may stem from the fact that throughout both seasons in his various strolls through Harlem, he fights against gangs from his own community, people that scrape together a living and, when faced with a lack of opportunity, turn to criminal activities as a means of survival, not prosperity. Luke appears angry when someone tries to shoot him or otherwise harm him; the resolution on his face as he counteracts attacks and subdues opponents is vaguely reminiscent of Batman's countenance in the comics and the Arkham games when he fights against criminals from his own city, Gotham. Other law enforcement characters such as Misty Knight and Jim Gordon from *Gotham* to have to apprehend people in their community, sometimes leaders in their community who have used the disadvantages of their people for their own self-indulging success. Luke's connection to Harlem plays out in the quiet moments in the first two episodes when he works at the barbershop with Pops and enjoys reading works by black writers and poets during his off-time. Luke imagines Harlem as a place where great artists and great thinkers can still thrive, and although his jobs require lower-level literacies, he still participates in a culture that thrives through spoken and written language, preferring to read about the movements of historical figures in Harlem and admire them as creators of aesthetic beauty that his crime-ridden community once created and promoted.

In "Unlocking the Cage: Empowering Literacy Representations in Netflix's *Luke Cage* Series," S.R. Toliver states, "Literacy stands out in *Luke Cage* because it is heterogeneous and counters ideologies about black male literacy, specifically because of the reliance on literature throughout the show" (4). In the opening of Season 2, Luke wears a hoodie with the words "African American College Alliance" in bold letters, wanting to inspire the youth of Harlem to go to college.[6] Mainly, he keeps the promise of the American Dream and the hope of prosperity as his mission; in the last episode of Season 1 after defeating hordes of criminals, he states, "Harlem is supposed to represent our hopes and dreams. It's the pinnacle of black art, politics, innovation. It's supposed to be a shining light to the world" (*Luke Cage* Ep. 1.13). For those hopes and dreams to have the possibility of actuality, Luke remains a beacon for the people of Harlem, an intersection of their reality and their optimism. When observing the range of Luke's actions through the two seasons—passive moments reading books to bullet-flying scenes of Luke breaking assailants' bones—students can witness the conflicts of the mind and the body as representations between ideologies of a community and the forces of reality that regularly erase, subjugate, or falsify those ideologies.

Misty Knight

As a counterpart to Luke, Misty connects to Harlem through her childhood years and her present-day police work in the community. As opposed to Luke whose superbody allows him to engage in brutal combat without fear, Misty has to rely on her instincts as a detective, utilizing her multiliterate abilities through a careful process of examination and logical structuring. Throughout Season 1, Misty sits in her office at the police station, staring at grouped photos of crime scenes and recreating the actual crimes visually. This recreation acts as her literacy event, grounded in visuals, but still reading for clues and meaning, thus enabling her to perform her job efficiently. According to Claudia Mitchell and Casey Burkholder in "Literacies and Research as Social Change," "To contextualize research for social change as a literacy practice, we acknowledge the New Literacy Studies' assertion that language and literacy are multiple, rather than singular and autonomous" (651). Misty's specialized visual literacy, one of her many literacies as a detective, intersects both message and meaning into the language of the photos. Often, photos are ignored as a part of literacy events, but they have significance in professional jobs, especially those in criminal justice where meticulous records must be taken and interpreted regularly.

Misty frequently seems at odds with Luke as his reactions to threats tend to be physical and immediate; her best detective skills lie in her ability to read a crime scene from pictures that of the scene. The narration of the show makes her literacy events ambiguous as to whether she has a superpower of observation or whether she has developed this literacy skill so finely to the point that she can recreate an image from pieces of evidence that connote a visual aftereffect of the crime. In Ep. 1.2, she can read the pictures of the gunfight crime scene (a shootout between Cottonmouth's gang and Colon's gang over territory) to the extent where she recreates the crime scene as if she were actually there when the violence occurred. The bleak police office falls away, and she stands in the middle of the street, watching the various victims and shooters move in slow motion as the bullets fly and bodies fall. With a blink of her eye, she returns to her office, and we as the viewer see the pictures fill up her walls, grouped around one incident after another.

We realize that her work as a detective requires a highly-specialized literacy: the ability to connect visual texts into actual movements and then to transfer that information into written reports. Work in the field of criminal justice results in deliberate literacy events, carefully planned and meticulously executed in every step of the detective's work, to keep social systems running. The paperwork compiles and details evidence of crimes, paperwork that must be filed into the court systems and used by the D.A.s and their deputies to prosecute criminals.

In Season 2, Misty returns to Harlem, coming back from the events of *The Defenders* with a missing arm and claims her police days are over. However, by the end of Ep. 2.1, she returns to her job as a detective, causing Luke to comment "It's good to see you back where you belong, Misty." Suspects, criminals, and even coworkers ridicule her disability, but her multiliteracies and detective skills remain just as strong.[7] In Ep. 2.5, she goes back to her office and sees a note from Danny and Colleen (characters from *Iron Fist* that also appeared in *The Defenders*). Misty unfolds a graph of paper and sees the schematics for a bionic arm, designed especially by Rand Industries.[8] By Ep. 2.7, she has returned to her early methods of reading images of crime scenes; her make-shift office in Luke's shop now has pictures and maps on the walls as she and Luke discuss Piranha, the new criminal mastermind terrorizing Harlem. In the last episode of Season 2, Misty reads the boards on the walls one last time; this time, the walls have police reports and crime-scene photos, letting Misty read the scene and recreate the sequence of violent movements. Unlike Mariah who spouts empty rhetoric, Misty actually wants to make Harlem safe and uses all of her powers of reading, observation, intelligence, and detection to achieve her goals. When surveying the extension of her multiliterate abilities, she stands in direct contrast to Luke and his skills: he has a penchant for the beauty of language in written prose and poetry, and she has keep insight into the visual representations of physical spaces, a spatial literacy.[9]

Enduring Literacy Myths

Usually when social and political institutions invoke literacy practices, these invocations involve beliefs about literacy acquisition that over-estimate the role the literacy plays in shaping communities, especially those socially-disadvantaged. **Literacy myths** are the beliefs that education generally and literacy specifically can lift individuals out of poverty and guarantee them success, ignoring the complex culture of modern American life that reinforces racial discrimination and stereotypes. Literacy and educational myths have proved the most challenging because of how ingrained and resilient they have been in their continuation, effect, and renewability for each rising generation. I stress, though, that to observe literacy events and practices in superhero TV shows, we must first arrive at the understanding that those events and practices and even the superheroes themselves are created through general perspectives of the literacy myth. In *Literacy Myths, Legacies, & Lessons* (2011), Harvey Graff provides a succinct description of the literacy myth:

> The Literacy Myth refers to the belief, articulated in educational, civic, religious, and other settings, contemporary and historical, that the acquisition of literacy is a necessary precursor to and invariably results in economic development, democratic practice, cognitive enhancement, and upward social mobility [35].

His research explores the distinction between what social institutional practices promise that literacy can do and what literacy actually does and the fallout when those promises about literacy education do not deliver socioeconomic prosperity.

Literacy studies parallels with American history, Graff argues, because "we cannot ignore literacy's history, one which intersects vitally with the course of social change and development—especially in the centuries since the invention and spread of printing. Nor can we neglect the relevance of that history has to modern social thought" (10). Elements of the literacy myth are rooted deep within the fabric and layers of American culture, and to counteract the myth would require, as Graff argues, "recognizing literacy and the literacy myth as ideology and also as culture, and criticizing that ideology and culture. It also mandates critical exploration of the relationships between and among material reality, social relationships, institutions, policy, expectations, and social theory" (2010, 638). According to Mike Rose in *An Open Language*, we should question the assumption that "literacy is the premium mobile in social-cultural changes" (225) and should instead view literacy as a part of "a complex interaction of economic, political, and religious forces" (225). Neither Graff nor Rose claims that literacy is not important, but that western, social tendencies to treat it as an independent but all important variable—to esteem it too highly, to credit its advantages too much, to overvalue the possibilities of its acquisition—results in hyperbole around literacy studies.[10]

As is demonstrated through both seasons of *Luke Cage*, the interplay between ideology and culture remains important in understanding the literacy myth; the ways we conceive of literacy both in practice and education become fundamental in deciphering the ways we understand and react to our culture's prescriptions about education as means of social mobility. In discussing literacy as linked to ideology, Don Kulick and Christopher Stroud stress, "The problem, however, is that by attributing agentive power to literacy, one tends to diminish or disregard the role which human agents play in the processes of acquiring and maintaining literacy" (251). In this acquiring and maintaining, literacy and its beliefs influence ordinary American lives from all aspects: top-down political movements such as organized national literacy campaigns, horizontally through our interactions with colleagues and peers that embody our beliefs about literacy acquisition, and bottom-up from concerns of poverty through grassroots organizations aimed at using literacy to counteract socioeconomic constraints as Linda Flower's *Community Literacy and the Rhetoric of Public Engagement* demonstrates. Flower defines literacy as "an action and a practice: a literacy action taken to support agency, understanding, and a justice; and a rhetorical act built on the social ethic" (7), and in doing so her views on the possibilities of literacy (namely a means to bring agency to silenced, impoverished communities) clash against Graff because she places too high expectations on literacy as an independent variable to elevate urban communities.

In *Luke Cage*, we see this struggle between binaries of literacy reverence and literacy limitations: characters want to escape their situations in lower-socioeconomic straits but education is not enough (all Luke's reading and pacifist ideology will not stop Cottonmouth's violence), and community opportunities cannot counteract the years of America's racist, gerrymandering, gentrification, and oppression of minority groups. Even if myths of literacy and education prove unreliable and faulty in its results, the myths endure because the belief in the American Dream persists as it is encouraged by the institutions which deny it to those desperate to achieve it. Graff in *Literacy Myths, Legacies, & Lessons* argues, "For better and for worse, *the Literacy Myth* reflects and grew from the unprecedented interest and concern about education's relationship with social inequality, declining cities, race, discrimination, poverty, and the radical analysis and prescriptions that accompanied them" (57).[11] The circular nature of the myths continues because American mainstream culture needs to believe in the certainty of literacy's power to keep reinforcing its dependency on its values and ideology. In the words of Gloria Ladson-Billings, "Is it possible, then, that more holistic, sociocultural approaches to literacy can hold some promise for the development of literacy among African Americans?" (381). Luke Cage offers students the opportunity to see the development of literacy, acting as S.R Toliver "a site of struggle that negates harmful ideological constructions of black male literacy practices by promoting empowering depictions" (Toliver 2).

In "The Literacy Myth at Thirty," Graff argues that the literacy myth is often misunderstand because it exists "apart from and beyond empirical evidence that might clarify the actual functions, meanings, and effects of reading and writing. Like all myths, the literacy myth is not so much a falsehood but an expression of the ideology of those who sanction it and are invested in its outcomes" (638). No matter how much Luke, Misty, Claire, or other characters develop their literacy skills, they still live in a place overrun and controlled by criminal activities. Many of the literacy practices and events in *Luke Cage* reflect tendencies towards the myth as characters share the beliefs that better literacy practices and learning skills will eventually lead to economic prosperity. In this venue of thinking, the myth becomes synonymous with the American Dream and all its idealized, middle-class, socioeconomic freedom. All of the components of the literacy myth—a pinnacle of perfection, the reliance on the hierarchy of institutional powers for success, the continued promise of what literacy development and growth can deliver despite what it actually does deliver—appear in superhero media, but they become even more overt and emphasized in *Luke Cage* as the show focuses a community fraught with poverty and criminal movements.

Markers of the myth are exaggerated and embellished, but they endure as possible potential simply by the existence of the superhero. We as the audience already must suspend our disbelief enough to believe in the realistic appearance of the superhero. Taking that disbelief one step further—superhero can become all powerful and heroic by sheer force of his own resilient will—is to follow most of the ramifications of the American Dream, that success and prosperity depend on one's will and efforts. Therefore, viewing the superhero as the embodiment of the myth lends believability to superhero skills. If we think, subconsciously or even unconsciously, that literacy can situate an individual into any avenue of success, the fact that superheroes use literacy in their quest to become superheroic fits neatly into the ideology of American culture's beliefs about pathways to prosperity. Through performing reading events and pushing themselves into greater literacy practices, superheroes develop their specialized literacies which require this supposed resiliency, durability, and persistence. Advanced and specialized literacies mean little in a world terrorized by violence and brutality, all controlled by powers that exist outside the social order by those acting in direct defiance of the social contract. Against the social pressures and external motivations of criminal enterprises, Luke and Misty's endeavors to assist the citizens of Harlem offer a means to escape poverty and violence, thus keeping the embers of the American Dream alive and glowing.

The circumstances of the myth in superheroic narratives mirror our investments in our educational and capitalistic culture, and the myth is particularly attractive in regards to superheroes because it implies that with enough effort, time, and money, we can all become superheroes. The literacy myth does not simply fit superheroes; they are the literacy myth. They become the embodiment of what self-instruction, funds, and perseverance can accomplish if one just commits to an ideal; just as literacy is "represented as an unqualified good, a marker of progress, and a metaphorical light making clear the pathway to progress and happiness" (Graff, 2011, 39), so superhero narratives continue myths about intelligence and assessment of information. These myths about possibilities of success, power, and control persist because "like all myths, the literacy myth is not so much a falsehood but an expression of the ideology of the those who sanction it and are invested in its outcomes" (5). In much the same way, we—the audience of superhero media—see our ideology infused in superhero media and thus the draw of such narratives becomes a vicarious, nearly voyeuristic portrayal of the pinnacle of American cultural achievement. The end of Season 2 demonstrates the futility of the myth: Mariah leaves Club Paradise to Luke, the deed made official with her last will and testament. Luke becomes the proprietor, switching out his hoodies and jeans for a tailored suit. On the stage of the club, a rap beats out as the singers retell the story of Luke Cage, and he looks down on the stage from the round window, the same window where Mariah pushed Cottonmouth to his death. The scene suggests that Luke might become the next kingpin of Harlem, pulled into a corrupt system that he could not fight from the outside. As originally expressed by Harvey Dent in *The Dark Knight,* Luke has not died a hero but has lived long enough to see himself become the villain.

Literacy Acquisition as Social, Political Capital

> We are living amidst major changes, changes creating new ways with words, new literacies, and new forms of learning. These changes are creating, as well, new relationships and alignments within, between, and among the spheres of family, school, business and science [43].
> —James Paul Gee, "New People in New Worlds"

Recognizing and understanding the literacy myth allow students to see the institutional forces that promote the myth, institutions responsible for much of the social inequality in the first place. Literacy access and restriction have been a toll of oppression such as lack of literacy in slavery, literacy tests during racist Jim Crow, and segregation in school. Jeffrey Brown argues, "Following the binary logic of the male/female, nature/culture, uncivilized/civilized, body/mind dynamic, blacks have historically and symbolically been represented as pure body and little mind" (1999, 30). Nowhere is this more striking than the lack of literacy in the 1800s for slave populations in the South; states even had decrees against teaching literacy:

> That any free person, who shall hereafter teach, or attempt to teach, any slave within the State to read or write, the use of figures excepted, or shall give or sell to such slave or slaves any books or pamphlets, shall be liable to indictment in any court of record in this State having jurisdiction thereof, and upon conviction, shall, at the discretion

of the court, if a white man or woman, be fined not less than one hundred dollars, nor more than two hundred dollars, or imprisoned; and if a free person of color, shall be fined, imprisoned, or whipped, at the discretion of the court, not exceeding thirty-nine lashes, nor less than twenty lashes [Johnson 112].

Almost all abolitionists agreed that literacy acquisition was the first step to freedom.[12] After emancipation, in the height of Jim Crow laws, literacy tests prohibited most blacks from voting.[13]

Graff in *Literacy Myths, Legacies, & Lessons* stresses the tight social and political grasp that American institutions have had on literacy over the last two centuries: "Limits of dependency on literacy, itself restricted and often poorly disseminated, set rigid constraints on the contribution from schools to polity and culture as well as economy" (92). This dependency and its consequential constraints led to literacy's currency changing rates, especially as multimodal multiliteracies have entered into our cultural capital in terms of financial access and social mobility, shaping what Graff termed "the role of social class and group-specific demands for literacy's skills, the impact of motivation, and the growing perceptions of its values and benefits" (102). The citizens of Harlem reflect those group-specific demands as they engage in literacy events, speaking to their community's social order and the specific hierarchies of their immediate surroundings. According to Mitchell and Burkholder, "Participatory visual methodologies help to illuminate the socio-cultural context of literacy practices, and how concepts of self and community are negotiated and represented by participants" (657). The participants who demonstrate literacy events as part of the large social practice must "work to promote individual and community engagement, which, in turn, looks to inform research for social justice, and social action" (657).

In line with Graff's view of literacy's significant place in American history, Morris Young states that "literacy has often functioned as a trope for citizenship that itself limited membership to those who could demonstrate specific levels of education, unaccented speech, or markers belonging that might exclude people of color, immigrants to the United States, or others deemed 'unfit'" (64). Through its usage in ordinary, everyday occurrences as normalized literacy events, literacy practices have engrained themselves in social practices, enabling citizens to work, play, thrive, and exist alongside their literacy events. In some nations, literacy practices have empowered groups of people to move forward such as European countries after the invention of the printing press and the wide dissemination of information. Usually, the impacted community is smaller, such as Victorian London or 1990s Silicon Valley, but the effects on the nations are still as strong, changing the ways individuals create and understand new literacies. However, limits and restrictions on literacy improvement or even literacy acquisition also have lasting effects. As the characters in *Luke Cage* demonstrate, the overall promotion of the individual and the community requires two objectives: the freedom to move through social spaces and institutions without fear of retribution, whether from personal or communal treats; and opportunities for advancements and self-improvement. When studying literacy events and practices in *Luke Cage*, students can observe the pervasiveness and persistency of the literacy myth: an idealization of education that neglects the very real needs of a community struggling to achieve safety and security for its most vulnerable citizens.

Chapter Conclusion

This chapter examines *Luke Cage* and the characters Luke and Misty as representations of urban, localized literacy practices that reflect ethnic literacy events in a high-poverty community. This chapter uses Graff's *literacy myth* to highlight beliefs about literacy as a means of elevation in socioeconomics living conditions. Luke's reading choices and nostalgia for past artists of Harlem differ from Misty's practical approach to detective work and skillset to solve crimes by reading photos of crime scenes. The chapter covers a binary of opposing ideas: the persistency of ideological optimism for change via education against the realities of living in a community fraught with crime, gang violence, and political corruption.

Class Activities

These class activities aim to inspire discussion and writing that focus on the triangulation between literacies, ethnic minorities, and communities as a means of expression, prosperity, improvement, and identity. Rather than narrow the scope of literacy and language to any one social group, these activities have the objective of expanding conversations about how our literacy events both belong to and differ from larger, communal literacy practices.

Activity 1: Literacies Shaped by Ethnicities

In this activity, students watch an episode of *Luke Cage* and then answer the following questions by writing short responses before tying their ideas together in a larger directive.

QUESTIONS FOR STUDENTS TO ANSWER:
- Within ethnic spaces and minority communities, how do we see literacy events as markers of personal identity?

6. Literacy in Luke Cage

- In communities where literacy practices are subjugated by violence or used with strains of the literacy myth, how do citizens work to overcome poverty and a lack of career choices and achieve personal autonomy?
- How do Luke and Misty use personal literacy events to counteract the oppression and limitations of their community?
- How do Luke and Misty work in different ways and through different careers to improve language and literacy acquisition for their friends, family, neighbors, and all citizens of Harlem?

SUGGESTED READINGS AND QUOTES FOR DISCUSSION:

Ivanic, Roz. "Bringing Literacy Studies into Research on Learning across the Curriculum." *The Future of Literacy Studies*, edited by Mike Baynham and Mastin Prinsloo, Palgrave Macmillan, 2009, pp. 100–22.

"The imperative to make Literacy Studies relevant to pedagogy raises up the question of whether vernacular practices can be drawn upon as resources for enhancing students' success" (Ivanic 109).

Heath, Shirley Brice. "What No Bedtime Story Means: Narrative Skills at Home and School." *Literacy Studies, Volume 1: Great Divides and Situated Literacies*, edited by Mastin Prinsloo and Mike Baynham, Sage, 2013, pp. 163–90.

"In some communities these ways of schools and institutions are very similar to the ways learned at home; in other communities the ways of school are merely an overlay on the home-taught ways and may be in conflict with them" (Heath 161).

DELIVERABLES OR WRITING PROJECT:

Students compose 200–400 words of a response that answer the questions and provide descriptions through a combination of their ideas and research on ethnic literacies.

Activity 2: Group Presentation on Urban Literacies

The goal of this activity is to generate conversation about reading and comprehension in a variety of urban communities. Harlem serves as an excellent opportunity for students to explore literacy events and practices as the seclusion of the community in a larger metropolis gives students a unique chance to review social mobility as a part of literacy studies.

GROUP ACTIVITIES:

For discussions, small groups explore these questions:

- How do language and literacy shape people inside communities?
- What types of contributions do spaces and institutions (home, extended family, school, work, religious groups, media) make to one's personal literacy events?
- How does the literacy myth have a role in these literacy events?

SUGGESTED READINGS AND QUOTES FOR DISCUSSION:

> Flower, Linda. "1: What is Community Literacy?" *Community Literacy and the Rhetoric of Public Engagement*. Southern Illinois University Press, 2008, pp. 9–29.

"America's rhetorics of change and its call to community is rooted in an attempt to confront the divisive and unjust effects of social disparity. The premise of community literacy is that such a rhetoric calls us to speak out *about* and *for* silenced voices" (Flower 9–10).

> Toliver, S.R. "Unlocking the Cage: Empowering Literacy Representations in Netflix's *Luke Cage* Series." *Journal of Adolescent & Adult Literacy*, vol. 61, no. 6, May 2018, pp. 621–630.

"Luke's racial and gender expression, his journey to and from prison, and his prominent wearing of a hoodie instead of a suit makes him the embodiment of common black male stereotypes: aggressive, scary, and uncouth. Instead of allowing the stereotypes to be bolstered by this representation, however, the writers and directors of the series showcase Luke participating in literacy practices that combat the static representation, promoting a more nuanced version of black male reading abilities" (Toliver 6).

DELIVERABLES:

Groups present on different approaches to community and urban literacy, demonstrating the difference between mainstream, dominant literacy instruction from educational institutions and the local literacy practices of insulated citizens in a particular community.

Activity 3: Multimodal Grouping on Urban Literacies

On a webpage, students post multiple quotes from authors about urban and minority literacies. They look for access to literacy and education across socioeconomic and political campaigns intended to improve the lives of those relegated to the outskirts, communities with high-poverty and high-crime, and those struggling for recognition. What types of language and literacy developments were suggested? How many came from voices outside the community and how many were made by voices inside the communities?

SUGGESTED READINGS AND QUOTES FOR DISCUSSION:

Richardson, Elaine. "4. African American-Centered Rhetoric, Composition, and Literacy: Theory and Research." *African American Literacies*, Routledge, 2002, pp. 95–113.

"As an African American centered teacher-researcher, my task is to connect students to these discourses, rhetorics, and literacies developed by African Americans, to describe historic and transformational literacies from the viewpoints of Black experiences, to interpret data from these subject positions" (Richardson 95–6).

Derry, Ken, et al. "Bulletproof Love: *Luke Cage* (2016) and Religion." *Journal for Religion, Film & Media*, vol. 3, no. 1, Jan. 2017, pp. 123–155.

"This focus on community is evident throughout the series, from the importance of Pop's barbershop as a refuge and meeting place, to the fact that Luke has no mask or 'superhero' identity: he is always Luke Cage and he openly helps, and often needs the help of, the people around him. He also tries to understand the people who are hurting Harlem, and the series itself slowly peels off the masks of the villains—Cornell Stokes, Mariah Dillard, Willis Stryker—to show us the painful histories that have shaped their current identities and actions" (Derry et al. 130).

MULTIMODAL DELIVERABLES:

A webpage with intersecting quotes from authors concerned with ethnic and urban literacies.

♦ ♦ 7 ♦ ♦

Daredevil and Disabilities

> In addition to the language we use, every day in our theories, our conception of disability, including intellectual disability, is shaped by mass culture, such as film and television [125].
> —Heather Keith and Kenneth Keith,
> *Intellectual Disability*

This chapter examines literacy practices as both able and disabled events in Season 1 and 2 of *Daredevil* (2015–16) for the examination of access of textual data across printed and multimodal platforms. *Daredevil* was the first MCU TV shows to premiere on Netflix; *Marvel's Agents of S.H.I.E.L.D.* was a weekly show in ABC, but *Daredevil* dropped as an entire season of 13 episodes (a shorter season than most TV drama seasons) all at once. In terms of visualization and tone, the setting—a gritty depiction of New York's Hell's Kitchen—resembles the city of Gotham in its various depictions (the TV show, the *Dark Knight* trilogy, and parts of *Arkham City*). The actual timeline of *Daredevil* fits into the MCU as New York is rebuilding itself after the alien attack in *The Avengers* (2012): Lea Garrido explains that "it is precisely this catastrophic incident in the shared Marvel universe which provokes renegotiations of space and identity through various lenses such as race (*Luke Cage*), (dis)ability (*Daredevil*), and gender (*Jessica Jones*) as depicted in Marvel's individual television series" (6).

The protagonist of *Daredevil*, Matt Murdock, was blinded as a child by chemicals which heightened his other four senses. By day, he works as the blind lawyer of Hell's Kitchen, representing poverty-stricken clients at the mercy of large social system and using the law to protect the helpless from criminals; by night, he lurks the dark alleys as a masked vigilante who enacts justice on those who have escaped the arm of the law. Unlike the *Daredevil* film (2003), this show remains deliberately elusive about Matt's abilities to "see" and navigate his environment, ambiguous as to whether his skills result from scientific mutation of the chemical spill or from his own training and extensive physical combat. Matt navigates between his profession as a lawyer and his vigilante work as the protector of Hell's Kitchen, and both occupations require literacy events to gather information. His lack of sight induces him to work around traditional literacy events (visually reading alphabetic print) and employ alternative methods of reading.

The plot of each season of MCU TV shows on Netflix follows a pattern of storytelling: the superhero uncovers and foils the plans of a main supervillain and squares off with a range of minor villains, smaller thugs, and muscled henchmen. In *Daredevil*'s first season, a group of four distinctive villains, headed by Wilson Fisk, seek to take control of Hell's Kitchen by illegal purchases of run-down tenements and underground drug trading, and Matt as the Masked Man (his first alter ego name) fights against them jointly as lawyer and vigilante.[1] By the end of the first season, he dons the iconic red leather suit; his heroic feats are witnessed by a police officer who gives an account of events to a newspaper reporter, and the next morning's issue titles him as Daredevil. In Season Two, Daredevil faces opposing threats from Punisher and Elektra who conflict with his vigilante ideology in responding humanely to criminals in Hell's Kitchen.[2] Louis Rosen emphasizes that *Daredevil* "has provided excellent opportunities to tell new stories about crusading, heroic lawyers despite its fantastical setting, contrasting Murdock and Nelson's burgeoning legal practice mostly representing indigent, hard-luck clients against the drama, action, and violence of gritty, urban superheroics" (386). Through all the action and physical feats, instances of specialized literacy events ground both of Matt's identities as well as the other characters'.

To sustain the significance of a disabled superhero in the Marvel Cinematic Universe (MCU), the show refrains from depicting what Matt sees, save for one quick glimpse. In Ep. 1.4, his confidant and medical aide, Claire Temple, asks Matt how he "sees" the world. For a split second, the screen enters Matt's POV: a world of fire with objects moving in and out of burning shape. Other than that brief glimpse, the show remains as third-person POV, leaving the viewer to wonder what various spaces and textual objects might look like to Matt as both a blind lawyer and a blindfolded superhero. His impairment does affect literacy activities that most of us would consider ordinary, especially those activities that help us gather information. In Ep. 1.3, after Daredevil subdues a mobster, he picks up the man's smartphone and runs his fingers over the flat screen. A second later, he tosses the phone away because he cannot "read" the information on the flat screen. Even his superheroic abilities that give him a 3-D impression of the world are not enough to give him an accurate description of 2-D, digital words on a smooth screen. This scene reflects Lars Ellestrom and Jorgen Bruhn's emphasis on the limits of multimodality in which "all media are at least slightly multimodal as far as the spatiotemporal and the semiotic modalities are concerned, whereas some media are multimodal on the level of all four modalities [solid materiality, visuality, spatiality, and iconicity]" (37). Daredevil cannot engage with digital technology as projected information on the screen, but his abilities to anticipate emerging conflicts and gather data around and from these conflicts remain multimodal as his abilities require discerning information that exists in modes other than alphabetic texts.

The importance of traditional, alphabetic data stays consistent throughout *Daredevil*. In multiple episodes, Matt sits with Braille sheets in front of him, running his fingers over the sheets, both hands moving from the middle of the page to the opposite edges in fast, smooth motions.[3] Rather than a visual activity, all his literacy events use touch as the first sense and then sound, smell, and taste as additional methods to provide him with the information he needs to function, both as a lawyer and a superhero. Because his texts are printed with the Braille alphabet, we as the audience cannot see what he is reading in the same way we can read alphabetic print in media like newspaper headlines or text messages. Ironically, his use of Braille reading makes us as viewers realize the extent to which we depend on our own visual abilities as, for most of us, our literacy events depend on sight. Other types of reading such as Braille and sign language require literacies that are not practiced by the majority of the American public. In *Death, Disability, and the Superhero*, Jose Alaniz stresses that the character of Daredevil becomes "a landmark for the depiction of disability in a notoriously ableist genre that celebrates idealized, hypermasculine bodies as a matter of course" (54). Against ableist expectations of superheroes, Alaniz also stresses, "Murdock's impairment does not stand in the way of having a brilliant career and earning the respect of his community as the most admired half of the Nelson and Murdock law firm" (54). Rather, his impairment reflects our culture's ableist perspectives of superheroes, a perspective about humans and skills that has far-reaching implications in a capitalistic, consumer-driven culture which consigns health and ableness as the norm.

The Ableist Culture of Superheroes

Before I examine Matt's literacy events, I highlight the ableist culture of superheroes because it is such a prominent part of superhero narratives. In most of these stories, superheroes are damaged, brutalized, threatened, or handicapped in some capacity along their missions.[4] The damage inflicted, physical and psychological, contrasts against their earlier states at the beginning of the story. Superheroes exist within an ableist culture because their narratives show most of the superhero's activities relying on the body: enhancing the body, reinforcing the body, and arming the body. In *Disability*

Studies and the Inclusive Classroom, Susan Baglieri and Arthur Schapiro argue, "Culture shapes our perspectives about the world and the people around as societal knowledge and beliefs about disability are communicated through media, entertainment, arts, laws, and language" (5). Much like the exaggeration of a superhero's intelligence and literate abilities, disabilities of a superhero are stressed in their narratives. According to Leonard Davis in *The End of Normal*, "If you want to make a film about disability in such a culture, then every part of the story has to do with that disability. The film has to be, in some sense, obsessed with that disability" (37). This state reflects what Davis identifies as "the economy of visual storytelling in an ableist culture" (36), and therefore if a character's disabilities limit his interaction in the modalities, his multiliterate abilities become limited as well.

A leading author in critical disability studies, Tobin Siebers notes in *Disability Aesthetics* that the merging of trauma studies with disability studies will "allow us to borrow the interest of trauma studies in global media to think about the disabled body as a product of the electronic age" (103). He notes the importance of the body as a space to create narrative and meaning because "The disabled body is at once a symbol of the trauma of modern life and a call to discover a more inclusive and realistic conception of culture, one that recognizes the fragility as well as the violence of human existence" (103). The study of disabilities in superhero stories has potential as most students can recognize the immense traumatization of superheroes as a reproduction of the mortal human condition, be those traumas physical or psychological. The superhero's suffering connects him or her to the viewer because, according to Siebers, studying disabilities "symbolizes human variation but also because it represents the fragility of human beings and their susceptibility to dramatic physical and mental change. The capacity to be wounded, injured, or traumatized is not always considered a feature of disability, but it should be" (102). The presence of a superhero with disabilities coincides with the constant theme of trauma in superhero narratives, a theme that spans all TV superheroes: Bruce Wayne loses his parents, Oliver Queen is kidnapped and tortured on the island of Lian Yu, Barry Allen suffers a radiation-laced lightning strike, and Jessica Jones is brain-washed. Out of the trauma arises the determination to survive, the will to fight back, and a righteousness of humanitarian concern for fellow living creatures. When these characters face their lowest human moments, they then make the decision to be more than human as a means of mediating their trauma.[5]

Yet, for all the trauma that superheroes suffer, blindness in *Daredevil* immediately roots the narrative in its critique of our ableist culture because Matt's blindness has an immediate presence to it. After all, although Oliver Queen returns from Lian Yu with scars and tattoos covering 25 percent of his body, he can hide his disfigurement with a tailored suit, keeping his face blank to hide any lingering physical pain. The murders of Thomas and Martha Wayne affect Bruce psychologically first and manifests secondly in his self-enforced training to become Batman, but that trauma is not immediately noticeable. The past trauma of many superheroes is hidden from other characters, only obvious to us the audience through flashback scenes or private conversations. Matt starts his superhero training after being blinded by the chemicals as a child and losing his father; those moments of trauma are the catalysts that ignite his turn towards superheroic endeavors.

Opposed to masked trauma, Matt's blindness has a notable presence to it, making other characters in *Daredevil* hyper-aware of his disability, and we as the audience can witness our culture's tendency to forget disabilities until they are marked and shown. According to Mark Jeffreys, both cultural studies and disability studies have "already done much to expose, historicize, and explain the constructedness of both the visible and invisible cripple" (38), a dual construction stemming from "anxiety, hostility, and hubris" (38). In their introduction to *Disability Studies*, Sharon Snyder, Brenda Brueggermann, and Rosemarie Garland-Thomson argue that "the disabled body is imagined not as the universal consequence of living an embodied life but rather as an alien condition" (2). The possibility that the body can be marked or disfigured seems a radical notion, seeped in our culture that sees disabilities as "an absolute state of otherness that is opposed to the standard, normative body" (2). To see this disparity more emphatically, I discuss Daredevil's literacy events in the next section and then contrast those events against other major characters in the following section.

Literacies for Daredevil/Matt Murdock

High-tech digital systems exist throughout the MCU, but Matt's literacy events center mostly on hardcopy print texts in Braille.[6] Others around him use cellphones, computers, and tablets, but he listens to the information that is derived from those technical modes because he cannot access them for himself. Like most superheroes, Matt has developed the ability to instantly memorize and recall all the information, knowledge, and intel that he has gathered through the texts he has encountered, both those written in Braille and those read to him by Foggy, Karen, and other characters. Matt's blindness forces him to rely on his memory for both the information he has learned and the physical vicinities he visits. According to Cesare Cornoldi and Tomaso Vecchi, the lack of vision in a narrative requires the viewer to develop "an understanding of the role of visual perception in generating and manipulating visuo-spatial images and, at the same time, an understanding of the specific characteristics of visuo-spatial mechanics developed in the absence of visual stimuli" (95). Traditional literacy events still affect Matt's life even if he cannot fully participate in them; outside of his apartment, a large neon sign flashes an advertisement that would bother a person with sight but that he cannot see. The intrusion of the sign lets him rent the apartment at a cheaper rate than he would be able to find normally, placing him in the center of Hell's Kitchen.

His disability emphasizes further how much literacy events are fundamental parts of American culture, both as a given—an "expectation of literacy" (Johnston 112)—and as an exaggeration in superhero media. Advanced literacies do not only lead to higher social aspects or more prosperous living, for superheroes. Their multifaceted literacy practices elevate them to elevated, powerful, and privileged statuses of vigilante decision-making; at this self-appointed level, superheroes control and direct the worlds in which they live and act with absolute impunity to make resolute decisions that they deem worthy by the information and resources they have gathered in their quests. Here perhaps, we have another embellishment of possible implications of the literacy myth, the expectation that we cannot only overcome our circumstances and situations, but that we can become even greater than the average, mainstream criteria for middle-class America.[7] In the process of his training, Matt does not just overcome his handicap and become a lawyer; he becomes a superhero, pushing past all limitations of his disability to a condition where his blindness no longer serves a stumbling block—he has for all intents and purposes overcome it. In the same way, we see the literacy myth in our culture as its implications suggest that learning literacy and engaging in educational endeavors will not only help one overcome poverty and limiting circumstances but will erase all markers of that poverty and limitations as it does with Matt's humble beginnings.

The central literacy sponsor in *Daredevil* is, ironically, Matt's working-class, divorced, boxer father—a poverty-stricken man living with his young son in a rundown apartment in Hell's Kitchen. Matt's superhero mentor/sponsor is actually a blind man named Stick who teaches him to use his four remaining senses to navigate the world, but for the most part, Jack Murdoch acts as the sole sponsor to his nine-year-old son, both before Matt's accident and afterward. Limping home after a particularly vicious boxing match, Jack returns to the apartment to get his son to sew up his open cuts; during the medical care, Jack asks if Matt has done his homework, and though Matt tries to shrug the question off, Jack insists that the boy completes the work before going to sleep. After the blinding accident, Matt accompanies his father to the practice ring and sits learning to read Braille while Jack trains in the ring. When Jack takes a break from training, Matt points out the difficulties in learning to read Braille, namely in the recognition of bumps as individual letters. The longer Matt explains the difficulty in learning to read Braille and the longer Jack encourages him to continue his studies, the discrepancy between the lives of the sponsor and child being sponsored becomes more apparent as the father encourages and promotes an ideal of literacy that he himself does not have and will not attempt to learn. In later years, as an adult practicing law, Matt shows the effects of that sponsorship as he reads Braille at rapid speeds and remembers what he has read with accuracy and precision. His high levels of literacy provide him with the confidence to move into superheroic vigilantism with similar levels of conviction and assurance that he developed through his educational endeavors.

Much of Matt's success from boxer's son to accomplished lawyer resembles the exaggerated promises of the literacy myth: insistence from a literacy sponsor and Matt's dedications to his studies move him from lower-class squalor at the mercy of the mob which controls the boxing tournaments into middle-class respectability and prestige as a lawyer. His literacy skills have erased all barriers that socioeconomic, familial, and poverty-ridden circumstances would create.[8] Even as a child, his aspirations of making something of his life contrast with his father's background or their immediate situation; already blinded, Matt sits reading Braille amidst the working-class boxers training in a grubby gym, and he has already risen above his father's class by his own determination to develop literacy skills despite his disability. In *The Myth of the American Superhero*, John Lawrence and Robert Jewett note, "The anti-elitist bias, expressed through the hint that anyone can become a superhero, embodies a respect for widely-distributed human potential, a worthy democratic theme" (358). This ties into the literacy myth as a part of that potential is linked to learned methods of research, investigation, and reading because "literacy or at least a minimal amount of education is presumed to be necessary and sufficient for overcoming poverty and surmounting limitations" (Graff 42). A central theme through the MCU superhero TV shows is the need to use education and self-reliance to get out of poverty and begin to achieve the markers of the American Dream: middle-class stability with agency in the power hierarchies of social institutions.

Multiliteracies in Daredevil

> Physical disabilities appear in the popular imagining in a variety of ways, notably as challenges or tragedies, and effect while cognitive disorders have a somewhat different role [31].
> —Leonard Davis, *The End of Normal*

The world of *Daredevil* does not have the glossy, digital glow to its narrative like *Arrow* and *The Flash*, but the characters in Hell's Kitchen have multiliterate abilities that feel real and actualized, much like ours in modern-day America. (The newspapers influence citizens' opinion, but no character hacks databases like Felicity or travels to other dimensions through technology-created portals like *The Flash*.) As of 2020, most American newspapers have online sites and offer digital subscription because print subscriptions have lowered significantly in number and outreach. Yet, the ideology of the press as a contributor to not only popular opinion but also a compulsion for the involvement of the police remains strident in the world of *Daredevil*, specifically in crime-ridden Hell's Kitchen, New York. This ideology mirrors Brian V. Street's understanding that we should be able "to view literacy practices as inextricably linked to cultural and power structures in society and to recognize the variety of cultural practices associated with reading and writing in different contexts" (433–4). While the superhero in the general has basic literacy skills to navigate his way through the boundaries of these written texts, the entire world of the superhero and its corresponding expectation of superheroics demand that the superhero step outside traditional literacy to enact justice. However, that demand necessitates high-levels of traditional literacy from the superhero first and foremost: he must be able to comprehend all information to use it effectively or, in Matt's case, use alternate forms of literacy. Literacy events and practices depend on the individuals that sanction and engage in their usage. The flow of activities always reflects the individual engaging in literacy events, and it is this flow that I direct attention to as practice for students to understand and engage in as a realization of determining their literacy events through an active understanding of the larger circumstances and individual needs that create those events.

Actual moments of reading and writing appear throughout *Daredevil* (usually with a character glancing quickly at a page or screen), but there are also implied moments of literacy events which shape the characters' choices and different narrative directions. The power of the press maintains its importance in the MCU which seems more of an idealized concept of how American culture should be than how it actually is. Earlier in the first season, Karen Page pressures Ben Ulrich to print the findings of their investigation about criminal mastermind, Wilson Fisk, in Ben's newspaper. The two discuss taking their information to an online blog or anonymous internet source, but they arrive at the conclusion that the newspaper itself is the best form of not only legitimacy but also audience outreach. Ben Ulrich writes an exposé for his newspaper to reveal Wilson Fisk's criminal acts, but Fisk hacks Ulrich's computer and steals the document. Fisk brutally murders Ben for his reporting, an act that indicates how strong a presence the written word still has with social and political broadcasting of information. Next, Fisk holds a press conference where he reads Ben's words, slightly altering them to make Fisk appear as the savior of Hell's Kitchen rather than the head of an organized crime syndicate. The stealing of the document, its alterations, and its public presentation act as the catalyst that leads to the final confrontation between Daredevil and Fisk, the climax of the first season.

Understanding the difference between events and practices can assist students in identifying individual events—acts of literacy indicative of the individual—as part of larger practices in particular communities, locations, and time periods. In "The Limits of the Local" that Brandt and Clinton emphasize, "Literate practices are not typically invented by their practitioners. Nor are they independently chosen or sustained by them. Literacy in use more often than not serves multiple interests, incorporating individual agents and their locales into larger enterprises that play out away from the immediate scene" (338). When students apply this understanding to *Daredevil*, the literacy events become more easily identifiable because of the range of characters literacy events as well as the fact that the main character, a blind lawyer, has events that differ from all other characters in the narrative. Unlike the *Arrow* which features Oliver Queen learning many different specializations of literacy including literacies of digital accessibility, weaponry, and machinery, *Daredevil* features one central specialized literacy, that of the law.

In terms of multiliteracies, the other characters' literacy practices resemble those of ordinary Americans. In between *The Flash* where multiliterate events are enhanced and over-exaggerated and *Gotham* where characters exist in a non-digital world, *Daredevil*'s setting reflects that of our actual world where characters engage with alphabetic texts and multimodal platforms as the average American does in our present time. Examining specialized literacy events—especially the contrast between the literacy events needed to navigate the profession of law against those needed as mainstream average Americans—allow students to see the difference between different types of events and practices. Students can also connect these varying perspectives of literacy with Brian V. Street's understanding of literacy events and practices which links "them to something broader of a cultural and social kind" (2003, 78) through their contexts and interlinking patterns.

Literacy Metaphors

When educators talk about literacy or most often lack of fluent literacy skills, they tend to use metaphors to describe literacy practices. This phenomenon occurs because actually defining literacy acquisition or deficiency becomes difficult. **Literacy metaphors** refer to the tendency to talk about literacy in analogies, usually comparing the lack of literacy to something negative. Illiteracy is usually referred to as a sickness or disease in a poverty-stricken community, and literacy acquisition is the cure. Metaphors of literacy appear throughout many areas of current American culture: organizations such as Aid for Africa have continual efforts to "end the book famine in Africa" (illiteracy as starvation) and educational programs such as Reading Recovery Council of North America that promises to help raise literacy levels in "Intervention" lessons (illiteracy as substance abuse) or Reading Rockets that aims to "Target the Problem!" (illiteracy as a military strategy…?). As David Barton states, "different metaphors have different implications for how we view illiteracy, what actions might be taken to change it and how we characterize the people involved" (12). The metaphors frequently empower a group or institution to then step in as the cure for the disease, the answer to the problem, or the saviors to the forsaken.[9] The language of the metaphors allows for individuals and groups to talk around literacy, to circumvent specifics of literacy events or practices, and instead create descriptions that rarely define or solve problems involving literacy. Metaphors influence perspectives of literacy throughout educational structures and political hierarchies; when students recognize metaphors of literacy, they can distinguish between appropriate analogies and discard comparisons that use hyperbole (illiteracy as a deadly disease!).

The language used to approach literacy consistently reinforces our deliberate attempts to marginalize it and redefine it in more-comfortable, more-familiar language. In much the same way, the literacy practices of superhero TV shows rely on these metaphors to highlight the high levels of traditional autonomous literacy for the superheroes and marginally low literacy for everyone else. The problem with metaphors of literacy is that they are using different descriptions to describe a concept that already has a shaky, somewhat unclear definition. The attempts to define literacy often result in us talking around literacy, describing what literacy is not and talking about approaches to literacy, rather than literacy itself. Mary Hamilton (*Literacy and the Politics of Representation*, 2012) argues that "metaphors are *always* part of discussions of literacy and no education or social policy or practice can proceed without a root metaphor that conceptualized literacy in a particular way" (45). This happens in composition as we use figurative language to define strong writing: writing that has a flow (writing compared to water), writing with emphasis (writing like an impact sport), or writing with abandonment (writing without any apparent effort). The more metaphoric the language used, the more difficult to define the activity at hand and its limitations, expansions, uses, and changes. The tendency to try to paint a picture of what it looks like when someone cannot read is more favorable (or perhaps just easier) than to describe someone reading.

Because literacy rates and levels frequently appear unclear and sometimes indefinable, we find it easier to talk about the lack of literacy rather than the evidence of it occurring. Yet, often the opposite is true in superhero media because the instance of literacy becomes paramount to the existence of a superhero; we need those high levels of literacy to enact the superhero ideal. Literacy itself is rarely described or defined in a straightaway fashion in these narratives. Rather it is talked about (or around) in metaphors because the concept of literacy or even the term *literacy* itself seems boring or mundane, a word rarely associated with anything superheroic. Instead, the superhero refers to literacy development or specialized literacy as training or as detection and camouflages the act of reading into networks of skill comprehension: the instance of close reading into exposure and scrutiny; specialized literacy into comprehensive patterns that align multiple databases, information centers, and historical evidence into intersecting networks that only the superhero can decipher.

Throughout *Daredevil*, literacy takes the metaphor of empowerment, a means for Matt to counteract his disability and enact his system of morality. The opening credits of each episode features red dripping wax/blood that creates figures, and the first figure that emerges is blindfolded Justice holding up her scales. Matt's non-traditional literacy development allows him to overcome the limitations of his blindness, to train himself to be greater and stronger than his blindness, and to access knowledge from a position in life where he is severely disadvantaged. Because of his blindness, he cannot access normal means of literacy activities (Matt could never develop the specialized and alphabet-heavy digital literacies that Oliver Queen has), and characters around Matt constantly give expositions of information and circumstantial details that he needs to know to function. Yet, rather than a disadvantage, his disability proves to be a double advantage as he gains information through 3-D physical objects but keeps up the pretense of being completely blind so that information he would gain from normal literacy events is communicated to him. Sylvia Scribner's metaphor of literacy as adaptation fits Matt's dependency on creating specialized literacy for himself because this metaphor is "designed to capture concepts of literacy that emphasize its survival or pragmatic value" (9). This metaphorical language reflects Scribner's argument that "functional literacy is conceived broadly as the level of proficiency necessary for effective performance in a range of settings and customary activities" (9).

A level of proficiency for a superhero means that the superhero must adapt constantly to literacy's broad spectrum of changes and new information, and Matt's continual literacy development lets him surpass his blindness through technologies that, Scribner insists, "are, in effect, new systems of literacy" (11). Matt's adaption to the challenges of superhero activities, perhaps, allows us the greatest understanding of the range in which literacy changes and adapts to fit the needs of both the individual using it and the community that endorses the particularities of its practice; we are shaped by our literacy practices indicative of our time, place, education, and socioeconomic background, but we also change our literacy practices by the investments we make into our unique events as well as the overarching practices that we partake in. When students from a low socioeconomic background first arrive at college, they must adapt their literacy usage to fit in with the larger practice of higher education, but at the same time, the institution does outreach to serve the needs of incoming students, creating a dual flow of expectation and changes between an individual's literacy events and the college's larger literacy practices.

Chapter Conclusion

This chapter focuses on *Daredevil* and its main superhero whose disability requires him to use alternative methods of reading to gain information. The term metaphors of literacy refers to the tendency in western culture to use exaggerated analogies in an attempt to describe (il)literacy and lack of literacy skills. Matt's alternate literacy events present new ways to understand and define literacy activities, and they contrast in performance to other characters' literacy events that rely on sight for achievability. The dependency and prominence of the news media in this TV show illustrates the importance of literacy in a community, but it also allows for commentary and caution about how news is gathered, produced, monitored, and interpreted.

Class Activities

These activities allow students to examine literacy events and practices through the lens of disability studies; students can scrutinize the ways that composition writing and reading encourages students to change their individual events and actively engage in a variety of literacy practices. I encourage readers to views these ramifications not as strict limits or boundaries of literate actions but rather as individual markers to what literacy can achieve for us and to what extent we can engage in a variety of multiliterate practices when we all have variations of particular abilities that empower us to engage with different modalities and texts. Ellis and Kent argue that "digital technologies are often presented in a way to eradicate disability as it is socially constructed, while issues regarding access are ignored or glossed over" (4); this discrepancy becomes obvious when students examine *Daredevil* as Matt's disabilities cannot be solved by digital technologies as he cannot interact with them effectively. Here I observe the limits to the events by observing the means in which students' abilities and disabilities construct the ramifications of how far they can engage through literate practices to external texts, including those of specialized language. The heightened sense of technology and robotics in *Arrow* and *The Flash* allow students to see literacy practices as expansive and all-inclusive, always accumulating and incorporating new knowledge, while the practices in *Daredevil* become grounded in actual events that reflect larger practices that correlate to our actual limitations in relation to our human bodies.

Activity 1: Understanding Literacy Events for a Blind Superhero

Students can contrast unusual literacy events with normal events in *Daredevil*: the Braille texts (which they can't read) against other types of alphabetic information shown (that they can read) such as newspaper headlines posted on Ulrich's bulletin board, a laptop screen that Karen reads, and the printed legal briefs that Foggy creates to help impoverished clients. By making this contrast between Matt's literacy events and the other characters,' students can understand how literacy events are not only shaped through an individual character's usage but also are facilitated and promoted throughout our current culture. The fact that Matt trains himself to read Braille also highlights our own work to train our literacy events to encompass more information and further our knowledge bases, both early in childhood at the beginning of our education and throughout our lives as we develop specialized literacy skills and multimodal multiliteracies through higher education and into lifelong careers.

Questions for Students to Answer:
- How is our culture designed around the promotion of particular literacy events that fit into prescribed literacy practices as a larger community activity?
- What different types of literacy events in *Daredevil* change the way we conceptualize the activity of reading? (Ulrich reading a newspaper left to right vs. Matt drawing his right-hand and left-hand fingers across the Braille pages)
- How do many literacy practices in superhero TV shows represent ablest culture?

Suggested Readings and Quotes for Discussion:
Ellis, Katie, and Mike Kent. "Universal Design in a Digital World." *Disability and New Media*. Routledge, 2011, pp. 13–28.

"The discipline of critical disability studies seeks to develop new ways of understanding disability. An emerging discipline, it is developed from now familiar base concepts of other instigations of the social construction of the exclusion" (3).

DELIVERABLES OR WRITING PROJECT:
Students write a short description of literacy events, both on and off campus, that include those of disabled persons and marginalized literacy events.

Activity 2: Group Studies on Literacies and Disabilities

In reflecting this culture, the characters of *Daredevil* engage with a variety of texts indicative of their character's needs and interests. Matt reads Braille through touch; Foggy reads hardcopy law documents and newspapers; Karen reads online information and read, writes, and talks in Spanish; as a cultured mob-boss, Fisk reads displays of artwork and descriptions to impress a female curator; Ulrich assimilates a pattern of crime through a network of police reports and newspaper headings. Minor characters read, write, and speak in Mandarin, intersecting English with Chinese words or written symbols, and information is spread through newspapers, online articles, and TV broadcasts that provide information to the public as well as controlling the news feed to the masses. Observing all of these idiosyncratic events allows students to create perspectives of literacy events that fit current American life which has a diversity of communal literacy practices.

GROUP ACTIVITIES:
Members of small groups examine different characters from *Daredevil* and other superhero media and identify ableist assumptions about literacy events and practices.

SUGGESTED READINGS AND QUOTES FOR DISCUSSION:
Baglieri, Susan, and Arthur Shapiro. "Why Consider Attitudes toward Disability?" *Disability Studies and the Inclusive Classroom: Critical Practices for Creating Least Restrictive Attitudes*. Routledge, 2012, pp. 3–19.

"The primary way that communities arrive at shared understandings about the world is through culture, which generally refers to the patterns of human activities and the systems and symbols that shape the meaning of these activities" (Baglieri and Schapiro 4).

DeWeerd, Katherine. "Understanding How Sensory Input Affect Children and Helps Them Cope." *Social Skills Deficits in Students with Disabilities: Successful Strategies from the Disability Field*, edited by Helen Myers, Rowman and Littlefield, 2013, pp. 79–100.

"It is important for professionals to understand that there are areas of our brain that keep us regulated throughout the day, calm us when the sensory input is overwhelming, organize us when we are overstimulated, and alert us to our surroundings when we are feeling tired and nonresponsive" (DeWeerd 82).

DELIVERABLES:

A presentation that highlights literacy events and practices in superhero media by examining disabilities and ableism in American culture.

Activity 3: The Spectrum of Able and Disable Literacy Events

Students, usually unaware of their own ableist projections, tend to project their circumstances upon academic knowledge; they may assume that discussions of literacy practices are referring to their literacy practices (e.g., students were educated in a middle-class environment so they assume that all people have the same literacy practices from middle-class environments) or they may define literacy practices too narrowly. In *Daredevil*, Matt's literacy events as a blind person contrast sharply with the others,' and the range of multiliterate events in *Daredevil* speak to a wide practice of multiliteracies in this current day and age. Students who recognize differences in literacy events, in both acquisition and practice, have more nuanced and complex understandings about the diversity of events inside a communal literacy practice and understandings about the particularities of disabilities studies.

SUGGESTED READINGS AND QUOTES FOR DISCUSSION:

> Murray, Pippa. "Being in School? Exclusion and the Denial of Psychological Reality." *Disability and Psychology: Critical Introductions and Reflections*, edited by Dan Goodley and Rebecca Lawthom, Palgrave MacMillan, 2006, pp. 34–41.

"This deep-seated failure to acknowledge their own internal experiences type defies societal attitudes to virtually all disabled young people, who were simply not seen as psychologically real by the majority. We deny the psychological reality of others, our capacity for empathy is forfeited: they cease to be human in our innermost representations of them" (Murray 38).

MULTIMODAL DELIVERABLES:

Students advocate for a variety of literacy practices that reflect actual ranges of events to become more mainstream throughout educational institutions and broader functions of American life, including disabilities and socioeconomic disadvantages.

◆◆ 8 ◆◆

Literacies for Evil Purposes
Villains and Antiheroes

> In effect, the supervillain makes the superhero a superhero. The presence of the supervillains creates the primary directive of the superhero narrative—the preservation of the status quo [86].
> —Frank Verano, "Superheroes Need Supervillains"

Where other chapters explore superheroes and their literacies, this chapter analyzes the "bad guys" of the shows and their literacy events and practices. Villains frequently have multiliterate skills that rival the superheroes,' and villains work to improve those skills to facilitate their nefarious plans. In the majority of superhero media, the villain acts as a mirror to the superhero and challenges him or her to improve to fight the villains' particularly-nefarious plans or superhuman strength.[1] According to Galen Foresman in his research about supervillain philosophy, "a great supervillain needs to have goals that people do *not* think are good. Often when we describe a supervillain as one of the best of the worst, we are evaluating that villain based on his or her goals" (28). Before I explore avenues of literacy practices for the villains, I note certain characterizations of these villains that rely on their intellectual capacity and their ability to navigate cultural, social, and capitalistic institutions for their edification and self-promotion. These characteristics, defined through sections in this chapter with four separate villains, empower villains to link their literacy practices to activities which have negative repercussions for particular individuals or vast communities in superhero TV shows. The four character archetypes I have chosen to represent the collective of villains belong to different socioeconomic classes and have different occupations that require different literacy skills: the gentleman of leisure, the mad scientist, the cutthroat mercenary, and the cold-blooded politician. By studying villains' literacy practices, we as literacy scholars and students of human behavior can understand that literacy, like most tools, can serve altruistic or destructive purposes. Literacy can be used to further a community (Linda Flower's *Community Literacy*); literacy can be used to destroy a community (Royster's *Traces of a Stream*). Ultimately, literacy as a tool serves and accommodates the interest of those in the community who employ this tool through self-direct literacy events.

Supervillains' literacy events belong to the larger social literacy practices from which they emerge, and these practices shape their literacy events towards particular motives that use a range of multimodal abilities. In "Multiliteracies and Language," Norman Fairclough defines multiliteracies with two central developments that have brought great change to current cultures as "first, cultural hybridity increasing interactions across cultural and linguistic boundaries within and between societies, and, second, multimodality: the increasing salience of multiple modes of meaning—linguistic, visual, auditory, and so on, and the increasing tendency for texts to be multimodal" (171). Using these two increasing attributes in their nefarious plans, supervillains have greater access to inflict more damage, more harm, and ultimately more death through multiliterate methods than they did decades before. Some villains seek disruption of an ordered system as a means of punishing communal injustice, sometimes even righting the wrongs of previous political systems. Some villains have personal destructive forces and enjoy physical violence while others prefer to watch from the distance, safe in the security of their own scams that provides them with anonymity from legal ramifications. Some villains are simply in league with the legal systems and pay off members of law enforcement and government agencies. Jason Bainbridge emphasizes that throughout superhero media, "the state has gone so far in its efforts to impose order, the line has blurred so much between these antagonists, that no one even notices the substitution of the supervillain" (381). Some villains like Slade Wilson, Eobard Thawne, and Wilson Fisk possess extraordinary multiliterate abilities that they use to navigate digital modes, and their multiliterate skills pose formidable challenges to their respective superheroes. Other villains rely on physical or psychological intimidations; superheroes often use literacies to combat brute force by building machines, enhancing their own skills, or assembling combative forces.

Supervillains' Multiliteracies

> The reader also needs the villain. We need to see the hero face adversity, and the villain supplies it [158].
> —Ivory Madison, "Superheroes and Supervillains: An Interdependent Relationship"

8. Literacies for Evil Purposes   153

In his breakdown of supervillains in media, Lee Easton states, "The supervillain's persistence in the face of indubitable failure reminds us of the structural negativity at the heart of the superhero film" (4). Generally, superhero TV shows feature an assemblage of villains with a range of combat skills that tends to improve with higher learning and higher literate skills. The low-level thugs that wander the streets in *Arrow* or protect supervillains *Gotham* rely only on physical combat skills, usually rudimentary guerrilla-style fighting that involves unfocused blitz attacks which the superhero deflects easily. Those with high intellect and sophisticated multiliterate skills such as Malcolm Merlyn from *Arrow* or Fish Mooney from *Gotham* present more dangerous and lethal threats against the superhero (and consequently large segments of the population) because the villains have been able to effectively read the superhero's body and demeanor and search for weaknesses; these villains have identified loopholes in the legal systems and power vacuums in the political arena, and they then aim to exploit systems and people for personal profit. Even if the opponent is not an immediate physical threat like the Riddler from *Gotham* or Jessica's mother from *Jessica Jones*, the villains' sharp intellect expedites their desire to create elaborate traps both physical and psychological to defeat the hero. The superhero uses intelligence to solve crimes; the supervillain uses intelligence in creating and sometimes hiding crimes.

Most of the supervillains in these narratives have manipulative personas that they use to influence those with lower IQs to become idealistic pawns in the villains' elaborate games; these henchmen, usually relegated to the background without names or speaking lines, work as the muscle to stop any outside threats to the villains' nefarious plans. Supervillains usually have high multiliterate skills across modalities: they access important information through complex digital databases, build nefarious machines, and make political and social allegiances that allow them to be more lethal than the average thug. Therefore, the superhero cannot rely only on his body and combat abilities; he has to have multiliteracies of advanced detective skills to counteract villains' multifaceted schemes. Villains create intricate webs of subterfuge, hiding criminal actions within multimodal texts of legal suits, business holdings, financial accounts, etc., and their confidence in their skills and intelligence makes them formidable foes for superheroes. The activities and plans of supervillains fluctuate from petty (robbery, extortion, embezzling) to full-blown acts of terrorism (mass killings, widespread poisoning, assassinations), but regardless of intent, literacy events are weaponized to assist villains in causing destruction and delivering death.

Though the superhero's strength and might pose problems for the villain, the more intelligent and multiliterate the villain, the more the villain can work around the immediate presence of the hero to scheme and plot. If superheroes are positive extremes of the human capacity for goodness and benevolence, the height of sacrifice and well-meaning, supervillains become the flipside of the good/evil coin, a mirror image of the superhero. Supervillains portray humanity at its most selfish, most egotistical, most destructive—the baseness of all our ids and dark desires. According to Nathan Miczo in her work on communities modeled on superhero ethics, "We see ourselves in the face of the supervillain, as in a looking glass, when we act mindlessly, proceed as cognitive misers using heuristics to make easy decisions, relying on violence and coercive reading" (121). Perhaps that is the attraction of the supervillain; we understand them because they act as we would if we did not have moral compulsions (or if we had a range of genius skills that would allow us to manipulate systems and people as easily as supervillains do). For example, in *Arrow*, when Moira Queen runs for office as mayor of Starling City, the language of her campaign's messages and press conferences comes under close scrutiny while the tangible evidence that she has engaged in covert criminal enterprises is hushed up; this situation occurs in our political system such as in most presidential elections when each political side focuses on the language of their candidates and their political appearance and works to diminish or brush over the past flaws of their candidates while exaggerating the unfortunate language and past flaws of their opponent. The political concerns of *Arrow* extend to situations for multiple supervillains to span the globe, featuring a range of powerful opponents that work from ruthless, self-promoting ideology that emphasizes a drive towards power, greed, or domination.

Supervillains often seem as varied and unique as the superheroes, displaying a spectrum of personality types and public personas. In *Arrow*, Oliver faces an array of villains that span socioeconomic, political, and capitalistic hierarchies: Malcolm Merlyn appears as an altruistic businessman, Slade Wilson remains mostly hidden but appears as a potential investor in Queen Consolidated, and Sebastian Blood campaigns to revitalize Starling City if he becomes mayor City by weeding out corruption.[2] In the first season, Malcolm works with Oliver's mother to arrange a series of bombing in the poverty-stricken Glades to rid the city of the homeless and poor and subsequently unite the survivors in a goal to rebuild and restore Starling City to its former glory. In his research on trauma in *Arrow*, Evan Gledhill clarifies, "Merlyn has a lust for power that extends to controlling nature itself, through the development of a machine that can produce an earthquake" (85). In the second season, Slade launches covert attacks against Oliver to destroy the Queen family, not because Slade wants to unite a community but to satisfy a personal vendetta against a decision Oliver made while on the island. Slade joins forces with Sebastian Blood to enact his revenge and together they engineer enhancing an army with Mirakuru. These villains present a different context of political maneuvering that Oliver has to identify and then counteract: respectively, destruction as economic cleansing, carefully-plotted revenge, and brain-washing to ascertain ideological legacy. Each of these *Arrow*-esque supervillains possesses multiliterate skills—some that rival Oliver's—and they employ their skills to facilitate their crimes into fruition.

Throughout superhero TV shows, superheroes' literacy levels set them apart from other characters, and main supervillains have similar literacy skills that elevate them beyond the citizens and henchmen of the places they live. In *Traces of a Stream*, Jacqueline Royster argues that "amid a complex system of communicative practices in the general culture, there are multiple literacies across sites and language boundaries, as well as across perceived needs, purposes, and communicative norm" (44). These complex systems are most obvious in superhero narratives where superheroes and villains exist in high levels of multiliteracies past those of the average American citizen. The implications of political skills as a part of multiliteracies may seem at first an unusual inclusion, especially for superhero narratives and literacy studies. However, the roles that political maneuverings play in superhero narratives are much more emphatic and devastating than many audiences realize; after all, superheroes step outside of the law, avoiding the restrictive arm of the institutions of law and order which cannot or in many cases will not deliver justice.

Many of the problems that arise in superhero narratives result directly from an inundation of crime, cronyism, bribery, and political greed: Daredevil faces off against Wilson Fisk who uses crime-ridden, poverty-laden world of Hell's Kitchen to enact social justice in the form of destruction, Oliver fights for Starling City where decades of wealthy families have corrupted and pushed the city to the brink of desperation between the haves and have-nots, and Luke Cage competes against Cottonmouth who runs guns out his nightclub front and has several corrupt policemen on his payroll. The implications of political struggles usually reflect either a desire for domination and control from the villains' standpoint or chaos and anarchy that result from failed policies or overly idealistic beliefs. Along with political maneuverings, the ability to read movements of power and control plays heavily in superhero TV shows as supervillains have to recognize the potential to create threats from different power structures to seize upon power vacuums.

The Gentleman: Kilgrave

The supervillain Kilgrave is a rapist through mind control. Kilgrave is unequivocally a rapist—the show's only contention with that interpretation comes from Kilgrave himself, and his protestations reflect the

ignorance-as-innocence epistemology of rape culture, as well as the specious reasoning that if physical force is not involved, it is not rape [81].
—H. Rakes, "Crip Feminist Trauma Studies in *Jessica Jones* and Beyond"

Kilgrave (aka Kevin Thompson) suffered from a brain malfeasance as a child, and his parents experimented on him with painful medical procedures in an attempt to heal him. Kilgrave reflects on the sociopathic experiments of his childhood: "That's my loving mum and dad, scientists, bent into turning me into a freak. Neurological exams, fluoroscopy, brain biopsies and my personal favorite, cerebral spinal fluid extractions" (*Jessica Jones*, Ep. 1.8). From these experiments, Kilgrave developed his thrall: the ability to brainwash and control others just by telling them what to do. Kilgrave's intellect connects with his ability to manipulate people; he understands the social structure of western life, and with his gift of manipulation, he can easily persuade others to do as he requests without hesitation or questions. Yet, because his persuasion is temporary, usually lasting no longer than 12 hours, he has to discern feasible plans that address his immediate needs, plans that can be enacted by those under his thrall quickly after he commands them to act.

At first, he seems indestructible, and as his powers make people act against their own self-interests, the likelihood of his villainy being recognized and persecuted remains low. Jessica has trouble convincing the authorities to believe she was brainwashed, and despite living in the MCU where New York has suffered an alien invasion, the general public does not want to believe that a man can convince people to harm others and even themselves just by commanding them to do so. While other villains seek to amass great political authority and wealth or to destroy the status quo, Kilgrave seems to have a lack of motivation beyond wanting Jessica to himself. His immediate needs are answered without hesitation by the people he controls, but in true Freudian style, he wants the one thing he cannot have: adoration and submission from Jessica. This intense need drives him forward, but he also seems to enjoy the play for Jessica, the hunt of the game, just as much as he does the act of controlling her in moments of physical confrontation. His literacy events demonstrate the petty, selfish needs of his character, rooted in his small, sadistic nature that enjoys inflicting cruelty with childish impatience.

Despite being British, Kilgrave easily assimilates into American culture, notably following the trend for amassing bigger and better things which speak to markers of the American Dream and its amassed wealth as a sign of privilege. David Bloome defines culture as

> a set of traditions and rituals; particular human ecologies, a homeostasis and social structures that function to meet the basic needs of a social group; a set themes that

8. Literacies for Evil Purposes 157

structure social life and its meanings; a set of shared and learned standards (expectations) for acting, feeling, believing, using language, and valuing [10].

Against these set values, Kilgrave works his nefarious plan, and as his powers of persuasion remain verbal, his literacy skills are only implemented when he needs information or wants to finalize a plan. In several episodes, he sits in public places, reading a newspaper, but these literacy skills are those of leisure, a gentleman in a suit with ample time to devote towards unhurried cultivation of his own pleasures. Scenes of him perusing a paper in a park contrast sharply against the frantic research Jessica does in the confines of her office/apartment. While he reads for entertainment, she reads to survive.

In Ep. 1.7, Kilgrave visits Jessica's childhood home, walking through the home as if he were on tour at an open house. He confronts the owner and begins to work his power of persuasion before stopping and offering the owner an obscene amount of money to vacate the house. Even though he could simply order the occupants out of the house where Jessica lived at one point, he offers the buyer money to sell him the house, utilizing large amounts of paperwork that gives legitimacy to Kilgrave's actions. The owner, tempted by the large amount, agrees, and in the next scene, the owner signs over the deed to the house, legalizing Kilgrave's ownership of the house. This literacy event speaks to the permanency of the documents and emphasizes Kilgrave's understanding of literate activities: he does not have to bother with the trifling details of documents that run and regulate the lives of the average citizen, but when he chooses to, he can use and manipulate the legal ramifications of imperative documents to his advantage. Through the lens of his cruelty and egocentrism, Kilgrave designs plans that allow him to legitimize his actions to keep them away from the suspicions of the authorities.

Supervillains' intellect and literacy skills for nefarious work are dependent on others' specialized literacy skills, manipulating legalistic cooperation to obfuscate crime. Kilgrave also hires Jeri as a lawyer to gain legal access to the plans that he wants. Because of the limited effects of his thrall, he knows that his superpower has short ramifications and no lasting action; he needs the permanency and legitimacy of actual documents to enforce his plans. Villains have literacy abilities and skills that challenge their corresponding heroes' skills in terms of intelligence and learning. The villains usually present some type of physical mode of destruction or chaos, but the emphasis that superhero TV shows put on the inner workings of the villains' minds points to the fact that these villains have high levels of not only learning and literacy but also adaptability and new forms of understanding to help them progress with their nefarious plans. Kilgrave possesses the ability to control other people's actions through his voice: whatever he tells them to do they have to do. The show explains this as his voice becomes a virus that impedes people's mental processes and forces them to act in accordance to his commands. The high IQs and advanced intelligence that gives villains the confidence to launch into crimes work well to supplement feasibility to continue crimes on larger scales. Despite this incredible power, his goals to control other people are not enough, and he fixates on gaining control of Jessica again and becoming a powerful political player in Hell's Kitchen.

Patrick Sullivan in *A New Writing Classroom* states that, being proficient readers ourselves, "internalized, reflective, inquiry-based reading in questioning process is something we do naturally and effortlessly, but this is because most of us have many years of practice at it and this way of engaging written work has become second nature to us" (86–7). In the same way, Kilgrave's reading of people and situations becomes second nature to him as he uses his intelligence to manipulate situations and opportunities for his advancement. He could have far-reaching, global aspirations, but he lacks the longevity of manipulation to achieve those resources as he controls the mind and the body of those in the immediate vicinity only. Because his effects wear off eventually, he is not able to motivate others to follow his commands as other villains do. In comparison to Wilson Fisk from *Daredevil*, Kilgrave's influence seems small and petty while Fisk acts as a kingpin with his mafia and business intertwined into a threatening conglomeration of influence and force throughout Hell's Kitchen.

Kilgrave's influence suits his personal vanity and egotism, and while his assault and control of Jessica are much more personally demeaning, his villainous actions do not have the same widespread, social implications as other villains do. Because of this, his literacy events remain focused on the sources of his control. He does not have to learn about the ins-and-outs of business negotiations, weapons manufacturing, drug running, or local crime which would require its own discursive language and resulting literacies. At the basis of cause and effect sequences, he orders other people to act, others who have those literacies and access to the specialized language, and he can remain a puppet master for short amounts of time, feeding on the submission of others. In studying this type of limited, short-termed villainy and Kilgrave's egocentric literacies, we can better understand literacy events as tied not only to the needs of a particular person but also occurring in the immediate vicinity of the person's geographical and circumstantial needs.

The Scientist: Eobard Thawne

> My fate was to become your greatest enemy. I was never going to be the Flash. So I became the reverse of every-

8. Literacies for Evil Purposes 159

> thing that you were. The more people you saved, the more you were loved … the more I had to take from you.
> —Eobard Thawne to Barry Allen,
> *The Flash*, Ep. 2.11

On the other end of the villainous spectrum, Eobard Thawne has advanced, specialized literacy skills that suit his degenerate purposes, and he works tirelessly to see his sinister plans come into fruition towards wide, collateral damages. At the end of the pilot episode of *The Flash*, we see Thawne as Harrison Wells first planning his diabolical scheme: to steal speed from the Flash. Ironically, Thawne decides to disguise his endeavors by remaining in a wheelchair and thus going slower than someone on two legs could move. He represses his thirst for power and lets his cold, calculating nature exact plans to move slowly against Barry, helping Barry increase his abilities both in speed and fighting practice. Thawne's movements, usually hidden from the rest of the team, speak to his ability to prolong his desires to enact a plan of careful calculation. His literacy abilities include both the technology and data from our world as well as the advanced digital machinery and systems of Earth-2. For Thawne, the future is not seen in moving images but projected newspaper articles that report the Flash is missing in 2024, a timeline that Thawne has to maintain to enact his plan.[3] His hidden room within S.T.A.R. Labs conceals a nearly-sentient machine called Gideon that reports on the future of Earth-2 and provides him with data that he reads and assimilates into his present knowledge as a way of manipulating and controlling his current environment. At the height off futuristic technology, Thawne's literacy events allow us to see someone using intelligence and scheming for nefarious purposes, rather than performing the altruistic detective work that Team Flash does.

Like many of the digitally-enhanced skillsets of superheroes, Thawne has developed scientific and technological literacies to monitor and manipulate machines. He steals the appearance of Harrison Wells of Earth-1 by arranging a car crash that injures the scientist and kills his wife. Thawne has developed an appearance-stealing device which steals Harrison's DNA and allows Thawne to duplicate himself as Wells on a genetic level and assumed his identity. Because of his work in the future of Earth-2 which also included scientific research such as the particle accelerator and further research that allowed him to travel through time, Thawne assimilates into S.T.A.R Labs and the scientific literacies used in 2014 on Earth-1. The hardest part of his scheme is keeping up his identity as the humble, paralyzed scientist rather than the master-planning megavillain that he actually is. He constructs the particle accelerator on Earth-1 to act as a potential time machine that can create a wormhole to visit other universes.

As a man in hiding and belonging to a different universe, Thawne has several specialized multiliteracies that allow him to act effectively in his plans against Barry and the rest of the team. The first is his ability to read signs and markers of time in Earth-1 and Earth-2 as both a linear progression and a circular influence. He originally travels back in time to kill Barry as a child before he could become the Flash, but due to Barry learning how to time travel, both Thawne and the Flash end up fighting each other at Barry's childhood home on the fatal night of the murder. While Barry rescues the younger version of himself, Thawne kills Nora Allen and frames her husband, Henry, for the murder. Once Thawne loses his connection to the speed force, the ability that he uses to travel in time, he becomes trapped in the early 21st century without a way of returning to his time on Earth-2 in the 2180s. Resigned to his fate, Thawne kills Dr. Harrison Wells, the director of S.T.A.R. Labs on Earth-1, and decides to pose as Wells to wait until Barry becomes the Flash through the freak accident of the particle accelerator. His next move is to work as a mentor to the Flash, helping Barry increase his speed through mentorship and scientific advancements that will ensure that Barry does become the Flash. Pretending to mentor the other scientists, Thawne is able to put his scheme into action through his readings of the future and therefore is able to stop obstacles that get in the way of Barry's improvement of his speed or that threaten to shut down S.T.A.R. Labs. Unlike other villains who seek mass chaos as vengeance, Thawne only wants to steal Barry's speed to return to his own time and universe where he will enact a plan to stop the Flash of the future.

Through his interactions with the other scientists on the team, primarily Cisco, Caitlin, and Ronnie, Thawne devises a device that will not only create the Flash but also the other metahumans as well as the particle accelerator jumpstarts the genetic mutations that allow ordinary people to develop superhero abilities through metahuman evolution. Throughout Thawne's numerous actions, his goal of returning to his time remains steadfast and fixed, and all of his abilities fostered on Earth-1 and created for Earth-2 facilitate his objectives and careful mapping of the future through the various technology and devices he has created that he alone can read and control. The destruction that he brings through metahumans and their crimes acts as a consequence for his actions rather than his direct intent, but he still shares blame for the creation and the misworkings of the particle accelerator. When studying ill-intended literacy practices of supervillains like Thawne, students and scholars can observe the range of technical devices, networked multimodals, and extensive literacy events of a person who travels interdimensionally. Even though his villainous actions are not possible in our present world, by studying Thawne's work, we can understand the broad capacities of literacy skillsets as multimodal tools to facilitate the work of evil purposes just as effectively as heroics intentions work to stop them.

8. Literacies for Evil Purposes   161

The Mercenary: Slade Wilson

Slade Wilson as Deathstroke has appeared in multiple Batman media—the comics, *Arkham Origins*, and *Teen Titans* cartoon—but his status in the DC universe remains that of a bad guy with redeemable possibilities: a questionable antihero. *Arrow* keeps his person ambiguous as he meets Oliver on the island and, after first trying to kill him, trains Oliver as his accomplice with the singular mission of getting off the island. A former mercenary, Slade kills to save himself from danger, and most of his survivalist skills echo his background—organized Australian military and later chaotic warmongering.[4] Other rogue characters are trained assassins such as Sarah, rescued and trained by the League of Assassins, but Slade keeps his status as a mercenary-for-hire, preferring to sell his savage skills to the highest bidder. Slade has advanced literacy skills along with trained combative physical abilities, strongly rooted in his self-sustaining instincts. Once he takes the drug Mirakuru on the island, he becomes stronger and more paranoid as the drug affects his senses and amplifies his physical abilities. The drug, a similar drug to the venom that Bane uses in Batman stories, changes Slade's body to let him act and react faster, empowering him in his revenge against Oliver. In the second season, we see the fruition of his careful planning and slow progression of ill will when he tracks Oliver down in Starling City; Slade not only aims to destroy Oliver but wants to be the major catalyst in the destruction of the city. His hatred against Oliver is personal as he blames Oliver for stealing Shado's affections and then choosing to save Sarah's life over Shado's when Ivo makes Oliver choose. Before his escalating feud against Oliver, Slade was more than willing to not only train Oliver but fight alongside him as he realized the younger man had practical, technical abilities that would help them leave the island.

During the island flashbacks, Slade seems willing (if not eager) to launch himself into mass combat including hand-to-hand, guerrilla-style brawling, but some of his multiliterate skills rival those of Oliver's. Slade easily tracks down adversaries and targets through jungle and urban landscapes, overcomes security systems, and moves with confidence in civilized society where high levels of literacies and low levels of physical abilities remain the norm. In Season 2 when he tracks down Oliver to his family home, Slade enters under the persona of a businessman wanting to donate to Moira's campaign. Dressed as a wealthy donor, Slade speaks with the confidence of someone who can control social situations and converse with language appropriate to his pretense, subtly mocking Oliver while charming Moira. His casual demeanor is undercut by menace and warning to Oliver, a danger signal we as the audience realize though Moira does not; Slade implies to Oliver that he could easily forge documents and other data to keep up his ruse because his career as a hired mercenary requires him to enter into discourse communities of privileged language. Unlike other assassins such as Deadshot who kills long-range targets with a sniper's rifle, Slade prefers to meet target up close, especially when he seeks personal revenge on enemies. For him, all his intelligence and literacy activities narrow down to two objectives: survive and avenge.

Throughout *Arrow*'s first two seasons, Slade proves himself a capable tactician with his intelligence and meticulous planning. One of the few people to actually outsmart Oliver, he aligns his plans for infiltration and ultimate destruction of the younger superhero by aligning himself with powerful players, both on the island and in Starling City. While trying to escape other mercenaries on the island, Slade demonstrates a range of combat literacies that include mathematics and aerodynamics: he calculates the trajectory of a missile launcher to hit Ivo's ship and later calculates the flight of a parachute to land on a freighter to infiltrate it. With his personal vendetta against Oliver, Slade executes a series of complex steps in an overall plan to keep Team Arrow confused and overwhelmed with conflicting data. While they struggle to find concrete proof of his plans, Slade concluded with Sebastian Blood, a government official, to begin to create an army of superheroes infected with the Mirakuru drug, an army that will unleash chaos and brute destruction throughout Starling City as a ransom coup. In each step of his calculation, Slade relies on his powers of deduction and his capacity to see both short-term and long-term missions as an extension of his intelligence and multiliterate abilities. Slade's intelligence and literacy skillsets help him to focus on the problems at the moment, in much the same way as Kilgrave's function. Slade's mercenary tendencies (and his lack of superpowers) prompt him to create alliances with those in power, and he stays effective because of his quick grasp of social, political power structures and their methods of communication. Whether Slade reads extensive legal documents or an oncoming physical attack, he can react appropriately, a chameleon with an extensive array of skillsets and multiliteracies.

The Politician: Mariah Dillard

> [Mama Mabel] put you in school and forced me to run the streets. [...] All that education, and you just as shady as me.
> —Cottonmouth to Mariah, *Luke Cage*, Ep. 1.7

With so much of the discourse in this project reflecting political and social powers of superhero TV shows—powers that use significant language and messages to disseminate information through hierarchies of class and education in these fictional worlds—I use this section to emphasize the importance of politicians who create and influence language and messages from the top of the hierarchy. Another choice for this section would be Moira Queen who has aspirations of becoming mayor of Starling City and launches a lengthy campaign, but I chose instead Mariah Dillard whose status as a congresswoman gives her considerable sway over her community. Along with her influence in Washington, D.C., Mariah has local ambitions for reinventing Harlem and inventing a green initiative that will help elevate the people of her neighborhood out of poverty and racial oppression. Poised, polished, and professional, Mariah stands in direct contrast to her cousin Cottonmouth; his criminal business activities and corrupt gun and drug enterprises put him at odds with the law enforcement and general goodwill of the neighborhood, much to her chagrin. Already tired of the violence he generates that results in political backlash against her, she snaps at him in Ep. 1.1, "Forget about all this noise. Politics is where the real power is."

Raised by a criminal matriarch (Mama Mabel), Mariah understands the complexities of life in Harlem, a community oppressed, repressed, and scapegoated by the larger institutions of New York City. She aims to secure a future for herself and her political aspirations as well as keeping all signs of her involvement in the criminal underworld from the public eye and keeping her hands clean. Her language reflects the morphing futility of politicians: engaging in rhetorical speeches that emphasize a future of flourishing lives and opportunities, a utopian dream that has little resemblance to her actual world overrun with poverty, extortion, gang intimidation, and drug activities which inspire impetus for survival and secrecy at all cost. Mariah's multiliterate abilities resemble those of Moira Queen from *Arrow* as both women come from money built from underhanded dealings and criminal enterprises and both have political aspirations to help a struggling system that they were implicit in creating. However, while Moira can rely on her privileged, white background as a safety net to shield her from any implications of criminal dealings, Mariah fights against the racial oppression that she has endured her entire life. Hating her nickname "Black Mariah" just as much as Cottonmouth hates his, she takes her identity from what she has accomplished as an educated, successful woman, rising above the oppression of Harlem by becoming a powerful player in the political arena.[5]

The first black woman to play a supervillain in TV shows, Mariah also stands in direct contrast to Luke Cage in terms of background and education as well as political and social influence. He has gone to prison while she remains untouchable; he has a lower middle-class background while she received the best education that money could buy; he is open about his superhero status and works directly to help people while she remains in the background of Cottonmouth's deals and works indirectly to keep the drug operation and criminal activities both secretive and continual. When they both become figures on the nightly news, the contrast in their social and economic standing is obvious: Luke Cage seems to be the everyman helping out those around his neighborhood while Mariah remains cold and distance, engaging with the average citizen only for a photoshoot or PR campaign.[6] Deborah Brandt in *The Rise of Writing* notes, "Through most of its history, mass literacy has meant a reading literacy. The value of literacy has rested in the perceived powers of reading to develop mind, improve character, and expand knowledge, among other attributes" (127). Mariah has latched on to those powers, aligning herself with the leaders of the community. Her first TV appearance lets her proclaim her vision for Harlem: "Since the days of Langston Hughes, Malcolm X, Zora Neale Hurston, Duke Ellington, Harlem has been the jewel of black America. It's a perpetual symbol of ... of hope and prosperity and excellence. For black lives to matter, black history and black ownership must also matter" (Ep. 1.1).

Ironically, her campaign entourage hands out pamphlets in the community, pretending to do outreach but actually forcing business owners to donate to her projects, implying that any business who does not donate will face retaliation from Cottonmouth's gang. The positive language of the pamphlet which starts with "I believe in the environmental and economic prosperity of our growing community" stands in direct contrast with the violence the entourage perpetrates. Despite her sharp reading of all social situations and her political connections, she eventually is arrested and tried for her involvement in the drug trade as well as multiple murders in Harlem. At her trial, she stands and makes a speech, utilizing the language that she has developed to manipulate spaces of privilege and power: "You need me out there. You want me out there. Because without me, God help Harlem. God help us all" (Ep. 2.13). She orders her lawyer to execute her entire entourage who might turn on her, believing herself safe once they are dead, but in the last episode of the second season, she is poisoned by her daughter. Spitting out blood, Mariah falls to the ground and speaks her last words to Luke, "We aren't finished, Luke Cage." Her words could be a metaphor for the work left to be done in Harlem, a continuation of a struggling community and dejected people.

Chapter Conclusion

This chapter observes literacy as a villain's tool for evil, nefarious, or selfish objectives. Supervillains tend to have high intellect and multiliterate skills which lets them perpetrate the law and the social contract among citizens, and the four villains selected for this chapter use literacy events to facilitate their movements towards power, wealth, and domination. Each villain has a unique background and purpose in committing crime: Kilgrave was medically abused and wants to punish others with petty malice; Thawne time-travels and wants to destroy the Flash whose future persona is Thawne's equal in speed and intellect; Slade felt betrayed by Oliver on the island and seeks revenge to destroy Oliver's family and community in Starling City; and Mariah was the daughter of a ruthless matriarchal crime boss and desires influence and authority over Harlem. Their intentions are empowered by their multiliterate abilities which allow them to wreak havoc and destruction towards their respective superheroes in particular and their community in general.

Class Activities

These activities facilitate students in their examination of how literacy can be a tool for malfeasance, social disorder, and destructive greed. Students focus on literacy's facilitation of selfish or vengeful pursuits of the supervillains as a means of furthering their own egocentricity and self-interest. The main objective is to observe literacy as a tool used to achieve certain goals and to reconsider the possibilities of evil intentions in literacy events and practices.

Activity 1: How Multiliteracies Can Be Used for Evil

Students research the ways that literacy can be used for nefarious plans and political control in a wide spectrum of human life. They research some of the most prominent supervillains that develop public and personal animosity against the main superhero; students then observe the ways that these villains' high levels of reading comprehension and deduction allow them to enact their deadly plans.

QUESTIONS FOR STUDENTS TO ANSWER:
- How do villains in superhero TV shows use their literate abilities?
- How do technology and digital devices further enhance their literate abilities?
- In the chaos and confusion of supervillainous attacks and plots, can normal literacy practices still remain a priority and a part of the myth of the American Dream?

SUGGESTED READINGS AND QUOTES FOR DISCUSSION:
> Graff, Harvey. "2. Many Literacies: Reading the Signs of the Time." The *Literacy Myths, Legacies, & Lessons: New Studies on Literacy*. Transaction Publishers, 2011.

"This includes recognizing literacy and the literacy myth as ideology and also as culture, and criticizing that ideology and culture. It also mandates critical exploration of the relationships between and among material reality, social relationships, institutions, policy, expectations, and social theory" (Graff 56).

> Thweatt, Jeanine. "Origin Stories: Superheroes, Cyborgs, Artificial Intelligences (and Other Humans and Posthumans)." *Christian Perspectives on Transhumanism and the Church*, edited by Steve Donaldson, Palgrave Macmillan, 2018, pp. 197–207.

"Superheroes are wrest from the trauma, never resolved and always ongoing, a determination to devote their superior powers to the common good in some way. [...] What makes a villain is the opposite: in the aftermath of the origin trauma, supervillains lose all sense of continuity with humanity, including their own human identity prior to the trauma, with the result that humans no longer merit moral status or regard" (Thweatt 199).

DELIVERABLES OR WRITING PROJECT:

Students compose a short description of the literacy events of a supervillain's day and how those events influence their evil intentions.

Activity 2: Examining the Many Literacy Events of One Villain

Groups of students compile literacies on one supervillain and do a compare and contrast to tease out distinctions of literacies: those altruistic, those neutral, and those with nefarious intentions.

GROUP ACTIVITIES:

In groups of 3–5, students spend a week compiling various scenes from a superhero TV show that display the supervillain employing different multiliterate activities with print and digital modes.

FURTHER READING AND QUOTES FOR DISCUSSION:
> Brandt, Deborah, and Katie Clinton. "Limits of the Local: Expanding Perspectives on Literacy as a Social Practice." *Journal of Literacy Research*, vol. 34, no. 3, 2002, pp. 337–56.

"And in perhaps the most direct confrontation, Scribner and Cole's *The Psychology of Literacy* (1981) used experimental designs to show how the claims of the Great Divide actually rested on a conflation between the impact of literacy and the impact of schooling. They demonstrated how the cognitive effects of literacy actually vary with the settings in which it is learned: what literacy does to you depends on what you do with it" (Brandt and Clinton 340).

DELIVERABLES:

A short group presentation that outlines the different literacy practices of supervillains. The collective presentations might showcase supervillains across a range of gender, ethnicity, age, class, education, and backgrounds.

Activity 3: Tracing Villainous Actions and Literacy Events

Students create a website that lists the different abilities of two particular supervillains and the corresponding literacy events through multimodalities that allow these villains to be effective.

FURTHER READING AND QUOTES FOR DISCUSSION:

Heath, Shirley Brice. "Prologue." *Ways with Words: Language, Life, and Work in Communities and Classrooms.* Cambridge University Press, 2009, pp. 1–15.

"Many analysts of the social and individual functions of literacy limits their analyses essentially to the development of expository prose and closely related phenomena, of those literacy requirements most valued in the school and often automatically associated with the workplace" (Heath 230).

MULTIMODAL DELIVERABLES:

A webpage with two split pages side by side. On each page, students chronicle a supervillain's education, literacy events, and different multimodal usage. This way, students can compare and contrast literacy practices of supervillains.

♦♦ 9 ♦♦

Sidekicks and Mentors
Literacies from the Sidelines

> You still need people to help you with all of it. That's the best part.
> —Barry Allen, *The Flash*, Ep. 1.2

The TV shows I have selected for examination feature superheroes who take others into their confidence and rely on the advice, multiliterate skills, and community connections that their friends and mentors offer. Most superhero films focus exclusively on the main heroes and the development of their physical and intellectual capabilities due to the time constraints of film, but superhero TV shows allow supporting characters ample time to grow and develop in their subsidiary capacities. Usually, supporting characters do not have as developed a range of multiliteracies as the central superhero but do have literacy skills in specialized areas such as data-mining, engineering, or digital investigation, specializing in a particular type of advanced literacy usually derived from their chosen careers and specialized fields of study. Sidekicks and mentors do not need to have the wide range of physical literacies and field literacies that require combative and attack methods to subdue a foe in hand-to-hand combat, but their specialized literacies empower them to assist others in areas of much-needed information gathering to serve superheroes and their missions through research avenues that the superhero alone could not access.[1]

Because of the importance of these specialized literacies, I stress the understanding that the contribution of multiliteracies along with specialized literacies have in forming team efforts in superhero TV shows. These group efforts encompass more intrinsic and deeper resources of knowledge and data-gathering then any singular effort could and compass. For instance, in the beginning of *Arrow*, Season 1, Oliver has middling success with his efforts in tracking down names from The List through his wide array of multiliteracy skills and impressive detective abilities. Yet, once he adds Felicity to the team, the team's far-reaching surveillance and digital data-gathering capacities are broadened with her superior hacking and monitoring skills that use a range of digital literacies to retrieve and monitor specialized information. By studying these supporting characters' literacy events, we can see how advanced literacies in specialized areas work in furthering superheroic missions and how the supporting efforts, direct and indirect, help superheroic work move towards fruition and completion.[2]

The supporting cast of sidekicks and mentors works well in superhero TV shows because of this modality: due to the extended runtime and longer character- and story-development, the superhero needs to have allies and team members to talk to and plan missions, often as a means of relating information to the viewer.[3] Superheroes rarely act alone anymore; those who do are portrayed in film where the arc of a superhero story—emerging hero, emerging villain, and escalating fights leading up to a climactic battle—can span two hours with relative ease.[4] For the lone superhero in the TV show, the narration begins to drag slightly when the hero spends too much time by him- or herself without speaking to others or indicating beyond physical activities the plans that he or she is making.[5] The TV show might start with the hero alone like in the case of Jessica Jones or Oliver Queen, but the expansive work of TV superheroes requires supporting cast members who grow and develop in their unique ways. The support and formation of a team around a sole hero or a team of heroes enforce a collective state of specialized literacies from discourse communities, and their specialized literacies act as gateways to complement and further the heroes' knowledge and detective abilities. The superhero's team often becomes a discourse community in and of itself as the team members develop their language and literacy activities around the particular missions they embark on as well as the villains they fight and the schemes they detect.

Specialized Literacies as Discourse Communities

> Members of a discourse community have developed conventionalized or standardized solutions both as writers and as readers to manage recurrent social tasks (both written and spoken) since texts respond to recurrent communicative needs [xi].
> —Julia Bamford and Marina Bondi,
> *Dialogue Within Discourse Communities*

One of the fundamental changes in NLS's perspective of literacy and the understanding of literacy activities is the inclusion of specialized literacies as grounded in discourse communities. James Paul Gee was the first to coin the phrase "discourse communities" and has written about the influence of these communities extensively through his research on the compilations between discourse and literacy, mainly observing how literacy events and larger social practices form in discourse communities and change discourse communities through literacy activities. Gee notes, "Any discourse (primary or secondary) is for most people most of the time only mastered through acquisition, not learning. Thus, literacy is mastered through acquisition, not learning, that is, it requires exposure to models in natural, meaningful, and functional settings" (1998, 261). Discourses must have communities in which they function just as literacy must have a text to read and interpret: according to David Smit in his work on composition theory, "The definition of a discourse community is largely dependent on a description of texts, and ascribing features of these texts to the influence of the discourse community is largely tautological" (88). The language and literacies used within the superheroic teams work towards the promotion and general growth of the superhero's needs and a successful mission as primary objectives, but the team members also experience growth as they become better in their particular discourses and literacy events as they engage in activities that promote both attributes. Often, like the superhero, supporting team members create new messages and texts that must be decoded in new innovative, insightful ways, promoting specialized and intrinsic multiliteracies which span multiple texts through varied and unusual platforms, both written and digital.

    Before I discuss sidekicks and mentors in superhero TV shows, I stress the collaboration between specialized literacies and the discourse communities that foster them. Gee also argues for wider usage and implementation of discourses in "What Is Literacy?" by stating, "Learning should enable all children—mainstream and non-mainstream—to critique their primary and secondary discourses. This requires exposing children to a variety of alternative primary and secondary discourses" (543). In criticizing a discourse, students must first have comprehension and realization of the particularities of language and messages for the community. The ability to fluctuate and navigate between seemingly-disparate discourses, especially those in higher education, seems a step forward in progress, but it, too, has complications in its implementation. Lisa Delpit argues against Gee's call for more discourses by pointing out that "an individual who is born into one discourse with one set of values may experience major conflicts when attempting to acquire another discourse with another set of values" (546–7). This switch often occurs when students enter higher learning for the first time and encounter new terminology for different disciplines, sometimes seeing that words change meaning depending on the field's usage.[6]

    When readers enter into a discourse community, the readers' literacy events reflect the body of knowledge within the community, created out of a need for specific language that fits epistemological usage. The literacy events become specialized within that discourse community because they include descriptive and analytical knowledge about the discourse past that of basic literacy events of general knowledge. The limits of discourse communities extend and contract, depending on the popular culture's appropriation of these communities through multimodal utilization. Gunther Kress and Theo van Leeuwen define a transformation of discourse throughout modes: "the design process in the multimodal world involves selection of discourses and selection of modes through which content-in-discourse will be realized. To use the mode of image to represent certain information means that the mode of writing is not used for that purpose" (64). Much like my reservations towards the use of technology as a solution in teaching rather than a tool, I see the merging of literacy studies in discourse communities and superhero TV shows in much the same way: the merging is meant to enact, encourage, and promote critical thinking about our culture and our means of reading it rather than to be another rote activity to fill up required class time or prescribed number of assignments.

Felicity Smoak, the Tech Wizard

Not a character from the original comics or any other Green Arrow media, Felicity became a regular character on the show thanks to fan appreciation and her "adorkable" personality which plays well against Oliver's cold, calculating vigilantism. Though sometimes distracted and perpetually saying the wrong thing, Felicity has the ability to manipulate digital texts and machines makes her a powerful player in the fight against villains as she often is the most supportive character in gathering information for Team Arrow. Felicity begins the show as an IT personnel at Queen Industries, and Oliver approaches her with a few hacking jobs to get information on potential targets from The List that he himself cannot access. When he is shot by his mother in Ep. 1.14 and in danger of bleeding out, Oliver hides in Felicity's car, and when she finds him, he directs her to take him to his workspace underneath the club Verdant to be treated by John Diggle who has some military medical training. After her initial shock at realizing the heir to the Queen fortune is the vigilante stalking Starling City, Felicity becomes a member of the team and proves her worth quickly by serving as the fastest, most reliable hacker and intel person that the DC TV universe has seen. Mark Warschauer in "Digital Literacy Studies" explains, "There is a wide societal recognition of the importance of new technologies in daily life and learning. Yet the precise nature of digital literacies is difficult to ascertain for those who hold the reductionist view that literacy can only mean phonetic decoding of a text from a page" (124). At the intersection of new technologies and digital literacies, Felicity does her best work as she can envision the patterns and language of digital spaces with relative ease, proving herself a valuable member who can find hidden information that no one else can.

Felicity's specialized literacy skills assist Oliver's detective work by affording him with information that he does not have the time or the skillset to gather himself. His multiliterate skills are more general and broadly based to cover a wide range of print and digital texts; Felicity can control, manipulate, and create the platforms that contain all the needed digital data. In Ep. 1.15, she and Oliver have a discussion in a diner about how to get information about a jewel heister:

> OLIVER: This guy, he's targeting a very specific type of jewel. We figure out why and that'll give us the idea how to catch him.
> FELICITY: I have an idea.
> OLIVER: Mm-hmm?
> FELICITY: Your crush object with a badge said they were working Interpol.
> OLIVER: Yep?
> FELICITY: Why don't I work a couple of little tech, you distract her with a little flirty flirt, slip said tech onto her phone? It will turn into a micro transmitter and boop! We'll learn everything she knows.
> OLIVER: Hm. It's not how I typically get my information.
> FELICITY: How do you typically do it?
> OLIVER: I find the person. And then I put the fear of God in them until they talk. But we can try it your way.

Later, once the bug has been planted, Oliver, Diggle, and Felicity all sit in front of the screens in the Arrow Cave and listen to the phone recording, watching the bars of a sound graph go up and down to measure decibels. With each new piece of information they hear, Felicity pulls up documents on another screen, verifying the information they have just learned and confirming with more details to flesh out their suspicions with concrete proof.

Her literacy skills belong to a digital discourse community, an understanding of cyber connections and digital platforms that intersect and can be manipulated to glean important knowledge from a spectrum of databases. Throughout multiple episodes, Oliver and Diggle and later a stream of supporting minor heroes on Team Arrow embark into physical alterations in dangerous situations or simply on the darkened streets of the city, and Felicity sits in the Arrow Cave, staring at multiple screens with intense concentration as her fingers fly over keys to control what she is reading and accessing. Her multiliterate abilities make her a formidable player on the team as she understands that, despite brute violence and physical force in the superheroes world, the ability to find and confirm data that no one else can find remains paramount. Her information-gathering skills are her greatest weapons, and her literacy skills consistently sharpen and hone that weapon, proving that superheroes need effective sidekicks with sharp detective skills in a digital age to remain combative. Specialized literacies allow for the reader/user to employ a range of technical approaches to solve problems through collecting information. Students may not have Felicity's hacker abilities, but they can identify her extensive skills and the methods that she uses: different dexterities for particular objectives. The tasks she is given change depending on the missions, but the repetitive structure of her work helps her navigate platforms and modes to remain invaluable to the other superheroes out in the field.

Joe West and Iris West in The Flash

> We're going to go through every scrap of evidence until we find something that helps us.
> —Joe West to Barry Allen, *The Flash*, Ep. 1.3

Compared to Felicity and her wizard tech skills, Joe West and his daughter Iris from *The Flash* feel more like ordinary people, grounded in middle-class education with basic literacy skills. Both have specialized literacies that enable them to be efficient in their careers, but their literacy events tend towards average, everyday use. According to Barton and Hamilton, "Many literacy events in life are regular, repeated activities [...] Some events are linked into routine sequences and these may be a part of the formal procedures and expectations of social institutions like work-places, schools, and welfare agencies" (2000, 9). Joe occupies a fundamental place in *The Flash* where he serves several purposes: part detective, part mentor, part father, and part team-member, he works inside the legal, criminal justice system and is a valuable member of Team Flash, often providing information assembled from his detective work or helping the scientists put together information with extraneous data. While he does not act as a direct mentor in improving Barry's superhero powers, Joe instead gives moral and ethical support, giving Barry someone to depend upon within the turmoil and frustrations of being a masked superhero in a city overrun by super-powered villains. Joe and Barry both have detective abilities rooted deep in literacy practices of research, discovery, and assimilation of data into coherent patterns that deliver appropriate meaning to any investigation task at hand. Throughout Season 1, when researching the fake Harrison Wells and the Reverse Flash as a way of solving the murder of Barry's mother, Joe relies on his literacy skills of careful observation and attention to detail, skills that have served him in his long career of law enforcement.

What distinguishes Joe's literacy from that of Ronnie's (a low-level officer) or of Patty Spivot's (another officer) is his advanced status in the police force. Rather than working petty crime cases, Joe acts as a supervisor to other officers and as a liaison between the police and other branches of government, particularly City Hall in Central City. The information he finds has significance in its details and documentations; in Ep. 1.6, the Reverse Flash steals all the files in an attempt to obfuscate the truth of his crimes when he thinks Joe might review files. The files contain textual evidence of the Allen murder, hiding clues about the truth behind Nora's death that the police have not uncovered or connected. Because of Joe's work in the police force and thus his access to vast stores of information, Team Flash does not have to search as thoroughly through police paperwork as Team Arrow does. In tandem with their work, Joe provides information from his specialized literacy events that reflect the overall process of literacy practices within law enforcement: collecting information from a variety of places and modes and then transferring the accrued data into alphabetic reports, numeric ballistics, or photo documents. He shares many of the same detective activities that Jim Gordon in *Gotham* has, but Joe has a wider expanse of information-gathering due to his multiliterate skills in a world with not only 21st-century technology but futuristic technology from other universes and other centuries.

Despite working extensively with the four main scientists on Team Flash, Joe does not have his own brand of scientific literacy. As a police detective, his specialized literacy skills reflect the fact that he works with the same detective pattern-formation that Barry and other superheroes do: assessment of a crime, searching for motive and suspects, and then final pronouncement of the guilt party—all activities that make the detective utilize literacy skills towards a common purpose. In much the same way that scientific literacies function, criminal justice literacy and law enforcement literacy require a job to perform: the literacy events do not exist simply for the thrill of themselves. Henry Jenkins argues, "There are other reading theories, however, that call for a rethinking of the concept of literacy, precisely because they maintain it is the reader who controls the reading process, not the text" (467). As with all literacies, the superhero as a reader must make these theories work, develop, alter, and reinforce themselves towards a purpose. The superhero aims to thwart the villain and uses all literate, physical, and strategic skills at hand; those in law enforcement must do the same for ordinary criminals. Joe's language and literacy events indicate an important aspect of specialized literacies: they do not have to be jargon-filled or confusing to the outsider; specialized literacies can designate commonsense, straightforward logic, and simplicity in accomplishing the task at hand.

New to adulthood and in grad school, Iris works at Central City Picture News where journalists manifest and present the findings of their investigations through multiple modes, and the company publishes information to the public through print and digital media. Iris, while not a government

9. Sidekicks and Mentors 175

employee, shares similar literacy skills with her father as journal investigating and reporting usually require the investigator to search for patterns, clues, information, and communication to report on a busy city. Iris has no legal prominence as a reporter, and the media center she works feels more second-rate than an actual newspaper or news station, but her literacy skills remain as sharp as those working in more-respected businesses. In Season 1, Iris begins her journalism by reporting on the Flash's activity, using resources to obtain pictures and videos of the Flash in action and creates a blog that follows the man in red. To be part of the action, she acts as an amateur investigator, relying on her journalistic instincts to find information about various criminal activities in the city and the way that the Flash has reacted to them. As the first season progresses and metahuman activity becomes more and more obvious to the average citizen, Iris's outlandish claims at the beginning about Central City's superhero seem more realistic and add credence to her theories as superhero and supervillain activities pop up all over the city. Once Barry reveals his secret to her towards the end of season 1, she protests against his involvement as a superhero but eventually accepts his alter-ego role, and by Season 2, she becomes an important team member of *The Flash*. Although she does not have scientific literacies like Caitlin and Cisco, she acts as a liaison between the language of the general public at large and the team itself.

Iris's most impressive literacy abilities stem from her skill to report through multimodalities on the inner workings of the Flash in action and provide the public with an inside look into their city's first superhero. Her blog has written descriptions of the activities and crimes along with photos and short video clips that give credibility and actuality to the ideas that she has written. Because her father does not want her involved in the dangers of police work, she chooses instead a mass-media career where she flourishes as a journalist in pursuit of the truth. (Her Earth-2 doppelganger went into law enforcement and has a different set of literacy skills.) Not only can she glean information from images and multiple sources as well as public sites and news articles, but Iris specializes in close readings of people and events to derive meaning. When she becomes part of the action whether as a hostage or as an instigator, she still is able to recall with detail events that she witnessed and can then transpose them into written documentation on the page or screen.

Her multiliterate skills involving digital recording and information gathering often rival her father's, using what Jenkins defines as a movement away from "older notions of passive media spectatorship. Rather than talking about media producers and consumers as occupying separate roles, we might see them as participants who interact with each other according to a new set of rules that none of us fully understands" (3). Joe's and Iris's literacy events point to larger practices in the superheroes' world, practices that are reinforced in our world and serve to guide us against the enormity of information of the digital ages, an age rife with political intrigue and intersecting networks of information. We must, like them, learn to navigate the overwhelming complications of information to arrive at pertinent knowledge that serves our real needs.

Foggy Nelson and Karen Page

> Nevertheless, superheroes are not merely disposable entertainment, but an important part of how society understands justice [52].
> —Ian Boucher, "Applying Suspense to Archetypal Superheroes"

Throughout both seasons of *Daredevil*, we see Foggy and Karen as supportive characters to the titular superhero and his human persona, Matt Murdock, and they work at a startup law firm, Nelson and Murdock. Both sidekicks have their separate strengths and bring distinct literacy practices to the show, grounding the series with their individual knowledge bases. From these career-driven literacy practices, their particular literacy events enable the audience to understand discrepancies that education and career choices have on literacy acquisition and development. Foggy, as the second partner of the law firm, has literacy practices like Matt does, meshed in the literacy law and legal structures which depend on language and interpretation of written and multimodal texts. Karen, on the other hand, has some literacy of law but only to the extent as a paralegal because her skills rely on her ability to see to the smaller aspects of a law practice: taking notes on prospective clients, filing and paying bills, interacting with existing clients, and tending to the everyday concerns of the firm as general office manager. Due to the show's realistic, often gritty depiction of Hell's Kitchen, access to digital devices and multimodal information remains low and underutilized. Standards computers and cellphones limit characters' options in research, and occasionally the work Foggy and Karen do to gather evidence for cases feels reminiscent of *Gotham* when they sift through thick stacks of printed documents.

At the beginning of the show, Foggy appears as an unordinary lawyer and typical goofy best friend to the main character. As the narration unfolds, we learn that Foggy and Matt have set up their own law practice and are looking to expand their firm in the crime-ridden, high-poverty sections of Hell's Kitchen. Although our first impressions of Foggy may seem to speak to his awkwardness and geeky persona, he proves himself to be a highly-capable lawyer with an extremely advanced specialty of the literacy of law. Matt's intellectual equal in every way as far as their profession is concerned, Foggy can negotiate with other lawyers and high-powered figures of Hell's Kitchen with relative ease and extreme confidence. His presumed, almost frumpy demeanor acts as a mask he wears to disarm other people from seeing his brilliance as a lawyer as he reads and assesses both situations and texts carefully to establish the best angle in which to attack. When gang members try to stab each other with scalpels in the hospitals, Foggy reads the situation and talks them both down in a clear, authoritative voice:

> FOGGY: I'm not going to ask if you know what happens when you get charged with assault. I got a hunch you got more mugshots than baby pictures back home.
> THUG: Who are you?
> FOGGY: I'm the pro bono suit you try'll to retain after you go down for this. Only not even my soft-hearted partner will take your case or any other self-respecting attorney in Hell's Kitchen. Not because you're so badass but because you're just that stupid.
> THUG: You got a big mouth, asshole.
> FOGGY: You forget, I do this for a living [*Daredevil* Ep. 2.03].

While Karen has more of the common-sense literacy practices, Foggy's intellectual base remains grounded inside the nuances and specifics of the legal system: its texts, its languages, and its influences. The social niceties of everyday existence—the polite exchanges with strangers and frivolous small talk—give Foggy problems, not the language and literacy of law.

Oddly enough, as Marvel's only superhero/lawyer, Matt becomes Daredevil to act outside the confines of the law when its institutions of enforcement (the police, the school system, journalism, or information flow) fail to achieve results. In Ep. 1.11, Matt informs his law partner, Foggy (who has recently learned of his secret identity), that he is going to seek revenge on Wilson Fisk as Daredevil. Foggy objects to using brute violence, insisting that they should act "By using the law. Like you told me and Karen to do." Matt sidesteps the accusation of hypocrisy, but his feelings are obvious to the audience: Daredevil can step outside the law to enact justice because he has proven himself smarter, more capable, more empowered, and more learned than Foggy and Karen. His literacy development and events have been achieved through extreme diligence and moved him beyond the average person. Foggy himself has to operate within difficult boundaries of the law, notably giving small bribes to a police officer to obtain information about potential clients who have been arrested and need a lawyer. However much Foggy doubts the ability of the law to rescue and save everyone, he still believes in the sanctity and possibility of the law to improve people's lives; he has not reached the place of disbelief and disillusionment with established institutions that Matt has.

Karen Page works well in the murky-gray morality of *Daredevil* and later *The Punisher* as someone not clearly defined as good or bad but lacking the deliberate definition of anti-hero. At first, she is a victim, framed for a coworker's murderer, and then later becomes a killer when backed into a corner by United Allied. Karen reacts to others threatening her with sudden violence and then regrets those actions; she wants to do more and then despairs at her own helplessness; and she finally rails against the system that she also works inside. While the other characters of *Daredevil* have clearly defined careers (Matt and Foggy are both lawyers, Ben Ulrich is a reporter, and Wilson Fisk is a criminal businessman) Karen's choices in livelihood appear more reflective on her current life situation than an actual intended career.[7] She starts as a secretary for United Allied but comes across evidence of money laundering, demonstrating that she has sharp literacy skills that help her recognize and decipher abnormalities in the world of land acquisition and construction building.

After the incidence of the murder of Daniel Fisher and being acquitted of the crime thanks to Matt and Foggy's legal aid, she becomes their office manager, almost a paralegal, for their law firm, but she does more than just manage an office and take notes for the two lawyers. She accompanies them on interviews, advises them on potential clients, and eventually becomes involved with Ben Ulrich in trying to bring down her old company and as a result bring down Wilson Fisk as well. Literacy skills enable her throughout these various jobs, and throughout the show, we are shown her literate abilities that demonstrate her sharp intelligence and keen eye. She probably works these lower-level, lower-paying jobs due to a lack of opportunity or educational chances, and while her specialized literacies do not have the advanced capacity for the law such as Matt and Foggy, she remains formidable in our understanding of news, politics, mass media, and access to information. Karen's quick reflects and sharp observations enable her to move into the discourse community of Matt and Foggy, and she adjusts to her job and its specialized literacies as she gains more knowledge about the interworking of the practice of law.

Most superhero stories support the same idealized depictions of social mobility. The literacy practices and detective skills enable the superhero to be more and overcome more obstacles than he or she could ever do with only body enhancements. Douglas McClenaghan and Brenton Doecke emphasize that "new multimedia technologies provide young people with ways to negotiate the social relationships and situations presented to them in their everyday lives" (225). This confidence in Foggy's own literacy skills is obvious in his meetings with another lawyer and at the end of the second season when he negotiates a job with Jeri Hogarth. Matt himself has a broad high-literacy spectrum that helps him smoothly transition between Braille readings of police reports to business documents to legal briefs. Foggy remains firmly entrenched in the literacy and specialization of law. Karen Page, who becomes their secretary/paralegal learns a little about law, but her background is in business so her literacy events consistently reflect business texts, language, reports, and accounts. The ability to read social interactions as pieces of larger movements creates a concept of interactions, namely dialogs, as texts which hold often the most important data. As his superhero ego, Matt amasses collections of written information, but he has to gather information through interaction with others, and we, the viewers, also read those interactions in the same way the superhero does: facial expressions, word choice, tone, body language, and pacing. Foggy has some of the same literacy events, but he depends on the language negotiation with and through legal texts. Our understandings of multiliteracies should include modes beyond print and digital discourse; they should expand to include a rich tapestry of many meanings across multiple platforms and through main and secondary characters who utilize these skills.

Mentors and Sponsors

> Connection, mind, body. The mind controls the body, the body controls our enemies.
> —Stick, *Daredevil*, Ep. 1.7

Despite the discrepancies in their inclusion of technology and digital platforms, *Arrow* and *Gotham* both feature the emerging superhero who has older sponsors of literacy who projects their view of appropriate literacy events and practices upon their young protégés. In *Arrow*, the sponsorship of literacy appears less defined because Yao Fei and Slade Wilson train Oliver in physical and combative practices, improving his combative skills more than his intellectual skills or literate abilities. The ability to combat and defeat a foe or multiple foes takes greater precedent in their minds than the detective work that Oliver does as a vigilante in Starling City. This is understandable because Oliver meets Yao and Slade on an island full of mercenaries where physical survival trumps literate events or practices. Emphasizing the particularities of sponsors, Brandt (1997) stresses, "Sponsors also introduce the instability in the worth of people's literacy. As various sponsors of literacy emerge and recede, and as their prospects rise and fall as part of economic and political competition, so go the prospects of those they sponsor" (27). This instability on the part of sponsors is certainly reflected in *Arrow* as Oliver's prospects ebb and flow under Yao and Slade mainly because both men are creating their own pathways to reach particular objectives, and Oliver must follow their methods to survive. Once free from the villains' hold, Oliver immediately establishes his own sponsorship of the literacies he deems important rather than those imposed upon him.

Though from vastly different, fictional worlds that practice different literacy events, Stick from *Daredevil* and Alfred from *Gotham* have similar literacy practices and abilities that they use in instructing their protégées. Stick is also blind like Matt, but Stick trains him in martial arts to use his other senses to read and then react with the world. Alfred acts as the butler to the Wayne family, but after the death of Bruce's parents, he becomes Bruce's guardian and takes over the role of mentor and trainer once Bruce has dropped out of school. Both men recognize their communities' shortcomings and the corresponding political movements, particularly crime and criminal activities which have spun out of control, thus necessitating the need for superheroes in the first place. For Stick and Alfred, their mentorship and stewardship of these two boys culminate in their protégés becoming stronger and more developed, both physically and mentally, then either man could be. Rachel Heydon and Jennifer Rowsell in "Phenomenology and Literacy Studies" stress the importance between "literacy as embodied and literacy as grounded in relationships. These understandings of literacy and our ability to come to them through phenomenology have implications for the practice of literacy research" (469). That is, we come to develop literacy practices due to our relationships with others, first through sponsors and then to others who have similar literacy practices.

Eli Goldblatt and David Jolliffe in "The Unintended Consequences of Sponsorship" argue, "Sponsors take risks, too. Indeed, sponsors can be harmed, altered, or even transformed by the population and the pedagogy they contract to teach" (127). Midway through the first season after Bruce takes time off from his education after the murders of the Waynes, Alfred insists that Bruce returns to school, a prestigious academy for the wealthy children of Gotham. After Bruce lands in a fight on his first day, Alfred removes him from the school and home-schools him in the quiet recesses of the manor where Bruce progresses at his own pace; as Bruce explains to Selena in Ep. 1.9, "I'm developing my own curriculum. It lets me move at my own speed, focus on academic areas that interest me." Though we do not get to see Bruce in those lessons, the characters imply that the material Alfred selects does not vary far from the selected curriculum of the academy. In his free time, Bruce reads over his company's reports and statistics, gathers information about his parents' death, and begins to track the criminal activity of Gotham. He begins to situate himself as his own literacy sponsor, but Alfred's insistence of traditional schooling, though done at home, reinforces Alfred's views of literacy: an appropriation of language, reading, and writing skills that follow the curriculum for most middle-school-aged teenagers.

Brandt (1997) insists that "sponsors deliver the ideological freight that must be borne for access to what they have" (3), and Alfred's sponsorship is constantly reflective in what Alfred thinks is appropriate for the orphaned son of Gotham's wealthiest and most influential couple rather than what

Bruce wants to learn. In Ep. 1.17, Alfred's old military friend, Reggie, shows up at the manor and offers to give Bruce a few fighting lessons. Alfred watches disapprovingly as Reggie pushes Bruce into aggression, daring the boy to tap into his inner rage that will empower him to fight more viciously. Alfred stops the fight, but Bruce protests that Reggie's methods are effective. Alfred replies shortly, "Not methods that fit into our curriculum, are they?" The disparity between the two men's teaching methods, one traditional and one more street-fighter, indicates the path that Bruce will forge as one which will take both men's approaches and merge them into a methodology of high literacy skills (careful detection and memorization) and extreme fighting methods (utilizing rage to fuel his animalistic tendencies). The struggle here between the two men that the growing child witnesses is reminiscent of Brandt's analysis of conflicting sponsors: "As sponsors compete with each other for dominance, they often use literacy as the ground of competition as they try to gain the upper hand. As a result, the sponsored can find the worth or reach of the literacy skills caught up in inflationary or deflationary spirals" (2009, 51). The instruction Bruce receives from Alfred will put him on the road to becoming a superhero, but it will not be enough, and therefore he will later turn to a new sponsor or begin to sponsor himself to develop new skillsets as the world's greatest detective.

Chapter Conclusion

This chapter explores sidekicks and mentors in superhero TV shows that aid or teach the main superheroes. Despite their position as regulated to the side or background in missions and explosive fights which require physical prowess, sidekicks and mentors have specialized literacy and multiliteracies that empower them to provide their teams with valuable data. The term *discourse community* encompasses the community of work or particular circumstances that create language specific to that community, and discourse communities usually require members to learn new literacy skills or moderate existent literacy events to discover information and texts inside the community.

Class Activities

These activities help students examine literacy events and practices of secondary characters in superhero TV shows. Amy Stornaiuolo argues that a "broader perspective on human activity and the connections between modalities, bodies, emotions, and artifacts can help make room for considering the emergent dimensions of meaning making within situated practices" (568).

In these TV shows, certain modalities are afforded more time and space to show the development of literacy than others, primarily the research found on screens through online databases. By realizing these reactions as a part of the process that superhero sidekicks and mentors undergo to keep their mind and cognitive process alert, students can understand the link between cognitive work and the mind in reacting to the information learned and the link's multiple messages and implications in reaching superhuman potentials with reading digital texts and information.

Activity 1: Supportive Literacies

This activity encourages students to think about supportive literacies as specialized literacy events that contribute to larger literacy practices. Individual literacy events often reflect the community's literacy practices, but the particulars of an individual's literacy event (what is read, how it is read, how it is understood, how long it takes to complete the reading, and what the individual does with the new information) depend on the needs and skillsets of the person.

Questions for Students to Answer:
- How do sidekicks' literacy events differ from their superhero's?
- How do sidekicks develop specialized literacy to aid in superheroic activities?
- What types of literacy events do mentors practice in teaching and training their protégés?

Suggested Readings and Quotes for Discussion:
> Bamford, Julia, and Marina Bondi. "Introduction." *Dialogue Within Discourse Communities: Metadiscursive Perspectives on Academic Genres*, edited by Julia Bamford and Marina Bondi, Tübingen, 2011, pp. vii–xxiv.

"Members of a discourse community can engage in various genres, some of which may be more central to their discipline than others'; in the case of academic discourse these may be research articles, textbooks, lectures, conference presentations, research proposals, seminars, workshops, faculty and departmental meetings and their agendas and minutes, letters of references, end of research reports, just to mention a few of the many professional genres the academic may engage in" (Bamford and Bondi viii).

> Murray, Mitch. "The Work of Art in the Age of the Superhero." *Science Fiction Film and Television*, vol. 10, no. 1, 2017, pp. 27–51.

"In these series' amplified depictions of superpowers, these powers can be understood as our own collective political formations seeking articulation and enactment. Matt's partners [Foggy and Karen] and the tenants figure out a communal remedy for housing inequality, while Claire in *Daredevil* and Malcolm in *Jessica Jones* come to embody an expanded healthcare sector, including mental health and wellness" (Murray 48–9).

DELIVERABLES OR WRITING PROJECT:

A short writing sample that examines sidekicks' literacy events and mentors' literacy events and the commonalities that they share in supporting a centralized superhero's mission.

Activity 2: Teamwork, Mentoring and Sponsorship for Superhero

In groups, students discuss the ways that teamwork and connective literacy practices are portrayed throughout superhero TV shows. They draw connections between the individual literacy events of specific characters and then collaborate those events into a larger literacy practice of the entire team. Depending on which superhero TV show students choose, the literacy practices may be highly multimodal and digital or may remain more traditional and based on alphabetic print.

GROUP ACTIVITIES:

Students spend time discussion and researching the following questions:

- What types of teamwork and connecting literacy practices are seen in superhero TV shows?
- How do mentors and sponsors help the main superheroes develop literacy and learning practices?

SUGGESTED READINGS AND QUOTES FOR DISCUSSION:

> Scribner, Sylvia, and Michael Cole. "Literacy Without Schooling: Testing for Intellectual Effects." *Literacy Studies, Volume 1: Great Divides and Situated Literacies*, edited by Mastin Prinsloo and Mike Baynham, Sage, 2013, pp. 91–106.

"The capacities generated by literacy are seen not merely as different, but as higher-order capacities because they resemble the abilities that psychological theories attribute to later stages in development" (Scribner and Cole 94).

DELIVERABLES:

A short presentation where students make connections between sidekicks and mentors in superhero TV shows to friends and sponsors in their own lives as their support network for their college and literacy activities.

Activity 3: Teamwork in Individual Missions

This activity allows a student to use digital spaces to research the teamwork and literacy events that go into a superheroic mission. Students can look at several members of the team and how each of their individual literacy specializations contributes to establishing a problem, researching suspicious characters, planning an attack, and then completing the mission by using their multiliterate talents and individual knowledge bases.

SUGGESTED READINGS AND QUOTES FOR DISCUSSION:

Mahiri, Jabari. "New Literacies for a New Century." *What They Don't Learn in School: Literacy in the Lives of Urban Youth*. P. Lang, 2004, pp. 1–18.

"Implications from the studies suggest that there do not have to be inherent discontinuities between young people's authentic life experiences and their experience of life in schools. Yet, some of the very perspectives and technologies that facilitate the sourcing of multitextual, multimodal, multicultural resources for learning are the ones least used or developed, especially in urban schools" (Mahiri 14).

MULTIMODAL DELIVERABLES:

A webpage that serves as a digital layout of intersecting literacy events through a visual medium, perhaps spider-webbing these events with a main mission at the center.

♦ ♦ 10 ♦ ♦

Places for Literacy Development
Caves and Workshops

> To see literacies as material is to see them as tied to space and place, and to a sensory experience [490].
> —Kate Pahl and Hugh Escott, "Materialising Literacies"

The main purpose of this chapter is to establish the different types of places and spaces in superhero TV shows that support, enforce, or help to develop specialized literacies for superheroes and their teams. Early superheroes in comics had spaces to facilitate their work: Batman had the Batcave, Superman had the Fortress of Solitude, and the Teen Titans had Titan Tower. The hidden, private places where superheroes work, train, surveil, gather data, and heal reveal the literacies of the heroes and sidekicks. The physical layouts of these workspaces contain access to multiple modes across many platforms that characters use to build superheroic weapons, computer screens, medical equipment, weapons modifiers, digital simulations, and combat enhancements. Often, most of the technological activities of superheroes are far beyond those of our current culture, but we can understand the multiliterate abilities needed to access such complex systems, a blending of cognitive processes and information intake.

Kathy Mills and Barbara Comber in "Socio-Spatial Approaches to Literacy Studies" explain that

> applied to literacy studies, spatial approaches to literacy often consider the social and spatial stratification of literacy practices, power, economy and literacy, and modes of ideology. Such approaches have addressed equity and the distribution of literacy practices, and spatial patterns of marginalization and domination in relation to literacy practices and societal structures [92].

The importance of these spaces in terms of detective work becomes evident when considering the amount of research performed, examined, and improved there. According to Sarah Bednarz and Karen Kemp in their work on nurturing literacies, "Spatial literacy is thus important in the workplace, for academic achievement, and broadly to modern society for the opportunities it affords individuals and societies" (20). Even though we as the audience do not always have a first-hand look at the superheroes doing research because that would slow down the fast-paced plot of most episodes, the physical setup of these spaces demonstrates the intensive research and study activities of the superheroes and their teams, linking literacy activities and intelligence with physical representations of strenuous detective labor.

The low-tech superheroes such as Matt Murdock, Jessica Jones, and Luke Cage have places in their apartments or businesses that support their superhero activities, but most of these spaces do not require literacies outside of normal everyday practices and those required in advanced detective work. Jessica Jones' office doubles as her apartment which regularly shows clients and mercenaries entering as welcomed and unwelcomed presences, seeking her out as a private investigator or as a superhero. Matt's law firm and his loft apartment provide him two spaces to utilize his detective abilities, but as he remains masked while acting as Daredevil, most of his work as a superhero does not connect to the places that he occupies. Luke Cage, who outs himself as a superhero early in Season 1 of *Luke Cage*, spends most of his time at Pops' barbershop which acts as a community gathering place for people needing help, but Luke's innovative literacy skills of detective work are not furthered or enhanced through his work at the barbershop.

So rather than discourse on the ordinary literacy events that transpire in normal spaces of American life, I instead focus first on places of enhanced, specialized, digital literacies and places where new literacies are being actively developed by the sharp minds that work there. By doing so, I emphasize the importance of connecting physical spaces to the literacy activities which are molded, altered, and progressed by these spaces. Sometimes, the space is relatively private: Jessica Jones's bleak office as a private eye, Wayne Manor's formal library in *Gotham* where Bruce spends his days learning, and Matt Murdock's loft apartment with a box of equipment to outfit his Daredevil activities. These lone heroes work to keep their literacy events private while those with teams (as in *Arrow* and *The Flash*) host spaces that display multiliteracies and digital platforms, suiting the demands of their particular vigilantism. These created and maintained spaces emphasize the importance of adaption, of change, of creating better, more efficient methods to learn and act with impunity.[1] In spaces where development takes priority in moments of respite, where the work never really stops, superheroes seem to gravitate towards their own workshops. Regardless of the superhero's quest, we need to provide equal energy in researching and understanding these developed space of literacy activities, especially those spaces generated for multiliterate, superheroic detective work. When understanding how spaces promote the work of defined specialized literacies, students can reflect on the tie between physical places and mental processes as significant in performing literacy events and developing multiliterate skills.

Material Literacies

> The materiality of writing is both the central fact to literacy and its central puzzle. This materiality is the central fact of literacy because writing gains its power—as a cognitive process, as a cultural practice, and even as a metaphor—by linking these two powerful systems: the material realm of time and space with the quintessentially human act of language [3].
> —Christina Haas, *Writing Technology*

In New Literacy Studies, extensive studies have researched and written recently about material literacies which ground literacy events to specific places underneath specific contexts. Pamela Smith defined material literacy as the activities in which one acquires "knowledge neither through reading nor writing but through a process of experience and labor" (76). Kate Pahl and Hugh Escott in "Materialising Literacies" argue that their approach makes "a case for a material cultural approach to literacy with a particular focus on writing. We argue that it is important to recognise how language and literacy practices intersect with the material world" (489). Their research on these literacy practices leads them to the conclusion that any discussion of literacy begins with a description of "the material nature of literacy. This approach sees material culture as informing literacy through the process of semiosis. A wider recognition of the materially situated nature of meaning-making practices opens up recognition of these affordances" (498). In identifying these affordances, we should first conceptualize of literacy as an activity directed to reading, comprehending, and responding to an exterior text, regardless of how that text is written, arranged, or changed. According to Cathy Burnett, "A focus on (im)materialising literacies prompts us to look differently at our understandings of the literacy event and of literacy situated. From this perspective, as soon as we identify a literacy event it dissolves before our eyes, connected in multiple ways to other materialities and imaginings" (526). Although the literacy event might disappear after the reading activity is complete, the spaces that afford and support the events, that enable multiple events to merge into a compilation of literacy activities that make up superheroes' literacy practices, offer us the opportunities to witness how superheroes create and access textual evidence in databases throughout these spaces.

With material literacies, the spaces that these literacies inhabit, control, and improve become signifiers of the work that takes place there, notably through the minds that house these literacies and use them as efficiently as possible. According to the New London Group, "In addressing the question of the 'what' of literacy pedagogy, we propose a metalanguage of Multiliteracies based on the concept of 'Design.' Design has become central to workplace innovations, as well as to school reforms for the contemporary world" (19). The more we recognize the materiality behind literacies as participation in various modes, the more we can grasp and develop our own literacy events that speak to and adapt with larger literacy practices. Many classrooms these days are organized to support not only traditional literacy activities but those of digitally-advanced multiliteracies as well, and often we see new venues of opportunity pouring money into these spaces to create the latest, state-of-the-art technology available, falsely believing that the tools of these spaces are the sole means of having these literacies improve. According to Rahat Naqvi,

> When young people are encouraged to analyze their surroundings and the content in which they are being instructed, they begin to form their own opinions and texts that will break the barriers that deny both the realities of difference and the possibilities for bridging those differences and begin to balance power relations between the dominant and subordinate cultures [57].

While I do agree that better literacies are enhanced with tools that enable more advanced in specialized literacy practices, I stress here the importance of literacy development as one's own personal objective first and then the materiality of the spaces themselves. While I look at a range of superhero spaces from the highly digital and enhanced to the low-tech and ordinary, it is not the spaces alone that make the superhero successful in his or her detective work or enabled the supporting team to do their work.

Rather, it is the effort put forth by the superhero—the superhero's drive and expanding intelligence, the superhero's insistence to learn more and do more—that makes the superhero's training and detective work effective, utilizing these places to their furthest potential. Oliver Queen has perhaps the highest level of digital devices available to his work as a superhero, and Bruce Wayne uses the least digital devices, but both of them utilize spaces of their work to the highest level of literate activities as superheroes. Print, alphabetic literacy practices depend on alphabetic texts, and when those practices expand to encompass digital texts, they still must have a platform to hold those texts for the reader. Texts can be digitally composed, digitally enhanced, and even digitally altered, but they require a material presence for representation. The superhero must decide how, where, and when to construct platforms for that representations; sometimes this construction results in intersecting databases, visual images on a wall, or a blend of print and image mapping on screens. All of these activities for superheroes and their detective work result from their protected spaces that support material literacy activities. Spatial literacy—involving the physical logistics of literacy events as part of large social literacy practices within communities—create possibilities for students to ground their own literacy events to physical spaces and perhaps to explore new literacy activities in new places with different platforms.

The Arrow Cave

Oliver's main workplace—the Arrow Cave as it is affectionately known—boasts gleaming lights and an impressive array of computer screens, monitoring equipment.[2] This place speaks of instant resources and immediate tools at hand for users with specialized literacies skills. In the first episode of *Arrow*, Oliver scouts out a space to use a headquarters for his superhero activities, and he finds an abandoned factory that used to belong to Queen Industries and utilizes the basement. After fixing the wiring and installing phosphorescent green reflectors to illuminate the area, he sets up state-of-the-art computers with an encrypted connection to the network. As the team grows, he begins to install more machines for surveillance, tools to improve weapons, medicinal equipment for healing injuries, and a series of minimalistic structures for training. The physical training in the Arrow Cave takes place on low-tech machines such as the salmon ladder or on padded floors where the superheroes and sidekicks fight against each other or improve their reflex times. The cave also contains a stretcher, defibrillator, first aid equipment, communicators, and chemical testing cart. After Felicity joins the team, she upgrades the computer system with more screens, faster software, and further surveillance that can hack any camera in Starling City. To keep the cave secret, the club and the cave connect via a ladder hidden behind a wall, and to be opened, the team members to pull a series of electrical switches. The first arrangement of Oliver's workspace seems fairly advanced, especially as *Arrow* was one of the first superhero TV shows to have a superhero with digital and technological innovations.

In "Digital Literacy of Students and Its Improvement at the University," Tatiana Shopova explains developments of technological and digital literacies that occur spaces of advanced research:

> The Internet and new media communication technologies with their interactive and increasingly individualized digital services change people's habits and behaviour,

building new value models and vital cues. They are becoming an irreplaceable source of education and self-education and important tool for the development of new literacy [26].

As a place of the development of new literacies for Team Arrow, the Arrow Cave is under constant improvements: new machines, new screens, and new devices for research, data collection, and medical testing crowd the edges of the workspace. Regular-sized computer monitors are replaced with touch-screen monitors that span three feet across and host multiple tabs to display information simultaneously as they link records across numerous databases. In Ep. 2.7, after realizing that flu vaccines around the city have been laced with the drug Vertigo, Diggle and Felicity try to track down the infection citizens. They use several screens, but the map of the infected in their homes do not show a pattern. Diggle stares intently at the screen and then asks Felicity if she is able to find the workplaces of the sick citizens. Scoffing at him "I'm really starting to wonder what it would take to impress you guys," she then watches the screen and types furiously. A second later, new dots appear on the digital map of the city, marking a trail through the streets which they realize is the route of a vaccine bus.

Responding to demanding missions, the Arrow Cave's aesthetics connotes a sense of futuristic design and improvements, a space in which the minds, bodies, and skills of the superheroes undergo constant renovation towards new and more efficient achievements. As the show continues and Oliver's abilities develop and improve, the Arrow Cave also progresses in its capacities for detective research and superhero surveillance. In Season 2, after Malcolm Merlyn causes an earthquake that destroys most of the cave, Oliver leaves his city to reassess his mission and rethink his approach in killing targets from The List. In his absence, Felicity remodels the cave with newer, updated technology: larger, brighter monitors that display cross- and intersecting data, white reflectors that highlight different workstations, and glass panels that showcase combat equipment, pristine suits, and arrows.[3] The new aesthetics of the Arrow Cave are streamlined and revolutionary, highlighted in blue that shines off the chrome and the reflective floor, suggestive of a space advanced in digital literacies, technological surveillance, and knowledge-gathering capabilities.

Team Arrow engages in physical fights with villains, using external weapons and their bodies as a means of subduing as opponent. These low-literacy, physical activities often take place outside of the Arrow Cave; inside the cave, high-technology activities take place on the multiple screens that Felicity uses to hack every social, civil, governmental, educational, financial, and political online database that she can find. Numbers constantly run up and down the screens, marking changes within Starling City that might indicate criminal activities such as an influx in stocks or bank accounts. Markers on digital

10. Places for Literacy Development 191

layouts of buildings and streets let Felicity and other members of the team watch team members out on the field through a variety of modes to help them complete their missions as efficiently and with little harm inflicted (to the superhero and the innocent bystanders) as possible. The first prototype of the cave works in Oliver's early days as a superhero, but as he continues his training—in physical action and reaction and in comprehensive detective skills—he and Team Arrow modify the cave to meet their needs. The better surveillance that the team creates, the better they can perform as superheroes to the fullest of their intellectual and physical capacities.

S.T.A.R. Labs in The Flash

In *The Flash*, we see the workspace of S.T.A.R. (Scientific and Technological Advanced Research) Labs as a place to experiment and work on far-out science. Originally created as a space to develop and monitor a partial accelerator, the lab acts as an intersection of literacies: science, robotics, media research, and communication. The white walls and gleaming equipment remind viewers that the characters in the lab (Caitlin, Cisco, and Wells as both of his alter-egos) are primarily scientists first and superhero teammates second. Experimentation and proving hypotheses remain their main concern, and even though the scientific methods that they practice are not actually possible in our reality at this current moment, the methods they use to research metahuman activity speak to their backgrounds as scientists. In their research on the changes that modern digital platforms brought for literacy development, Julie Coiro et al. note, "No previous technology for literacy has been adopted by so many, in so many different places, in such a short period of time, with such profound consequences" (2–3). The entirety of S.T.A.R. Labs reflects a need for uncovering the truth: the truth about scientific laws in the universe (and across the multiverse). While the Arrow Cave has a dark, secretive atmosphere to its solid walls and dim lighting, S.T.A.R. Labs has overhead windows that permit natural light to stream in and paint the lab in translucent brightness. The open glass windows to the adjourning rooms imply the openness of the scientists' attitudes towards their work: an embracing of forward momentum and freedom of research within scientific fields.[4]

In the first episode of *The Flash*, the camera zooms in on Barry's unconscious body after the accident, lying on a hospital bed and attended by Caitlin and Cisco. This is our first look into the space of S.T.A.R. Labs, and the screenshot shows a curved desk station that has three large touch-screen monitors on that. Above Barry's hospital bed, five blue-tinted monitors track his vitals, and on both sides of the bed, multiple monitoring screens rest on IV stations, waiting to be used by the scientists in this technical place. Fueled by digital screens and natural light, the scientists work to create the optimal conditions for their superhero as well as monitor the activities of their large metropolis. Here, the connection between scientists and digital information drives most of their activities, and throughout both Season 1 and Season 2, scenes in S.T.A.R. Labs often begin with one of the four scientists looking up from a screen to relay information, posit a hypothesis, or object to a proposed procedure from one of the other scientists. Riddled with complex formulas, the screens support new scientific literacies and are created by those with the highest of advanced, specialized scientific literacies. In this main room as well as the side rooms blocked by glass walls, the main actions of Team Flash revert back to the information gathered there, giving them a space to set forth new hypotheses, test new theories, and design new (and in Cisco's opinion, cooler) machinery made from these hypotheses and theories.

Spaces that support multiliterate activities and advancements have significance because they ground any literate action or event with a particular goal: a set objective for the hero or the sidekick to achieve in relatively quick time and with a broader expanse of capacity for gaining fresh knowledge. These places may support a variety of individual literacy practices as well as intersecting multimodal practices. We see this in S.T.A.R. labs when Caitlin and Cisco use monitors to watch the Flash's activities including a map of the streets where he runs, detailed summarizations of his vitals, and instant news reporting, all providing them with a third-person, near-omnipotent perspective of the activities occurring in Central City. By examining these activities, we can understand how literacies grow and develop in this high-tech spaces, how they empower the abilities of superheroes to flourish and improve, and how they encourage expansion of multiliteracies rather than limit them. In these material spaces, superheroes' identities and abilities are shaped by the technologies that they use as well as the new creations of technologies and tools that support their superheroic endeavors. When observing these in action, we see how our own literacies form around and through multimodal tools and digital texts; our literacies develop and expand to encompass new information gathered through multimodals advancements, improving as we add activities to our repertoire to learn more, read more, understand more, and do more.

The importance of both *The Flash* and *Arrow*'s spaces speak to the need to develop team literacies and team responses that use a wide range of multimodalities and multiliterate events to accomplish a goal. Whether improving scientific literacies or monitoring a city through multiple screens, the reliance on the team and its material literacies emphasizes how superheroic communications are enforced, created, recreated, and improved. It is these interactions and these quick responses with both written and digital texts that allow superheroes to respond with appropriate information to perform a task; according to Gee, "Multiple tools, different types of people, and diverse skill sets are networked in ways that make everyone smarter and make the space itself a form of the emergent intelligence" (2013, 174). These places afford superheroes the reliability to depend upon the information they receive in there, and the ways that information shapes and alters their missions is reflected by the reliability of the superheroes' actions. New villains may arise, new threats may occur, and the superheroes may pause momentarily from the enormity of these new threats, but in moments of crisis, they fall back on their abilities and skills. They must rely on the training that has been ground into their reactions, both mental and physical: training that prods them to aspire to higher levels of heroism, reaching pinnacles of superhuman endeavors. Students who observe the spaces of these high-digital, specialized literacies can identify the literacy events that take place, literacy events promoted by the logistics of multimodal research and networked detective skills.

Low-Tech Workspaces for Detectives

> Much of the popularity and pervasiveness of digital media is linked to the ability to overcome temporal and spatial boundaries and it is difficult to see a literacy event in terms of a particular time and locations if literacies straddle what we do on-screen/online and off-screen/offline [522].
> —Cathy Burnett, "(Im)Materialising Literacies"

As opposed to the high digital and technology-infused spaces of *Arrow* and *The Flash*, other TV superhero shows indicate that their main hero is able to do detective work efficiently in places absent all the digital devices and technical toys. The workspace of *Jessica Jones* expresses Jessica's abilities as a detective with very few tools at her disposal. She converts the living room of her apartment into an office with the main pieces of furniture being a wooden desk and a few chairs. Her laptop, which she carries into various rooms of the apartment, serves as her main research tool, but she has enough advanced literacy skills to utilize that one digital device to find all the information she needs to continue working, if not thriving, as an independent detective. A few various papers and sometimes photos frequent the inside of her office, but the space itself is kept nearly blank and clean without books on the shelves or multiple monitors for her to look at. Studying the office space reveals a utilitarian mind and spatial simplicity where she gathers evidence and connects ideas. She does not need fancy gadgets and digital projections to be able to do her job which relies on her cognitive skills as a detective to track people down and, as her contract work for the law firm specifies, serve them papers and other legal documents.

Jessica's workplace reflects her personality: sparse, cold, and neutral with an emphasis on functionality. In her office, she mediates between her job and her vice of drinking as both serve as distractions to her PTSD and smoldering rage. Without the computer, this could easily be an office from a hard-boiled detective story at the height of noir; the aesthetics of Jessica's space reflects her ability to focus and be mindful when working. Ellen Carillo argues for the need of mindfulness in literacy events: "while various definitions of *metacognitive* and *mindful* often overlap and *metacognitive* is already widely used, the concept of mindfulness highlights not just the task that one does 'mindfully,' but also the individual, the reader, who is learning *to be* mindful" (191). Any literacy activity Jessica performs as a detective will be methodical and focused, observing documents and pictures on her laptop, but limited by the sparse setting of an office that speaks to basic detective skills. The technology available in her space of work is basic, but mindful and metacognitive literacy events still take place to empower her work.

In *Luke Cage*, Misty Knight's workspace in the police station also resembles the utilitarian conditions of Jessica's office. While the police do have more tools to survey the city and have access to multimodal documents and digital resources to help them catch criminals and compile evidence, the actual physical space of Misty's office remains fairly blank and uncluttered with personal details. Misty best performs as a detective by putting up pictures of crime scenes on the walls of her office and staring at them intently to recreate the crime scenes in her head. The images of the crimes provide her a variety of perspectives of a singular crime scene from different spatial angles, and they emphasize the point of view that a person would have when reading the scene and gathering clues in real time. Unlike other detectives' work boards such as Barry Allen's research on his mother's death and Ben Ulrich's research on the kingpin of Hell's Kitchen, Misty's walls only house pictures, no written reports or hand-scribbled notes. The evidence of the crimes lay on her table or in compiled closed files, but her most important literacy events happen with the visual images that she stares at for—what the show indicates—countless hours.

These images in their bright, crisp visualizations almost act like panels of a comic book for her that she has to read through, creating a mental cause-and-effect analysis. She sees the end results of the crime, and she has to assemble meaning by working backwards through time. Regardless of the groups of pictures on the walls, the rest of her office clearly works as an area for police business, an organized space where advanced literacies of criminal justice act to compile data and neat, methodical ways. Misty's movements in the office as well as the actions of her bosses and her partner reflect the department's need for simplification and clarity, not massive amounts of strenuous data that would only serve to distract the police officers from their work. Detective work in Misty's office stays mostly a cognitive process rather than an externalized display flashed on multiple, colorful screens like in the Arrow Cave.

Like Misty, James Gordon is also a detective working in a police station, and the office workspace of the Gotham police resembles many of the hallmarks of the classical police station with desk and chairs grouped for officers to interview and take statements from witnesses and suspects alike. Because *Gotham* operates in a low-tech, nearly digital-less environment, this workspace consists almost entirely of printed, alphabetic documents and pages. The wooden desks and wooden swivel chairs along with the stacks of paper on individual desks and small decks lamps feel reminiscent of noir detective fiction, emphasized by the typewriters at the corners of the workspaces. One or two small computer monitors accompany desks in later episodes, but the whole of the space relies on traditional literacy events, mainly those restricted to alphabetic print. Rather than digital screens and intersecting technologies, this place reflects the cold, detached detective work that is limited by information rather than enhanced by it. Yet, because our current technology does not yet exist in this world, the sharpest, most capable things in the police station are the minds of the detectives that assimilate the information.

In many ways, this highlights the importance of understanding a detective's specialized literacy: no matter how enhanced or expensive the technology becomes in surveillance or accumulation of data, the detective's mind and his or her ability to read information and assemble it into patterns remain the most important elements about the detective. *Gotham* features some of the most low-tech environments seen on superhero TV shows, but the role of the detective and the emerging superhero reflect that of careful, methodical literacy events that search for reliable, important information and compile it into meaningful data. Studying low-technical places allows students to compare literacy events in those simplistic places to places of high-digital technology usage, and students can also discuss the dependencies of the brain's logical and cognitive processes to connect information instead of relying on digital devices.

Aesthetics Throughout Literacy Practices

Whether with basic tools or crowded technical machinery, private spaces of superhero training and detective work have aesthetics to their physical makeup. In "Looking Good: Aesthetics, Multimodality, and Literacy Studies," Theo van Leeuwen puts forth the connection between aesthetics and literacies: "To be literate in contemporary aesthetics is to be literate in style as identity, and to be able to understand the multimodal communicative potential of aesthetic signifiers" (432). We see aesthetics in literacy events in these superhero places that are kept meticulously clean and support vast platforms, providing access to multimodal information through a range of databases, collections, historical accounts, and digital mapping. This streamlined, sparse approach to gathering information empowers superheroes to act as researchers and detectives, having immediate resources to the information they use: these spaces function as almost military barracks combined with science labs and information portals to streamline the intake of information and the output of superheroic activities as neatly as possible. Sometimes a villain may attack the lab, or the cave gets momentarily damaged, but as quickly as they can, the characters work to redesign and replace all tools and information devices to get back to the team's overall mission, equipping the superheroes and supporting team members to function at the height of their intellectual and physical capacities. Theo van Leeuwen states that "aesthetic literacy also means being able to discern and create identities, similarities and oppositions of composition, shape, color and texture, and knowing how this can create meaning" (436).

The spaces of work in superhero TV shows reflect the literacies of their respective characters, but they also stress the personal aesthetics of their main heroes. Jessica and Oliver like places of sparse functionality and brooding. Bruce studies in a library full of books, reflecting the superhero he will become: Batman who memorizes vast amounts of data and recalls it immediately with near photo-like memory. Barry, Cisco, and Caitlin have a lab full of light that mirrors their optimism of the future, a time when scientific advancements will lead the human race towards prosperity. In their research on aesthetics and places, Jennifer Rennie and Annette Patterson posit "It is common now to think about reading as a socially, culturally and historically located practice, and these aspects of reading have been explored extensively by scholars" (209). The act of locating the spaces that reading takes place in proves difficult in this digital era as many of these spaces have become mobile thanks to the versatility of electronic devices that aid users in accessing information when and wherever they please.

The presence of a designated space to improve superheroic abilities in superhero TV shows has implications for our own world as we still have designated spaces that promote literacy acquisition, improvement, and multiplicity. The library and the school seem like obvious places designated to literacy outreach, but other places such as religious institutions and business conglomerations also encourage specialized and advanced literacy development across a multitude of platforms. The space may have advanced technological interfaces or remain simple with mostly alphabetic, print texts, but the reader must put forth effort in understanding literacy practices on social, educational, familial, and economic levels. The markers of these superheroic spaces as hideouts and private domains demonstrate to the audience that the work that takes place here operates with a higher level of human endeavor and intelligence than other places, and that that work is not only valued but set apart from other places in the superheroes' and the general teams' lives. When studying aesthetics of spaces and the literacy events within those spaces as prompted and defined by the aesthetics, students can recognize the effects of the superhero's ideology on the space just as the reader affects the space of individual's reading activities. Whether deliberately or unconsciously, the reader engrains the space of the reading activity with ideology about the functionality of literacy and multimodal multiliteracies.

Chapter Conclusion

This chapter examines the collective spaces on superhero TV shows in which the superheroes and their teams work: researching information, improving weapons and technology, collecting data, and planning missions. The term *material literacies* define how the physical materials of texts and spaces help shape literacy events and larger literacy practices. The high-digital space (the Arrow Cave and S.T.A.R Labs) promotes different literacy events than low-technical spaces (Jessica's office, Misty police office, and Jim's desk space). The chapter concludes by exploring aesthetics of superhero spaces in articulating the types of literacy events that occur within the physical confines of the spaces.

Class Activities

These activities focus on the physical, specially-created spaces of superheroes and aim to widen perspectives about the connection between spaces of human existence and their resulting literacy practices. I stress here the importance of thinking of spaces and places used by the superhero as extensions of the superhero's literacy practices. That is, the superhero and the team have created places to use to assist them in their missions; these places are meant for use and superhuman activity, not just for the sheer coolness of their aesthetical appearance.

Activity 1: Defining and Identifying Spatial Literacies

Students reflect on spatial and material literacies and debate on the methods that particular spaces enforce with specialized, advanced literacy events and collective literacy practices.

QUESTIONS FOR STUDENTS TO ANSWER:

- How do physical spaces, both private and public, reinforce superheroes' literacy practices?
- How do the workspaces of superheroes reflect particular literacy events that take place in them?
- Do limitations in these spaces limit the literacy activities that take place?
- How do technology and digital platforms promote multiliterate events?

SUGGESTED READINGS AND QUOTES FOR DISCUSSION:

Ryan, Mary, and Tony Rossi. "The Transdisciplinary Potential of Multiliteracies: Bodily Performances and Meaning-Making in Health and Physical Education." *Multiliteracies and Diversity in Education: New Pedagogies for Expanding Landscapes*, edited by Annah Healy, Oxford University Press, 2008, pp. 30–57.

"The multiliteracies notion of spatial literacy incorporates a 'reading' of the physical space and conditions of any context to derive meanings. It follows, then, the spatial meanings must have an impact on understandings of sport and physical activity in the curriculum" (Ryan and Rossi 34).

DELIVERABLES OR WRITING PROJECT:

Students compose a short essay (500–700 words) about how spaces and places in superhero TV shows are designed specifically to produce multiliterate events.

Activity 2: Comparison and Contrast of Superhero Workspaces

This activity invites students to work in groups to research and define all literacy events that are enacted in the workplaces of superhero TV shows. Group presentations will cover a range of TV shows, encouraging students to explore different literacy practices in different places.

GROUP ACTIVITIES:

Groups discuss these questions among themselves:

- How do the superhero and the team arrange their spaces to navigate superhero activities and detective skills?
- How might one understand a superhero better through reading the workshop spatially?
- How do physical, spatial literacy events contribute to the whole superhero team's literacy practices?

10. Places for Literacy Development

SUGGESTED READINGS AND QUOTES FOR DISCUSSION:

    Bednarz, Sarah, and Karen Kemp. "Understanding and Nurturing Spatial Literacy." *Procedia-Social and Behavioral Sciences*, vol. 21, 2011, pp. 18–23.

"Spatial thinking, then, was seen as an amalgam of concepts, skills, and cognitive approaches that allow individuals to use space to model the world, real and imagined, in valuable and productive ways. Spatial thinking defined in this way, as a functioning process, facilitates the development of spatial literacy" (Bednarz and Kemp 20).

    Street, Brian V. "Introduction." *Social Literacies: Critical Approaches to Literacy in Development, Ethnography and Education*. Taylor and Francis, 2016, pp. 1–12.

"Recently, however, the trend has been towards a broader consideration of literacy as a social practice and in a cross-cultural perspective. Within this framework an important shift has been the rejection by many writers of the dominant view of literacy as a 'neutral,' technical skill, and the conceptualization of literacy instead as an ideological practice, implicated in power relations and embedded in specific cultural meaning and practices" (Street 1).

DELIVERABLES:

    Groups present on the superheroic spaces. Here, I advise having students use lots of still images and moving clips so they can visually walk the class through superheroic spaces in the presentations. As superhero spaces have physicality and dimension to them, the more the presentation can lay-out the reality of the space, the better other students can conceptualize the literacy events enacted there.

Activity 3: Designing a Webpage to Map Literacy Activities and Spaces

    This activity lets students design spaces to help them improve their digital literacies and multimodal multiliteracies. Often, spatial designing is appealing, and students might already have experience with spatial designing through different modes: videogames (The Sims), TV (*Tidying Up with Marie Kondo*), or instructional books (Exner and Pressel's *Basics Spatial Design*).

SUGGESTED READINGS AND QUOTES FOR DISCUSSION:

    Luke, Carmen. "Cyber-Schooling and Technological Change: Multiliteracies for New Times." *Multiliteracies: Literacy Learning and the Design of Social Futures*, edited by Bill Cope and Mary Kalantzis, Routledge, 2000, pp. 69–91.

"These industrial-model, print- and book-based practices of schooling will become less relevant in the age of virtual classrooms, hypertext, and online communities of learners. [...] In an electronic digital and networked information environment, however, teaching spaces and practices must undergo profound shifts" (Luke 81–2).

> Sullivan, Patrick. "Deep Reading as a Threshold Concept in Composition Studies." *Deep Reading: Teaching Reading in the Writing Classroom*, edited by Patrick Sullivan, Howard Tinberg, and Sheridan Blau, NCTE, 2017, pp. 143–71.

"Define reading not simply as a way to decode text or to encounter received ideas but rather as the valuable process of constructing knowledge and meaning" (Sullivan 165).

MULTIMODAL DELIVERABLES:

Students showcase their new spaces on their webpages. This could be a 2D or 3D design, screenshots of a room from a game or online design creator, or a hand-drawn sketch.

♦ ♦ 11 ♦ ♦

How the Average Citizen Reads in Superhero Worlds

> [Literacy studies] is an approach to the study of reading and writing which starts out from what people do in their lives. It starts from people's social practices, noting that many of these involve texts of some sort, that in carrying out many activities in life people use texts [39].
> —David Barton, "Understanding Textual Practices in a Changing World"

This chapter, the last of my book, details the literacy practices of the average citizen living in a superhero world. This chapter moves beyond literacies of superheroes, villains, and secondary characters to present literacy practices of the everyday person in superhero TV shows, people that live in communities of heightened tension and global threats from superhuman forces. Often the average citizen is relegated to the background of the scenes, but their presence still implies the importance of learning, language, and literacy in their respective fictional settings. The push for multiliteracies as a communal movement in superhero TV shows demonstrates the demands of the viewing audience who has come to expect the spectacular and the amazing in superhero narratives but still want to see remnants of our own world in them. The current-day portrayal of superheroics establishes high expectations in visual texts: the story has layers of complexity and character development, the music is epic and grandiose, the stakes are high, and the special effects of fighting and physical feats heighten the tension for the viewer. Yet, for all the dramatic displays of superheroics, in the background people of the cities (New York, Central City, Gotham) live lives that reflect the majority of America's average citizens, falling into a wide spectrum of socioeconomic classes. When observing fictional depictions of class, we can come to more-accurate understandings about how our own social, economic, educational, and communal situations align with our literacy practices.

I emphasize the importance of literacy development and literacy practices as the norm for average citizens in these superhero TV shows because, according to The New London Group, a broad range of perspectives on literacy "account for the context of our cultural and linguistically diverse and increasingly globalized society; to account for the multifarious cultures that interrelate and the corality of texts that circulate" (9). The more diverse and multimodal the literacy practices of a community become, the more they are able to disseminate information, promote democracy, and improve the lives of all people in the communities. Rachel Heydon and Jennifer Rowsell in "Phenomenology and Literacy Studies" state, "Literacy research tends to emphasize the cognitive activities involved in reading, writing and communicating and seldom do literacy researchers venture into more embodied interpretations of literacy praxis" (457). In this chapter, I explore the embodied praxis of literacy events in superhero TV shows on a larger scale: moments of reading and responding to print and multimodal texts for the average citizen. Mostly this means observing the worlds that the superheroes live in and exploring these fictional spaces through the eyes of an ordinary citizen. Because *Arrow* and *The Flash* share the same DC universe as do *Daredevil*, *Jessica Jones*, and *Luke Cage* in the MCU, I'm aligning my research to the combined universes of those shows.[1] *Gotham* takes place in another DC universe, one outside of our localized time and history.

Influence of Culture in Creating Material Literacies

This chapter looks three different TV shows' universes and their respective literacy practices for the average citizen: DC universe, MCU universe, and Gotham universe. In all three universes, media in written, digital, and spoken modes affect the citizens within them. In his significant, sociological research of the relationship between power structures and education, *Pedagogy of the Oppressed*, Paulo Freire notes, "Reading the world always precedes reading the word, and reading the word implies continually reading the world" (10). This reciprocal affiliation, in which the word and the world influence each other, connotes a circular dependency of ideas and real-world events. As I have discussed in earlier chapters, literacy practices shape cultural norms and expectations just as the resulting cultures guide and alter literacy usages throughout social contexts and needs, creating a circular influence. During superhero TV shows, the culture and literacy practices of that culture seep through the background, embodied in the expectations of each show's setting and location and grounded in a collective representation of the average citizen. The main emphasis for this chapter lies in the understanding that any culture's literacy practices have ties to the material world, and the material world dictates the types of literacy practices used within world, including fictional worlds that present hyper-realistic, superheroic versions of our own world.

According to Kate Pahl and Hugh Escott in "Materialising Literacies," "Linking up a study of literacy in the community with wider disciplines enriches and develops ways of knowing across disciplines and can open up literacy studies to possibilities for emergent sites of scholarships that are rooted in the material social world" (500). Because literacy practices always arise from a need to interact with the material world, literacy events cannot be divorced from the social, material setting which fosters them. As John Duffy argues in "Other Gods and Countries," "While conceptions of literacy as embedded in cultural practices are by no means uniform, they are typically characterized by ethnographic observations of literacy use within the culture" (39). Superheroes improve their own literacy events to sharpen their detective talents and combative abilities in their quests for justice, but the average citizen, who has not sworn a vigilante mission to restore the world to order, follows the literacy trends of the culture in which they live. The media usage in superhero TV shows reference these cultural practices as indicative of the physical world and its manifestations of meaning that create spaces and general requirements for texts and literacy skills by the people and for the people.

In "Understanding Textual Practices in a Changing World," David Barton states that "literacy can be a powerful lens for examining changing social practices, including the impact of new technologies, the growing audit culture and the growing textualization of life" (50). Different types of multimodalities involve the merging of texts and platforms across different types of meaning and information to please, entertain, or interest the audience as well as presenting different modes of learning opportunities. With these multimodalities, we see an influx of learning opportunities that speak to multiple audiences through new methods and means of learning and efforts. Bronwyn Williams and Amy Zenger in "Popular Culture and Literacy in a Networked World" argue, "The literacy practices shaped by popular culture online are also influenced by the ways in which popular culture images, ideas, and references are read across borders" (2). These borders become less pronounced the more information is disseminated and reviewed because, according to Williams and Zenger, "as students from around the world read and write with popular culture, their literacy practices raise important questions about the interplay of rhetoric, power, technology, and global capital" (2). Because superheroes create their own literacy events, they sometimes feel outside the influence of their culture, but average citizens in the superhero's world conform regularly to its practices.

The presence of newspapers and online blogs as news outlets has some significance for disseminating information in the MCU and DC TV universes, but newspapers are most prominent in the universe of *Gotham*. Bruce receives most of his information through newspapers, Jim reads the headlines of the paper to see how the news media reports on the activities of the police, and other citizens in the background read newspapers that report on the criminal enterprises of the decaying city as well as political and legal efforts to clean up the street. Iris in *The Flash* has an online blog which reports on superheroic activities, and citizens read alternative texts online that fall outside of major conglomerations of news reporting, mostly blogs and guerrilla-style film clips. Often the TV in the background will show a news broadcast, as often happens in *Arrow*, and main characters and background characters stop to huddle around the screen, reading carefully the images and the lines of reporting to gather information about current events. Billboards and advertisements appear in all three universes, rooting the citizens of the fictional stories to American consumerism specifically and capitalism in general. From all these aspects of media comes a rooting of external texts as influential for the people living, working, and sometimes just surviving in these crime-laden spaces, resulting in critical literacy practices for citizens.

Rebecca Rogers and Katherine O'Daniels define critical literacy as "the practice of using technologies (from print to digital technologies) to analyze, critique, and redesigned structures that influence daily life. The potential of critical literacy is reflected in the diversity of topics, methodologies, and educational levels represented in the field" (62). In viewing the media of the average citizen, we see a variety of interests and needs of the communities being expressed on the page and the screen. Williams and Zenger stress the importance of popular culture as discourse by stressing that "many young people are in contact with text and people around the world through the lenses of popular culture: popular culture provides the rhetorical, linguistic, and semiotic building blocks through which they engage into cross-cultural discourse" (3). All this media usage and cross-cultural discourse speak to literacy practices across socioeconomic class, education, and prospects, and the citizens of these three fictional universes belong to socioeconomic classes which dictate their literacy events as part of larger literacy practices.

Literacy According to Socioeconomics

> It is problematic, then to claim that literacy necessarily causes a transformation of culture, society, or mind or that societies without high levels of literacy are barred from the mental activities that some theorists have come

to associate with literacy: verbal self-consciousness, abstraction, etc. [228].
—Mike Rose, *The Mind at Work*

Kim Donehower in "Connecting Literacy as Sustainability" argues, "Literacy levels have long been considered the markers of the health of a community" (98). As was seen with Graff's examples of the literacy myth, many problems of small groups and diverse communities across cultures have been laid at the feet of illiteracy and lack of education. According to David Bloom and Judith Green in "Social and Linguistic Terms," "Literacy practices and events are embedded in and constitutive of cultural ideologies. That is, a cultural ideology informs, and is informed by, what literacy practices are used in what social situations when, by whom, with what meanings, and with what social consequences" (20). In all three universes, we see similar breakdowns of class through the markers of wealth and opportunities (or the lack thereof): the upper wealthy class, the lower working class along with the ultra-poor and/or homeless, and the middle class stuck in the middle. The lives that divide these classes are not always obvious—and a true socio-economic study would make further distinctions: upper middle class, lower upper class, etc.—but generalities along class help students observe trends in individual usage of literacy events.

Throughout episodes of *Arrow*, *The Flash*, and *Gotham*, the wealthy citizens of their respective cities (Starling City, Central City, and Gotham) gather for a ritzy gala or ball to fund a charity, to lend political support to a candidate, or even to announce a new business venture that will garner the super-wealthy even more money and prestige. At these lavish parties, we see the upper-class citizens of the cities "glammed out" in formal dress, jewelry, makeup, watches, and fancy footwear as markers of the upper class. Within those crowds of people, the standards of the upper class seem most prominent as these citizens have access to large amounts of money and with this access have gained prestige and recognition in their communities. The level of specialized literacies that they have developed usually speak to profitable undertakings recognized in capitalistic endeavors as those of financial success, reaping in vast rewards. They are lawyers, doctors, businessmen, and venture capitalists along with bankers and politicians. Noticeable literacy events rarely happen in these collective spaces because the members of the upper class are celebrating or supporting worthy causes.[2] The literacy practices of the upper class usually are those in which language controls large segments of the population such as those involved with the government or those in business where language and the benefits of written and printed material enable large capitalistic endeavors: contracts for buildings, mergers between companies, accounts of investments, and stocks for shareholders in large companies.

Sometimes, the superhero belongs to these classes such as Oliver Queen or Bruce Wayne; sometimes, the supervillain belongs to these classes such as Wilson Fisk or Mariah Dillard. To hide his superhero activities and the Arrow Cave, Oliver creates and runs Verdant, a club for the young elite of Startling City to socialize and party, and while most of the literacy events in the club involve cellphones, the markers of wealth and prosperity are clearly written on his young, attractive clientele. In *Gotham*, Alfred insists that Bruce attend glamorous soirees to carry on his parents' legacy, and Bruce meets several political players who control politics, finances, or crime in Gotham. Outside of his criminal activities, Wilson Fisk is as a major player in the art world where he meets his love interest, Vanessa Marianna, who works as an art curator, and they share a conversation about the aesthetics that a painting can bring to a room and to a person's temperament, a cultured discussion that contrasts with his physical brutality in beheading his associate in a later scene. Abigail Hackett in "Multimodality and Sensory Ethnographies" notes, "The key literacies are now those that facilitate movement towards local goals, the literacies of social design and innovation in each present local context" (323). The social design of the wealthy and privileged gives them access to the innovations of their society and culture, and even though their wealth and importance cannot protect them completely from the random attacks of supervillains, they still have more access to the forces of control that move their communities through media and power plays.

Those at the mercy of the capitalistic systems tend to be those at the lowest level of socioeconomic prosperity, usually the homeless and low-level criminals that wander the street and exist in dangerous situations. According to John Duffy, "We stand within a history that has alternately marginalized and ignored the knowledge of the powerless and then (when we must listen) domesticated and assimilated that experience into mainstream and middle-class schemas" (172). Throughout all of the superhero TV shows, the powerless tend to suffer the most at the hands of reckless supervillains or collective gangs that commit crimes throughout large cities. Often the people on the streets are former criminals and are eager to join these gangs and become muscle to enact a villain's plan rather than remaining homeless and destitute. Occasionally, the homeless are used in the mad scientist experiments such as the insane inmates in *Gotham*'s Arkham Asylum or the prisoners in *Luke Cage*, serving as lab rats in bizarre science experiments. The lower class routinely are treated as disposable because they do not have agency through any wealth and lack the means to begin the near-impossible climb up the social ladder.

Although we champion education as a means of escaping poverty, the literacy practices of the poor and destitute in superhero TV shows reflect the actual realities of people at the bottom of the social ladder where the social amenities afforded to the middle and upper class often are out of reach. Proper identification, bank accounts, vehicles for transportation, family and friends as social networks, and a range of literate and multiliterate skills that are valued in today's marketplace often fall short for the people who have become homeless or been incarcerated. The superhero's actions and the supervillain's plans often seem as arbitrary and heartless as the conditions that led to their despondent situations in the first place. When you are living on the streets and are subjected to the elements, assaults, and physically-detrimental crimes nightly, a superhero fighting against a supervillain underneath the bridge where you live does not seem that much more threatening than a night plagued by petty thieves, strung-out junkies, and sewer rats. (At least you have something interesting to watch when the superhero and supervillain fight.)

Between the super wealthy and the super poor of the superheroes' cities exists the middle class which often is caught in the middle of the war between good and evil. Not powerful enough to affect the city positively or negatively, yet not despondent enough to suffer without agency, the middle class folks often stand at the edges of the war for the control of the cities or, for some ambitious supervillains, the world. The middle class are not likely to enlist in the roving gangs that frequent Gotham and Harlem which Jim Gordon and Luke Cage must fight; the middle class rarely go to prison in large enough droves to become a significant part of the population to be experimented upon; and the middle class do not have enough money to tempt a small-time supervillain seeking to rob those of their goods and personal wealth at banquets, balls, or impressive galas. Instead, the middle class tend to find themselves in their cars or in their offices when supervillains attack and often watch the action from fairly-safe but still close proximity. They are not as exposed as the homeless, but they do not have the armed guards or muscled goons for protection that the super wealthy have either. These middle-class groups usually produce most of the sidekicks and mentors, allowing them to live with comfortable homes and bank accounts but not the wide access to funds that the very wealthy superheroes and supervillains enjoy. These types of characters tend to rely on mass media such as newspapers and broadcasts for general information about their cities, and most superhero and supervillain activities are reported to them rather than witnessed firsthand.

At the edge of three well-established classes, there also exist citizens for hire who tend to be low-level criminals: mob thugs, gang members, goons to provide muscles, henchmen to hijack banks, armed vehicles, and museums, or toadies following supervillains around for loot. Criminals for hire mostly come from low-literacy, high-poverty areas and rarely engage with written or digital texts as they exist to follow their leaders' commands. Most of these criminals work as goons and hired muscle for a criminal mastermind, creating opportunities for the superhero to utilize his or her impressive fighting skills.[3] Sometimes, a henchman will hack computer databases to control surveillance feeds or to empty bank accounts, and they need higher levels of multiliterate skills than a beefed-up goon who holds people hostage at a bank robbery or throws punches at the superhero. Across the classes of citizens in the background of superhero TV shows, we see a representation of our own current socioeconomic classes and the ways that these citizens interact in social and cultural spaces. The literacy practices employed by each of these groups speak to individual needs as well as community demands on people's intelligence, comprehension, and responses to information.

Literacy Metaphors and Myths for the General Public

> Reading, associated early on with proper conduct and right belief, as well as the exercise of civil rights and duties, still enjoys a nearly sacred status in many societies. It is nearly universally regarded as wholesome and uplifting, an avenue to moral development and responsible citizenship [57].
> —Deborah Brandt, "Writing Over Reading: New Directions in Mass Literacy"

In all three universes, literacy metaphors and myths in educations still have prominence for the average citizen who does not get to decide their destiny as definitively as the superhero or supervillain does. Routinely, in all three fictional universes, children and teenagers are told to stay in school, finish their education, and make something of their lives to escape poverty or to have a range of opportunities. In *Luke Cage*, Pops tells all the young men who visit his barbershop to focus on school and stay out trouble with the gangs and the police; the wealthy of Gotham sent their children to private school where Bruce attends shortly after his parents' deaths. Throughout these fictional worlds, as in our worlds, education and literacy are seen as an inoculation against poverty, and prescribed education acts as the ladder to success and the securing of the American Dream. Karen Dooley notes, "Equity is one of the ideals of the multiliteracies education" (106), and this ideal reinforces literacy myths for enabling and empowering citizens. The background characters of the TV shows imply that multiliteracies and diversity work well in all advanced, digitally-infused societies.

Multiliteracies also sanction the frenzied flow of information that thrives in our current digitally-obsessed culture. According to Dooley,

Difference and diversity are the very core of multiliteracies thinking. The case for multiliteracies education has been argued with reference to, among other things, increasing flows of people across national borders, proliferation of variants of English, the emergence of digital, multimodal knowledge-making capabilities and preferences, and multiplication of life—worlds within popular, consumer, and digital cultures [104].

However, within these diverse cultures, metaphors and myths of literacy still exist because the average citizens have not traded an autonomous, traditional view of literacy for an advanced, digital view of multimodal multiliteracies. Those new views can expand the role of literacy but many of these problems still persist. "Just as we would not traditionally assume that someone is literate if they can read but not write, we should not assume that someone possesses media literacy if they can consume but not express themselves" (Jenkins 170). Throughout the different socioeconomic classes of the average citizen of superhero TV shows, the role of literacy as a system of taking in information and expressing oneself through that information becomes central in understanding how literacy practices shape and are shaped by the communities in which people foster them. A crucial metaphor we see in these shows is that of literacy and intelligence as developed states of awareness, the ability to read one's surroundings and multiple texts to receive meaning from multimodal signs, symbols, messages, and bodies. This metaphor has implications for students studying literacy practices, demonstrating the methods for improving one's skillsets within spaces of language, texts, and community discourses towards greater intellectual and cognitive processes.

Literacy as a mass practice allows for recognition and remembrance of major language patterns, influencing citizens to learn through interactions and leading to enlightened states of awareness and self-reflection. Saskia Stille argues, "The field of literacy studies has long been associated with critical work, situating literacy within the dynamics of the social world to reveal its contested and ideological dimensions" (612). These ideological dimensions shape cultures and the activities of people inside of them, emphasizing "the sociocultural context of literacy learning rather than the individual ability or performance, conceiving of literacy not as a neutral skill but as a practice that must be understood in relation to social conditions and power relations" (612). Most of these social conditions and power relations result from the institutions that create them, the institutions that both use and restrict access to literacy and therefore limit access to the institutions themselves that ultimately define power and privilege. In "The Legacies of Literacy," Harvey Graff stresses "the primary users of literacy—the state, the church, and commerce—have remained in effect, regardless of the degree of the social restrictiveness that regulated the supply curve of popular diffusion of literacy" (152). In studying these fictional institutions in superhero TV shows and the literacy practices that they regulate, endorse, and reinforce, students can arrive at better insights into their own institutions that detail the majority of sanctioned literacy events into patterns of social literacy practices.

An Accommodationist Model of Literacy vs. Great Divides

> The accommodationist model of academic literacy differs from the foundationalist model in its recognition of the presence of a plurality of different sets of linguistic and notational conventions and procedures for academic reading and writing [113].
> —Bruce Horner and Min-Zhan Lu, "Towards a Labor Economy of Literacy"

Great divide concepts of literacy as a representation of literacy usually use the binary between literate and oral or between literate and illiterate, but in this instance, the division is between views of literacy: traditional autonomous views of literacy versus digital multiliterate views. When literacy is seen as a social practice, Harvey Graff argues, an autonomous view of literacy necessitates an immediate hierarchy: "The 'oral,' 'preliterate,' and 'illiterate' serve as marked and subordinate terms, whereas 'literate' and 'literary' assume the status of superior terms. Such hierarchies reinforce the presumed benefits of literacy" (2011, 58). In "Autonomous and Ideological Models of Literacy" (2006), Street extrapolates that such hierarchies promote America's cultural contemporary reliance on autonomous views of literacy which both confine literacy to a narrow space of educational domination and overvalue literacy by labeling it as the sole criterion for achieving social, financial, and personal success. The divide between views of literate and illiterate groups has developed into further concepts which separate literacy understandings—mainly that of autonomous literacy and multiliteracies—but it also appears between academic literacy and mainstream literacy as well as between alphabetic, print literacy and visual literacies.

As opposed to the great divide binary that endeavors to label literate groups as vastly different from oral culture groups, accommodationist models of literacy include the broad perspective and general flow of literacy which matches to what the average citizen uses literacy events for: to understand and establish information towards a purpose. This works against the foundationalist model of literacy, what Horner and Lu describe as a model that treats academic literacy as "a universal, uniform, and fixed set of linguistic and notational conventions and procedures that writers are to follow" (112). Older, outdated literacy perspectives and instructions tended to have narrow, autonomous views of literacy that limited not only how citizens conceived of literacy but also limited how citizens used literacy as a tool, a criterion for gathering knowledge and expanding one's information base. Horner and Lu further explain that

> indeed, the continuing power of foundationalist and accommodationist models of academic literacy and their residual presence in at least some of what we have termed "translation" models of literacy [...] can be understood as manifestations of not just conceptual inertia but also of an ideology of technocratic literacy aligned with neoliberalism [121].

Ideally, definitions of literacy should remain fluid so that they can adapt to expanded views or new changes of individual or cultural procedures.

Possible fluidity is often impeded by the demands of cultural ideology and authority which proscribe certain literacy instruction and expectations. In *Literacy in Theory and Practice* (1984), Street criticizes western education systems by the ways that writers write their own culture and ideology into the texts that endorse/sanction these systems. The lofty and usually impossible aims of higher education exist because "the claims for literacy can be described as 'ideological.' They are part of an armory of concepts, conventions, and practices that give meaning to and protect the writer's own social formation and specifically their own place within it" (38). As scholars with our own strident interests of various areas in the humanities, our tendencies to write our own beliefs about literacy into our mediums of instruction become apparent, especially in the fact that higher education often struggles to adapt to new changes in cultural and social constructs. It is not that we as academics do not want to change; rather, our values are so deeply entrenched with the beliefs about the traditional merits of education that we become blind as to the possibilities of new innovations and approaches of literacy that can expand higher learning into in-depth forms, pedagogies, and practices of critical thinking and academic analysis.

Great divide understandings of literacy appear in education usually through autonomous, traditional perspectives regarding how a culture reads and comprehends external messages. Thus, the binary of academic vs. popular/mainstream/colloquial/anything non-academic emerges. Students who recognize and can identify tendencies to simplify understandings of literacy and to impose overly simplistic binaries to those perspectives are able to have a richer appreciation for the complexities of literacy acquisition, usage, patterns, and improvement. To compare the literacy activities of these TV shows and their respective citizens allows students to survey perspectives of cultural practices, examining two cultures that resemble their own, yet still appear different in regards to literacy practices. Most students have fully embraced multimodality of the digital age, but the overly-exaggerated multiliteracies of *Arrow* are not available to our culture at this time, nor have we began to develop the spectrum of specialized literacy that would allow us to interact with the vast array of modalities that Oliver uses.

At the opposite end of the spectrum, *Gotham* features a world devoid of multiliterate skills in which characters are limited by a lack of multimodality and therefore do not have access to knowledge and information through digital interfaces the way that students do in their current lives. Students can apply a typical academic activity of their own such as a research paper to the worlds of both *Arrow* and *Gotham* and compare the literacy events in both. Researching and gathering information in the world of *Arrow* is almost too easy because the digital and technical databases and information centers are so vast and overreaching that students would be depending on technology to perform the work for them, relying too much on digital platforms. At the other extreme, using literacy skills to research in the world of *Gotham* is overly difficult and complicated as one must analyze and read vast amounts of information one page at a time rather than depend on databases or research tools online as a way to gather data. As I continually emphasize throughout pedagogical approaches, identification of evidence and then analysis/exposition of evidence provide students the opportunities to establish context and logic patterns to give exemplification to the theories they are learning. According to Williams and Zenger, "Understanding convergence culture as a social practice is vital if we hope to gain insights into how and why young people engage in participatory popular culture" (2012, 4). Critical thinking requires students to not only accumulate knowledge but be able to reassemble that knowledge in their own words, for their own uses, and to serve their own learning objectives.

Chapter Conclusion

This chapter explores literacy events for the average person in a superhero world and the larger social literacy practices that dictate literacy usage and perspectives of it through large social institutions that mediate these practices through prescribed, educational methods. This chapter also classifies socioeconomic groups of people in superhero TV shows and their typical literacy practices. The terms *accommodation model* and *great divide binary* define two perspectives of literacy events and practices: the ability to see literacy as accommodating the task as hard for the individual to read and the tendency to divide literacy activities into overly-simplistic binaries.

Class Activities

These activities allow students to see literacy skills in a range of improvement, action, adjustment, and speculation that include more accurate portrayals of how people read, comprehend, and interact with texts. This specific directive gives students an active role in creating their own perspectives of literacy that center on important aspects of how each student identifies literacy events and understands larger practices of literacy from the narratives rather than trying to make the definition fit the narratives. By observing the differences between these classes and how average people navigate, communicate, and learn through the limitations or the expansions of multiliterate practices in superhero TV shows, students can see how their own learning abilities can expand their knowledge bases and acquire a variety of multiliterate skillsets that depend to some extent on the communities and social settings as well as the time and socioeconomic stratosphere that they occupy.

Activity 1: Ordinary Literacy Practices in Extraordinary Worlds

Students describe an average citizen in a superhero world and then define that person's literacy events throughout a day.

QUESTIONS FOR STUDENTS TO ANSWER:
- What types of texts and modes does an average citizen encounter in a superhero TV show?
- How do the citizen's career, family, socioeconomic class, and friends contribute to his or her literacy events?
- What routine reading activities might the citizen do that would normally be overlooked but contribute to their ethnographic literacy practices? (writing a grocery list, composing a text message, liking a Facebook post, checking bank accounts, responding to a Twitter post)

SUGGESTED READINGS AND QUOTES FOR DISCUSSION:
> Juliano, Stephanie. "Superheroes, Bandits, and Cyber-Nerds: Exploring the History and Contemporary Development of the Vigilante." *Journal of International Commercial Law & Technology*, vol. 7, no. 1, Jan. 2012, pp. 44–64.

"The average person has at the very least an understanding of what he or she considers justice. Regardless of how an individual's view of justice fits into the constructs of law, the motivation behind this view is based primarily in matters of morality, sculpted from societal and familial influence" (Juliano 44).

Street, Brian V. "New Literacy Studies." *Language, Ethnography, and Education: Bridging New Literacy Studies and Bourdieu*, edited by Michael Grenfell et al., Routledge, 2012, pp. 27–49.

"Whereas dominant approaches to literacy in education tend to conceptualise literacy as a set of skills and study it through cognitive based theories of learning and activity, New Literacy Studies adopts an ethnographic approach to the study of reading and writing in varied social contexts, both in and out of education systems" (Street 28).

Deliverables or Writing Project:

A list of literacy events that an average citizen in a superhero would perform. For example, a 35-year-old corporate business associate might read a news blog in *The Flash*, watch the stock market to see numbers fall in the market because of supervillains' attacks, watch a news program that reports on superhero activities, and vote locally on laws to curb vigilante movements.

Activity 2: Literacy Practices of Socioeconomic Communities

This section demonstrates the ways that literacy events—those of traditional practices or those expanding into multimodal multiliteracies—affect superhero narratives and the characters within their respective worlds. However, as ordinary citizens in superhero TV shows demonstrate, though our literacy and multiliteracy events may reflect people's current social situations, they are not absolute and all defining in their potential to limit or aid citizens. The citizens of *Gotham* construct other systems beyond that of multimodalities to achieve their results; the citizens of *Arrow* are not all-knowing and omnipotent because of their multimodalities.

Group Activities:

A group of 3–5 students represents different classes or socioeconomic roles in a superhero TV show. For example, if a group of 4 were to do a short presentation on the socioeconomic classes in *Gotham*, one student could represent a board member from Wayne Enterprises, one student could be a teacher from a Gotham school, one student could be a homeless person watching gang members recruit goons for the Penguin, and one student could be a patient in Arkham Asylum.

Suggested Readings and Quotes for Discussion:

Bianco, Joseph. "Multiliteracies and Multilingualism." *Multiliteracies: Literacy Learning and the Design of Social Futures*, edited by Bill Cope and Mary Kalantzis, Routledge, 2000, pp. 92–105.

"The Multiliteracies Project aims to develop a pluralistic educational response to trends in the economic, civic and personal spheres of life which impact on meaning-making and therefore on literacy. These changes call for a new foundational literacy which imparts the ability to understand increasingly complex language and literacy codes" (Bianco 92).

> Mor, Walkyria Monte. "Learning by Design." *A Pedagogy of Multiliteracies: Learning by Design*, edited by Bill Cope and Mary Kalantzis, Palgrave Macmillan, 2015, pp. 186–209.

"As learners acknowledge the theories implicit in their daily social practices, they are able—and eager—to mingle/weave knowledge that previously used to be separated into intra- or extra-school contexts" (Mor 207).

Deliverables:

A group presentation that explores socioeconomic classes in a particular superhero TV show and the ways those classes employ literacy events into a larger communal practice.

Activity 3: Broadening Accommodationist Understandings of Literacy

The actions designed in this section work to tease out ramifications of this examination and to allow students the opportunity to see their own literacy events as both reflective of their current situations and extraneous of them simultaneously. Through this self-examination, they also can research accommodationist models of literacy.

Suggested Readings and Quotes for Discussion:

> Gee, James Paul. "20. Synchronized Intelligence: Getting Out Minds and Tools in Synch." *The Anti-Education Era*. Palgrave Macmillan, 2013, pp. 171–190.

"Collective intelligence where people contribute to a problem as a group is but one type of synchronized intelligence. […] It is about finding multiple spaces where we can share lots even if we don't share everything and where different people can share different things and different spaces" (Gee 178).

> Harries, Patrick. "Missionaries, Marxists, and Magic: Power and the Politics of Literacy in South-East Africa." *Literacy Studies, Volume 1: Great Divides and Situated Literacies*, edited by Mastin Prinsloo and Mike Baynham, Sage, 2013, pp. 331–61.

"The interaction between literacy and other societal forces determines the way in which the skills of reading and writing are both acquired and perceived" (Harries 329).

MULTIMODAL DELIVERABLES:

A webpage that ties the larger theory of accommodationist literacy to actual instances of citizens engaging in literacy events and how an average citizen in a superheroic world would share our real-world events. The webpage could include links to academic articles, memes, and images to break down complex ideas, including clips of background characters reading in various superhero media.

Conclusion

The scope of my research here has over-viewed several superhero TV shows in search of literacy practices and teased out literacy elements in various characters and story arcs to demonstrate the way that literacy as an ability and a skill is heightened and super-powered for superhero TV shows. As the activities have demonstrated, by no means have I presented an exhausted list of even superhero TV shows or an exhaustion of literacy elements in any one show. Most of these TV shows have more than two seasons, and other superhero TV shows have possibilities for teasing out more skilled and specialized literacy activities, but the purpose of this book was not to create an exhausting list of literacy moments in superhero TV shows. It was to begin the research and further investigation of these literacy activities that will hopefully spur others on to studying not only literacy events but the connection between all superheroes and their literacies.

Part of my focus is to take the emphasis off of the superhero's body and physical activities which often lead to ableist conclusions about the affordances of physicality and instead stress the importance of the superheroes' mental activities, primarily those connected to the act of reading and comprehension. While so much of college focuses on writing as a process, writing as a product, writing as a skill, literacy and the active reading often is neglected or simply dismissed as a given because students are expected to read on higher levels that sometimes have not been demonstrated and if demonstrated have not been practiced. The reason I look at superhero TV shows and their literacies is because the literacy events in the shows follow a pattern of repetition and finesse from all characters, an assiduousness of effort all students would do well to follow. In "From Screen to Screen: Students' Use of Popular Culture Genres in Multimodal Writing Assignments" Bronwyn Williams notes, "While it shouldn't surprise us that students are familiar with popular culture genres, it is not clear that we engage their knowledge effectively when it comes to multimodal literacy practices" (111). In *Travel Notes from the New Literacy Studies*, Pahl and Roswell observe

Conclusion

> New Literacy Studies represents a tradition of considering the nature of literacy not as a neutral set of skills that we acquire, in school or in other learning contacts, but instead is how people use literacy in different contexts for different purposes. What this implies is a belief that literacy functions in all contacts in different ways guided by different discursive practices [3–4].

Just as current portrayals of superheroes are always looking to expand their forms of learning, reaction, combat, skills, machinery use, and physicality, so must our understanding of multiliteracies in these fictionalized spaces also shift to include broader, more diverse multiliteracies because our culture reflects the age of new media and digital information as the driving factors in higher learning and successful living.

Over the last two decades, increasing at an exponential rate, digital and technological media has consumed the college student's life; the individual use or preference of this multimodal media may be unique to the student, but the overall saturation of media in what Shaun Moores calls "a mediated culture environment" (7) remains all-consuming. In their 2000 research, Hawisher and Selfe promise, "The computer, the latest development in writing technology, promises, or threatens, to change literacy practices for better or worse, depending on your point of view" (70). However, they also caution, "Computer communications are not going to go away. How the computer will eventually alter literacy practices remains to be seen" (83). Depending on the student's cultural, socioeconomic background, interests in cultural media may be limited, specific, broad, or collective. Young urban students have different perspectives of what constitutes art and entertainment than returning students in a small rural town, leading to the condition in which, as Street states, "a particular group of people become associated with a particular literacy; another group of people become associated with another literacy" (9). Yet, shifting the focus of learning to understanding the multimodal multiliteracies needed to access and engage with art and entertainment moves the focus of the class from insistence on the qualities, even legitimacy of art and entertainment into rhetorical analysis of how we use and interact with media.

Bronwyn Williams and Amy Zenger note, "Much has been written about the ways in which digital technologies have change the perceptions and engagement with popular culture; there has been a great deal of attention paid to the ways in which new media are changing the concepts and practices of reading and writing" (5). However, despite these changes, students' reading, comprehension, and writing as a response have often fallen short of expectations. In her push for reading in writing centers, Muriel Harris argues that

> student writing in college is most often a compilation or response to what the student has read—as source material for research papers, as literature to respond to, as information gleaned from textbooks, and so on. Students who have not adequately

understood what they read do not constantly write informed papers that draw what they have read [229].

Another important aspect of improving literacy practices lies in the understanding that literacy development remains a long-term goal that can stretch through multiple semesters. Catherine Compton-Lily in "Longitudinal Studies and Literacy Studies" explains, "Literate identities, practices, and affiliations are not constructed in six months, a year, or even three years. The ultimate goal of our work as literacy educators is to enhance people's lives by enabling them to use literacy for the things that matter to them" (228).

By identifying these representations of literacy, we hold a mirror up to and arrive at better understandings of our culture and its time and place in American history. Henry Jenkins in *Convergence Culture* argues that we witness the intersections of "media convergence, participatory culture, and collective intelligence" referencing "the flow of content across multiple media platforms, the cooperation between multiple media industries, and the migratory behavior of media audiences who will go almost anywhere in search of the kinds of entertainment experiences they want" (2). As an overarching depiction of American values, these representations of literacy are exaggerated in their skills, capacity, abilities, and rate of success; the fact that literacy practices are so ingrained in the superheroes demonstrates the extent to which we desire to have similar methods of comprehension, memorization, and pattern formation. It becomes important that we recognize their exaggerations and their prominence in our culture and media because they reflect our ideas and ideals of perfection.

By critiquing those desires through external representations of our culture, students in composition and in the larger field of rhetoric and composition cannot only develop larger, broader, more complicated views of literacy, NLS authors, and representations of literacy elements, but they can also develop richer skills through critical thinking and academic writing that seek to explain human communication and knowledge through concepts of reading and comprehending. The recognition of the events and practices of traditional literacy are easier to see, observe, and critique when they appear in superhero narratives; when surveyed in a range of multimodal superhero narratives, they present a variety of differences—unique flavors in an array of storytelling—with which to better understand our own literacy events and practices, and through showing rather than telling, students can better understand literacy studies as well as expand and enrich their perspectives of literacy. It becomes important that we recognize their exaggerations and their prominence in our culture and media because they reflect our ideas and ideals of perfection. We see superheroes as what we desire to be, our utmost potential displayed before us and embellished to its utmost appeal.

Chapter Notes

Preface

1. Other superhero TV shows (*Iron Fist, Supergirl, Black Lightning,* and *Legends of Tomorrow*) have garnered acclaim and/or critical appreciation, but these shows have similar literacy events as the six I have chosen and do not offer deeper analysis or insight into representations or usage of literacy.

2. See *Ages of Heroes, Eras of Men: Superheroes and the American Experience* (2013), *Enter the Superheroes: American Values, Culture, and the Canon of Superhero Literature* (2013), *The Law of Superheroes* (2012), *The Myth of the Superhero* (2007), *Superheroes and Superegos: Analyzing the Minds behind the Masks* (2010), and *Our Superheroes, Ourselves* (2013).

3. Some of the research on literacies and multimodalities comes from writers using British Standard English rather than American Standard English. Because of this, I use their original spelling rather than correcting it: colour, materialising, etc. I also use their original punctuation usage which do not always follow the standards of America sentence patterns (the Oxford comma, commas after introductory phrases).

Introduction

1. Scholars have studied ways that superheroes represent American ideology: *Ages of Heroes, Eras of Men: Superheroes and the American Experience* (Chambliss, Svitavsky, and Donaldson 2013), *American Theology, Superhero Comics, and Cinema* (Mills 2014); our values: *Enter the Superheroes: American Values, Culture, and the Canon of Superhero Literature* (Romagnoli and Pagnucci 2013), *The Law of Superheroes* (Daily and Davidson 2012), *Demanding Respect: The Evolution of the American Comic Book* (Lopes 2009); our desires: *The Mythology of the Superhero* (Bahlmann 2016), *Superheroes and Superegos: Analyzing the Minds behind the Masks* (Packer 2010), *Our Superheroes, Ourselves* (Rosenberg 2013), *What Is a Superhero?* (Rosenberg and MacFarland 2013), *Do the Gods Wear Capes? Spirituality, Fantasy, and Superheroes* (Saunders 2011); our fears: *The 21st Century Superhero: Essays on Gender, Genre and Globalization in Film* (Gray and Kaklamanidou 2011), *The Meaning of Superhero Comic Books* (Wandtke 2012); and our futures: *Superhero Synergies: Comic Book Characters Go Digital* (Gilmore and Stork 2014), *Superheroes! Capes, Cowls, and the Creation of Comic Book Culture* (Maslon and Kantor 2013).

2. As one of the largest and oldest franchises, DC stands for Detective Comics, created in 1939 with the start of the Batman comics.

3. Throughout this project, I use the term "reader" to connote an individual interacting with texts, regardless of multimodality. "Reader" implies viewer, gamer, listener, and user at will.

4. Different disciplines and career fields place value on the modes best capable for disseminating information: the humanities might produce archival research in a written report while the sciences produce quantitative data about empirical studies.

5. Some modes like Matt Murdock's Braille sheets or Gorilla Grodd's ape language are not available for viewers to read, but they still contain important information for the characters.

6. The forms of communication have proved of more interest and opportunities for research whereas before language occupied the prominent place of study.

7. Platforms refer to larger systems that express a variety of multiple modes: TVs, videogame consoles, projectors, cellphones, etc.

8. As new college students, we lived in fear of Type 1 errors. Good writing meant avoiding Type 1 errors, primarily subject/verb disagreement and comma splices. An A-paper was one without grammatical errors, regardless of good content or complex ideas.

9. Early drafts of writing might take place on notepads, handwritten through brainstorming or freewriting. But polished, professional writing for academic or capitalistic purposes usually employs technology in editing, revising, and disseminating.

10. Great divides are common in the early days of most humanities' studies as humans have a tendency to use a binary to simplify life: good and bad, educated and uneducated, rich and poor, literacy and illiterate. When sectors of the humanities grow and develop as established fields, scholars recognize the complexities and move away from over-generalized binaries.

11. Other scholars throughout this project stem from pop culture, digital learning, and superhero studies.

12. Studies on the superbody have already been done. See *The Superhero Costume: Identity and Disguise in Fact and Fiction* (Brownie and Graydon), *Superhero Bodies: Identity, Materiality, Transformation* (Haslem et al.), *The Physics of Superheroes* (Kakalios), and *Uncanny Bodies: Superhero Comics and Disability* (Smith and Alaniz).

13. Some of the difficulty in defining literacy practices result from a lack of teaching reading in college. In his work discussing writing and reading in community college, Howard Tinberg states, "It has always struck me as odd that even as we college faculty—especially in English—often complain that our students either are not reading what we assign or simply not up to the task of reading at the college level, we rarely spend instructional time explicitly teaching what it means to read in our discipline and beyond" (244).

14. The particularities of the student set the events apart from the practices. All students might read the instructions (a literacy practice), but an individual student might read the instructions, not understand them, email the professor, go back and read them again, start the assignment, and finally write with instructions to the side of the screens (all literacy events). Another student might start reading the instructions and decide to tackle the assignment with his/her own understanding of what the instructions imply.

15. Gee extrapolates on literacies as a necessity of discourses in *An Introduction to Discourse Analysis: Theory and Method* (19990 and *Social Linguistics and Literacies: Ideology in Discourses* (1990). I discuss the impact of discourse communities at length in Chapter 9.

16. Some of the literacy practices depend on the place of the narrative: superheroes in cities have different literacy needs than those isolated by geographical boundaries like Oliver on the island or Luke Cage in prison. Also, the needs change depending on whom the superhero has to fight, work, or align with, including enhanced humans, aliens, metahumans, clones, or shapeshifters.

17. Street notes that "the 'autonomous' model of literacy works from the assumption that literacy in itself—autonomously—will have effects on other social and cognitive practices. The model, however, disguises the cultural and ideological assumptions that underpin it and that can then be presented as though they are neutral and universal" (2000, 1).

18. "We use the term multimodal literacies to refer to those events and practices in which the written mode is still salient yet embedded into other modes" (Heath and Street 2).

19. For the creation of a website, I suggest having students use Weebly or Wix. Most sites that host websites have tutorials, short video clips, and templates that students can work through on their own time.

Chapter 1

1. With the expansion of digital devices, literacy events have risen at an exponential rate: every time a person checks a cellphone for a text, email, Facebook update, Instagram post, etc., a literacy event has occurred.

2. The superhero's world usually is prone to much more chaos and mayhem then ours is, but the methods of analysis that the superhero uses have great value in our own

world. We may not be attacked by aliens from a parallel universe, but we have to make sense of vast disciplines, social institutions, clamoring media, and financial planning, all activities aided by strong literacy skills.

3. These abilities require reading across multiple modes and platforms, reflecting Maureen Kendrick's understanding of multiliteracies: "Literacy studies are now dependent on understanding relationships between and across communicative modes. Literacy studies have become *multimodal studies*, and written language can no longer be privileged" (630).

4. I often witness this in teaching research in college composition as students get lost in the absolute dearth of knowledge, both academic and popular, which fills thousands of search pages in most online library databases.

5. This willing suspension of disbelief is often referred to as verisimilitude, the act of truthfulness in simulations.

6. Like most action movies, superhero TV shows like *Arrow* and *Gotham* tend to culminate in climatic scenes that feature physicals feats of danger and daring, usually between the hero and the villain of the week. Literacy events may lead the superhero to the final confrontation, but they are rarely prominent in the apex of action.

7. For example, in the Iron Man films, Tony Stark constantly works to improve and further his technology and suits, but the films skip over the numerous hours spent working, limiting the screen time he works to montages or quick summations.

8. In several episodes of *Arrow* and *The Flash*, the scene opens at the end of a training session, after the superheroes have pushed themselves physically and mentally to new heights of accomplishment.

9. Throughout college, concerns about the extent and thoroughness of research are often matched with concerns about accessing and comprehending the highly-dense academic language. Not only are students developing new, specialized literacies, but then they also must survey fields of unknown data, theory, and history.

Chapter 2

1. Brian Street characterizes traditional views of literacy as autonomous, the conceptualization of "literacy in technical terms, treating it as independent of social context, an autonomous variable whose consequences for society and cognition can be derived from its intrinsic character" (2012, 431–2).

2. Andrew Goodwyn and Kate Findlay stress that traditional literacy instruction "remains singularly divorced from the social experience of children. It pays very little attention, for example, to the whole area of media and electronic text, especially to the multi-modal world of the Internet and interactive technologies" (34).

3. In Season 2, the criminals that Oliver subdues go to prison instead of dying with an arrow in their chests.

4. Much of this stem from tenants of the literacy myth that I discuss in length in Chapter 6.

5. Diggle believes that The List limits Oliver's opportunities, and he rages to Oliver, "You can make a difference if you think beyond the scope of those pages" (Ep. 1.6).

6. See Chapter 4 for more on literacy stewards.

7. The social contract of civilized life does not exist on the island. Instead, a kill or be killed credence is the norm for everyone unlucky enough to embark on Lian Yu.

8. The actor who plays Oliver, Stephen Amell, practice parkour and free running, and he performs more of his own stunts on the show, proving that some superhero skills are physically possible.

9. Detective Lance hunts Oliver in Season One, Slade kills his mother in Season Two, and Ra's al Ghul forces him into becoming the head of the League of Assassins in Season Three. Each of these older men attempts to control both Oliver and his superhero persona through illegal, violent, and torturous methods.

Chapter 3

1. The main characters end up traveling from Earth-1, which is designated as our earth in our universe, to other earths in other universes, each called by a number of the order that the show introduces them: Earth-2, Earth-3, and so on.

2. Although the characters refer to him as Harrison Wells in the first season, for the purpose of this project, I will differentiate the two characters thusly: when discussing the duplicitous character impersonating

Earth-1 Harrison Wells in Season 1, I label him Eobard Thawne, and when discussing the character from Earth-2, I label him Harrison Wells. Thawne is discussed fully in Chapter 8; Wells is discussed in this chapter.

3. In most standard episodes where Barry faces off a metahuman (the monster of the week), usually his first attempt to subdue the villain results in failure with the Flash outmaneuvered, overpowered, or simply too slow. This first futile attempt sends the team at S.T.A.R Labs back to the drawing board, including an actual glass marker board, to research other methods to combat the metahuman's superpowers.

4. For example, a 1st-grade teacher has state-sanctioned criteria directing what counts as literacy to students, the teacher's sponsorship might not meet the needs of minority or rural students; the sponsorship might reflect a narrow, autonomous view of literacy.

5. Most schools have reading lists of "appropriate" texts for each grade.

6. Many narratives in sci-fi fiction feature a rendition of the Frankenstein story where the creator/scientist wants to recreate or reimagine life and then is plagued, hunted, or destroyed by his/her creation.

7. Thawne's literacy events and skills are discussed in Chapter 8.

Chapter 4

1. The various characters had to be altered slightly to work in *Gotham*'s storyline: in the comics, Edward Nigma (Riddler) is usually several years younger than Bruce, but in *Gotham*, Edward is in his mid-twenties, at least ten years older than Bruce.

2. In the second season of *The Flash*, characters visit Earth-2 through universe-connecting portals.

3. Often sponsors and stewards can be the same such as fundamental religious sects that approve of reading sacred texts but only through narrow, guided perspectives which the leaders endorse. For example, a reader in this case would be taught to read the Bible for instructional purposes and not as a means to criticize Biblical content.

4. Harrison Wells for Earth-2 and Eobard Thawne are both sponsors and stewards of literacy for Team Flash.

5. The movement of knowledge reflects old methods of instruction which feel outdated because of the ways knowledge and data are dispersed—horizontally through new media and across multimodal platforms.

6. At 12, Bruce has not yet developed specialized literacy of legal and corporate texts like Oliver Queen has.

Chapter 5

1. Freezers were not produced on a national scale until the late 1940s.

2. The legitimacy of her work, particularly how she gathers evidence and serves documents, often falls below ethical and probably legal standards as she routinely uses her super-strength to enforce her business activities.

3. Much like Oliver, Jessica uses technology to provide evidence in her detective work. The Arrow Cave hosts better digital devices and surveillance apparatus, but Jessica has developed the skills of adaption, much like Oliver, and uses whatever she can find to assist her.

4. Kilgrave's thrall (another term created by the fan community) is finally discovered to be a virus that affects the brain of those he speaks to directly. I discuss the full effect of his powers in Chapter 8.

5. She notices burn marks of Stinson's wrist; she follows the paper trail of evidence in Season 2 to find Alisa, her mother, who was experimented on like Jessica.

6. Her mother's obsession over Trish's looks lead to her abusing Trish: hitting her with a People's Choice Award and making her vomit to lose weight.

7. For those interested in a division of gender responses and participation in a classroom, read David Moore's article, "Some Complexities of Gendered Talk about Texts."

Chapter 6

1. Most superhero movies and TV shows often follow the trope of having one black character, rooting the story in a white-washed America that does not reflect urban diversity.

2. This contrasts with superheroes like Iron Man and Captain America who live in Malibu (*Iron Man* 2008) or DC (*The Winter*

Soldier 2014) but who do not interact with average citizens of those places.

3. The use of the community center as a holding place for the cartel's money is one of the strongest ironies of the show: the place that should unite Harlem is used to house activities that put the people of Harlem in danger.

4. Physical punishment remains a common retribution for questioning authority for the supervillains in *Luke Cage*. In a flashback scene, Mama Mabel cuts off a finger of a gang member who disrespects her; Mariah stabs one of her gang members in the eye when he taunts her.

5. Diaz had killed one of Cottonmouth's gang members and fears retaliation.

6. Sadly, this hoodie, like all his hoodies worn in during crime-fighting, eventually is riddled with bullet holes. Luke is bulletproof; his clothes are not.

7. Throughout their mockery, the connection between discrimination from racial and ableist oppressors is solidified: those with minority and disable status face double oppression from hegemonious forces

8. The bionic arm she receives seems reminiscent of Bucky's from *Captain America: The Winter Soldier*. Both of their replacement arms allow them to act and react with more speed and resilience than before, and both use their arms as weapons in hand-to-hand combat.

9. For more on spatial literacy, see Chapter 10.

10. The literacy myth tends to share exaggerated descriptions like metaphors of literacy.

11. We see this in the staggering loans college students amass to pay for an education that promises higher salaries and better financial rewards, an education that forces students into poverty before "relieving" them of it. Any financial difficulties that arise after college are decided as the student's fault for a lack of effort or poor choices made in college for choosing the wrong major.

12. Fredrick Douglas was accredited with the saying "knowledge is the pathway from slavery to freedom."

13. One version of this is the infamous Louisiana Literacy Test. Consider the instructions of number 5: "Circle the first, first letter of the alphabet in this line." How is a reader supposed to know what a first, first letter is?

Chapter 7

1. The naming of superheroes by outside media or public groups is a recent trope in current narratives. Both *Arrow* and *Daredevil* have more ordinary names for the first appearance of their main superheroes (The Hood and The Masked Man) before establishing their better-known titles (The Arrow and Daredevil).

2. While Matt refuses to kill a foe outright, both Punisher and Electra kill without hesitation. Reflecting their respective backgrounds of the U.S. military and marital arts, Punisher favors military sniper shooting while Elektra wields a pair of bladed sai.

3. His literacy activity has a visible presence to its task; as we watch him moving his fingers swiftly, we understand the process of turning text into cognitive recognition because Matt is using a different sense to read.

4. Tony is paralyzed in *Iron Man*, Superman is infected with kryptonite in *Batman V. Superman*, and Spider-Man is crushed under a building in *Spider-Man Homecoming*.

5. In her critique of superheroes and their super egos, Sharon Packer states that personal and physical trauma often drives their stories forward and defines their motivations for action, providing "graphic details about ways to grapple with trauma" (235).

6. *Agents of S.H.I.E.L.D.* illustrates the high-tech world of the MCU which follows in the digitally-enhanced patterns established in *Iron Man* and *Avengers*. However, other MCU TV shows such as *Jessica Jones* and *Luke Cage* present more realistic use of technology and their resulting literacy practices.

7. For a more-thorough description of the literacy myth, see Chapter 6 which uses Harvey Graff's definition.

8. Because of the usual storylines of superhero media, the audience expects that the superhero will rise above his early circumstances. Matt stays in Hell's Kitchen as a choice rather than because he has no other options. Both he and Foggy are offered jobs at a prestigious law firm, but they chose instead to open their own practice to help the people of Hell's Kitchen.

9. In "Literacy: An Instrument of Oppression," D.P. Pattanayak describes the binary in which America culture places literacy/illiteracy: "Illiteracy is grouped with

poverty, malnutrition, lack of education, and health care, while literacy is often equated with growth of productivity, child care, and the advance of civilization" (105).

Chapter 8

1. Often the superhero and supervillain will share traits such as self-aggrandizement, frustration at the social system, or the need to see things balanced out in their own personal favor, but the original narrative pattern remains the same: heroes do good things, and villains do bad things.
2. For each villain, Oliver has to gain information through separate modalities: business personal accounts, legal rulings, private conversations with associates or henchmen, and publicity events, all modes offering unique forms of information that Oliver has to assemble into a collective to be able to counteract each villain.
3. Throughout the first season, Thawne checks the news reports of the future to ensure that he is stabilizing the timeline.
4. In almost all Batman media, the character has a military background and works as a mercenary for hire.
5. The supervillains in *Luke Cage* have names suggesting deadly, poisonous animals: Cottonmouth, Diamondback, and Piranha. Even the name Black Mariah implies a snake: black adder or black mamba.
6. In Ep. 1.1, she gives a televised speech while talking to and embracing young people on the street to show she identifies with her community. Once the cameras are off, she moves to talk with her criminal entourage and smears Purell on her hands.

Chapter 9

1. Even if the superhero could discover the information alone, he or she would spend more time in hunting down pertinent data for missions where time is of the essence. The superhero moves faster, physically and mentally, when he or she is supplied with information from another person or several people researching and gathering data.
2. Usually, sidekicks and mentors join the team if they stay on the superhero TV show long enough, but their early appearances may only support the superhero as an ancillary assistance: Felicity gathers information for Oliver for several episodes in Season 1 as an IT personnel before she joins Team Arrow.
3. Unlike books that can tell the reader information directly in an exposition paragraph, visual media often relies on characters' dialogue to relay information.
4. These films include most of superhero origin stories: *Batman Begins, Black Panther, Deadpool, Dr. Strange, Iron Man, Man of Steel,* and *Wonder Woman.*
5. In comics, the lone superhero sometimes gets a junior partner mainly so the superhero has someone to talk to: Batman has Robin, Superman has Superboy, and Aquaman has Aqualad.
6. For example, *theory* in the humanities speaks to methods of interpreting knowledge (feminism, new historicism) while *theory* in the sciences refers to knowledge gained from tested and affirmed hypotheses (theory of gravity, kinetic theory).
7. She shares some of Jessica Jones' traits: a young woman working at the bottom of a big business who connects disparate pieces of information together to uncover crimes.

Chapter 10

1. Characters in *Arrow* and *The Flash* have relative ease in their access to their superheroic workplace: members of the team stroll in and out while evidence of superhero activities are on full display. Perhaps there are locks or keypads that keep out intruders, but frequently new members of the teams (Iris, Roy, Thea) come and go with relative ease, mimicking the style of literacy activities that the heroes employ: effortless and without thought.
2. The term Arrow Cave is obviously a play on the Batcave from Batman media. The nomenclature feels appropriate for the world of *Arrow* as it suggests a dark, secluded place, and (as fans have pointed out), Oliver Queen/Green Arrow often comes off as Bruce Wayne/Batman-lite.
3. She explains to Oliver, "I've made a few improvement down here just in case, you know, you decided to come back" (*Arrow*, Ep. 2.1).
4. Even the marker board that Wells writes out his theoretical physics equations on is made of glass, allowing him to literally see through his work to the other modes in the lab's workspace.

Chapter 11

1. The tone of *Arrow* and *The Flash* have different aesthetics; *Arrow* is darker and more nihilistic than the upbeat, sometimes quirky *The Flash*. Yet, they share the same space and have crossovers each season where the characters team up and have included characters from *Supergirl* and *Legends of Tomorrow*.

2. Occasionally, someone will look at their cellphone for a missed message, or the person presenting will glance over papers they hold that contain the speech he or she will give.

3. In *Daredevil* Ep. 2.3, Matt has to fight his way through a hallway and a stairwell with an empty gun tapped to one hand and a heavy chain tapped to another, incapacitating mobsters as he moves forward.

References

Acu, Adrian. "Time to Work for a Living: The Marvel Cinematic Universe and the Organized Superhero." *Journal of Popular Film & Television,* vol. 44, no. 4, Oct. 2016, pp. 195–205.
Addison, Joanne. "Researching Literacy as a Lived Experience." *Rhetorica in Motion: Feminist Rhetorical Methods and Methodologies,* edited by Eileen Schell and K. J. Rawson, Pittsburgh: University of Pittsburgh Press, 2010, pp. 136–51.
Akinnaso, F. Niyi. "The Consequences of Literacy in Pragmatic and Theoretical Perspectives." *Literacy Studies, Volume 1: Great Divides and Situated Literacies,* edited by Mastin Prinsloo and Mike Baynham, Newbury Park, CA: Sage, 2013, pp. 107–46.
Alaniz, Joseì. *Death, Disability, and the Superhero: The Silver Age and Beyond.* Jackson: University Press of Mississippi, 2014.
Arkham Asylum. Written by Paul Dani, voice performances by Kevin Conroy and Mark Hamill, London: Rocksteady Studios, 2009.
Arkham City. Written by Paul Dani, Paul Crocker, and Sefton Hill, voice performances by Kevin Conroy and Mark Hamill, London: Rocksteady Studios, 2011.
Arkham Origins. Written by Dooma Wendschuh, Ryan Galletta, and Corey May, voices performances by Kevin Conroy and Mark Hamill, London: Rocksteady Studios, 2013.
Arnove, Robert, and Harvey Graff, eds. *National Literacy Campaigns and Movements: Historical and Comparative Perspectives.* New York: Plenum Press, 1987.
Arrow. Created by Greg Berlanti, Marc Guggenheim, and Andrew Kreisberg, performances by Stephen Amell and Katie Cassidy, Atlanta: CW, 2012–9.
Avengers. Directed by Joss Whedon, performances by Robert Downey, Jr., Chris Evans, and Scarlett Johansson, Burbank, CA: Marvel Studios, 2012.
Baglieri, Susan, and Arthur Shapiro. *Disability Studies and the Inclusive Classroom: Critical Practices for Creating Least Restrictive Attitudes.* Abingdon, UK: Routledge, 2012.
Bahlmann, Andrew. *The Mythology of the Superhero.* Jefferson, NC: McFarland, 2016.
Bainbridge, Jason. "Beyond the Law: What Is so 'Super' About Superheroes and Supervillains?" *International Journal for the Semiotics of Law,* vol. 30, no. 3, 2017, pp. 367–88.
Bamford, Julia, and Marina Bondi. "Introduction." *Dialogue within Discourse Communities: Metadiscursive Perspectives on Academic Genres,* edited by Julia Bamford and Marina Bondi, Tübingen: Niemeyer, 2011, pp. vii–xxiv.
Barton, David. *Literacy: An Introduction to the Ecology of Written Language.* Hoboken, NJ: Blackwell, 1994.
Barton. David. "Understanding Textual Practices in a Changing World." *The Future of Literacy Studies,* edited by Mike Baynham and Mastin Prinsloo, London: Palgrave Macmillan, 2009, pp. 38–53.
Barton, David, and Mary Hamilton. "Literacy Practices." *Situated Literacies: Reading and Writing in Context,* edited by David Barton et al., Abingdon, UK: Routledge, 2000, pp. 7–15.
Barton, David, and Mary Hamilton. *Local Literacies: Reading and Writing in One Community.* Abingdon, UK: Routledge, 1998.
Batman Begins. Directed by Christopher Nolan, performances by Christian Bale, Michael Caine, and Heath Ledger, Burbank, CA: Warner Bros., 2005.

References

Batman V. Superman. Directed by Zack Synder and Joss Whedon, performances by Ben Affleck, Henry Cavill, and Gal Gadot, Burbank, CA: Warner Bros., 2016,

Bauerlein, Mark. *The Dumbest Generation: How the Digital Age Stupefies Young Americans and Jeopardizes Our Future (or, Don't Trust Anyone Under 30)*. New York: Jeremy P. Tarcher/Penguin, 2008.

Baynham, Mike, and Mastin Prinsloo. "Editor's Introduction: Literacy Studies." *Literacy Studies, Volume 1: Great Divides and Situated Literacies*, edited by Mastin Prinsloo and Mike Baynham, Newbury Park, CA: Newbury Park, CA: Sage, 2013, pp. xxv-xli.

Bednarz, Sarah, and Karen Kemp. "Understanding and Nurturing Spatial Literacy." *Procedia-Social and Behavioral Sciences*, vol. 21, 2011, pp. 18–23.

Belt-Beyan, Phyllis M. *The Emergence of African American Literacy Traditions: Family and Community Efforts in the Nineteenth Century*. Westport, CT: Praeger, 2004.

Bergman, Daniel. "The 'Marvel'-ous Nature of Science: Using Superhero Movies to Teach Methods and Values in Science." *Science Teacher*, vol. 86, no. 9, July 2019, pp. 20–25.

Bezemer, Jeff, and Gunther Kress. *Multimodality, Learning, and Communication: A Social Semitic Frame*. Abingdon, UK: Routledge, 2016.

Bianco, Joseph. "Multiliteracies and Multilingualism." *Multiliteracies: Literacy Learning and the Design of Social Futures*, edited by Bill Cope and Mary Kalantzis, Abingdon, UK: Routledge, 2000, pp. 92–105.

Black Lightning. Created by Salim Akil, performances by Cress Williams, China Anne McClain, and Nafessa Williams, Burbank, CA: DC Entertainment, 2018–9.

Black Panther. Directed by Ryan Coogler, performances by Chadwick Boseman, Michael B. Jordan, and Lupita Nyong'o, Burbank, CA: Marvel Studios, 2018.

Blau, Francine, and Anne Winkler. *The Economics of Women, Men, and Work*. Oxford, England: Oxford University Press, 2018.

Bloome, David. "Classroom Ethnography." *Language, Ethnography, and Education: Bridging New Literacy Studies and Bourdieu*, edited by Michael Grenfell et al., Abingdon, UK: Routledge, 2012, pp. 2–26.

Bloome, David, and Judith Green. "Social and Linguistic Terms in Studying Language and Literacy." *The Routledge Handbook of Literacy Studies*, edited by Jennifer Rowsell and Kate Pahl, Abingdon, UK: Routledge, 2015, pp. 19–34.

Boucher, Ian. "Applying Suspense to Archetypal Superheroes: Hitchcockian Ambiguity in *Batman v Superman: Dawn of Justice*." *Mise-En-Scene*, vol. 3, no. 1, Spring 2018, pp. 52–67.

Boudreaux, Armond. "Introduction, Part 1: Superheroes as Myth." *Titans: How Superheroes Can Help Us Make Sense of a Polarized World*, edited by Armond Bourdreaux and Corey Latta, Eugene, OR: Cascade Books, 2017, pp. xi–xxi.

Boyd, Fenice, and Cynthia Brock. "Preface." *Social Diversity within Multiliteracies: Complexity in Teaching and Learning*, edited by Fenice Boyd and Cynthia Brock, Abingdon, UK: Routledge, 2014, pp. xi–xiv.

Boyd, Fenice, and Cynthia Brock. "Reflections on the Past, Working within the 'Future.'" *Social Diversity within Multiliteracies: Complexity in Teaching and Learning*, edited by Fenice Boyd and Cynthia Brock, Abingdon, UK: Routledge, 2014, pp. 1–10.

Brandt, Deborah. *Literacy and Learning: Reflections on Writing, Reading, and Society*. New York: Jossey-Bass, 2009.

Brandt, Deborah. *Literacy as Involvement: The Act of Writers, Readers, and Texts*. Carbondale: Southern Illinois University Press, 2011.

Brandt, Deborah. *Literacy in American Lives*. Cambridge, England: Cambridge University Press, 2000.

Brandt, Deborah. *The Rise of Writing: Redefining Mass Literacy*. Cambridge, England: Cambridge University Press, 2015.

Brandt, Deborah. *The Sponsors of Literacy*. Educational Resources Information Center, 1997.

Brandt, Deborah. "Writing over Reading: New Directions in Mass Literacy." *The Future of Literacy Studies*, edited by Mike Baynham and Mastin Prinsloo, London: Palgrave Macmillan, 2009, pp. 54–74.

Brandt, Deborah, and Katie Clinton. "Limits of the Local: Expanding Perspectives on Literacy as a Social Practice." *Journal of Literacy Research*, vol. 34, no. 3, 2002, pp. 337–56.

Brooker, Will. *Batman Unmasked: Analyzing a Cultural Icon*. London: Continuum, 2001.

References

Brooker, Will. "We Could Be Heroes." *What Is a Superhero?*, edited by Robin Rosenberg and Peter Coogan, Oxford, UK: Oxford University Press, 2013, pp. 11–8.

Brown, Jeffrey. *The Modern Superhero in Film and Television: Popular Genre and American Culture*. Abingdon, UK: Routledge, 2017.

Brown, Jeffrey A. "Comic Book Masculinity and the New Black Superhero." *African American Review*, vol. 33, no. 1, Spring 1999, pp. 25–42.

Brownie, Barbara, and Danny Graydon. *The Superhero Costume: Identity and Disguise in Fact and Fiction*. London: Bloomsbury Academic, 2016.

Burnett, Cathy. "(Im)Materialising Literacies." *The Routledge Handbook of Literacy Studies*, edited by Jennifer Rowsell and Kate Pahl, Abingdon, UK: Routledge, 2015, pp. 520–31.

Burns, Gary, and Megan Morris. "The Very Real Work Lives of Superheroes." *Our Superheroes, Ourselves*, edited by Robin Rosenburg, Oxford, UK: Oxford University Press, 2013, pp. 139–58.

Canagarajah, A. Suresh, ed. *Literacy as Translingual Practice: Between Communities and Classrooms*. Abingdon, UK: Routledge, 2013.

Captain America: The First Avenger. Directed by Joe Johnston, performances by Chris Evans, Tommy Lee Jones, and Sebastian Stan, Burbank, CA: Marvel Studios, 2011.

Captain America: The Winter Soldier. Directed by Anthony Russo and Joe Russo, performances by Chris Evans, Scarlet Johansson, and Sebastian Stan, Burbank, CA: Marvel Studios, 2014.

Carillo, Ellen. "Preparing College-Level Readers to Define Reading as More Than Mastery." *Deep Reading: Teaching Reading in the Writing Classroom*, edited by Patrick Sullivan, Howard Tinberg, and Sheridan Blau, Urbana, IL: NCTE, 2017, pp. 188–209.

Chambliss, Julian C, William L. Svitavsky, and Thomas C. Donaldson. *Ages of Heroes, Eras of Men: Superheroes and the American Experience*. Newcastle upon Tyne, UK: Cambridge Scholars Publishing, 2014

Cloonan, Anne. "Integrating by Design." *A Pedagogy of Multiliteracies: Learning by Design*, edited by Bill Cope and Mary Kalantzis, London: Palgrave Macmillan, 2015, pp. 97–114.

Coiro, Julie, Michelle Knobel, Colin Lankshear, and Donald Leu. "Central Issues in New Literacies and New Literacies Research." *Handbook of Research on New Literacies*, edited by Julie Coiro et al., Abingdon, UK: Routledge, 2014, pp. 1–22.

Cole, David, and Darren Pullen. "Introduction." *Multiliteracies in Motion: Current Theory and Practice*, edited by David Cole and Darren Pullen, Abingdon, UK: Routledge, 2010, pp. 1–14.

Collins, James, and Richard K. Blot. *Literacy and Literacies: Texts, Power, and Identity*. Cambridge, England: Cambridge University Press, 2003.

Compton-Lily, Catherine." Longitudinal Studies and Literacy Studies." *The Routledge Handbook of Literacy Studies*, edited by Jennifer Rowsell and Kate Pahl, Abingdon, UK: Routledge, 2015, pp. 218–30.

Cook, Kelli Cargile. "Layered Literacies: A Theoretical Frame for Technical Communication Pedagogy." *Technical Communication Quarterly*, vol. 11, no. 1, 2002, pp. 5–29.

Cook-Gumperz, Jenny. "The Social Construction of Literacy." *Literacy Studies, Volume 1: Great Divides and Situated Literacies*, edited by Mastin Prinsloo and Mike Baynham, Newbury Park, CA: Sage, 2013, pp. 191–206.

Cope, Bill, and Mary Kalantzis. "New Media, New Learning." *Multiliteracies in Motion: Current Theory and Practice*, edited by David Cole and Darren Pullen, Abingdon, UK: Routledge, 2010, pp. 87–104.

Cope, Bill, and Mary Kalantzis. "The Things You Do to Know: An Introduction to the Pedagogy of Multiliteracies." *A Pedagogy of Multiliteracies: Learning by Design*, edited by Bill Cope and Mary Kalantzis, London: Palgrave Macmillan, 2015, pp. 1–36.

Cornoldi, Cesare, and Tomaso Vecchi. *Visuo-Spatial Working Memory and Individual Differences*. London: Psychology Press, 2003.

Corteìs, Guido, Nir Jaimovich, and Henry Siu. *The "End of Men" and Rise of Women in the High-Skilled Labor Market*. Cambridge, MA: National Bureau of Economic Research, 2018.

Cushman, Ellen. "Elias Boudinot and the *Cherokee Phoenix*: The Sponsors of Literacy They Were and Were Not." *Literacy, Economy, and Power: Writing and Research After "Literacy in American Lives,"* edited by John Duffy et al., Carbondale: Southern Illinois University Press, 2014, pp. 13–29.

References

Dagostino, Lorraine, and James Carifio. "Achieving Proficiency in Various Specialized Literacies." *Work*, vol. 13, no. 2, Sept. 1999, pp. 83–8.

Daily, James, and Ryan Davidson. *The Law of Superheroes*. New York: Gotham Books, 2013.

Damaske, Sarah. *For the Family?: How Class and Gender Shape Women's Work*. Oxford, UK: Oxford University Press, 2011.

Dantzler, Perry. *With Great Literacy Comes Great Responsibility: Rethinking Popular Culture and the Literacy Practices of Superheroes*. 2016, Georgia State University, PhD dissertation.

Daredevil. Created by Drew Goddard, performances by Charlie Cox, Vincent D'Onofrio, and Deborah Ann Woll, Los Gatos, CA: Netflix, 2015 and 2017.

Daredevil. Directed by Mark Steven Johnson, performances by Ben Affleck, Jennifer Garner, and Colin Farrell, Los Angeles: New Regency Pictures, 2003.

The Dark Knight. Directed by Christopher Nolan, performances by Christian Bale, Michael Caine, and Heath Ledger, Burbank, CA: Warner Bros., 2008.

The Dark Knight Rises. Directed by Christopher Nolan, performances by Christian Bale, Gary Oldman, and Tom Hardy, Burbank, CA: Warner Bros., 2012.

Davis, Lennard. *The End of Normal: Identity in a Biocultural Era*. Ann Arbor: University of Michigan Press, 2013.

Deadpool. Directed by Tim Miller, performances by Ryan Reynolds, Morena Baccarin, and T.J. Miller, Los Angeles: 20th-Century Fox, 2016.

The Defenders. Created by Douglas Petrie and Marco Ramirez, performances by Charlie Cox, Krysten Ritter, and Mike Colter, Los Gatos, CA: Netflix, 2017.

Delpit, Lisa. "Acquisition of Literate Discourse." *What Counts as Literacy?: Challenging the School Standard*, edited by Margaret Gallego and Sandra Hollingsworth, New York: Teachers College Press, 2000, pp. 241–51.

Denison, Rayna, Rachel Mizsei-Ward, and Derek Johnston. "Introduction." *Superheroes on World Screens*, edited by Rayna Denison and Rachel Mizsei-Ward, Jackson: University Press of Mississippi, 2015, pp. 3–16.

Derry, Ken, et al. "Bulletproof Love: *Luke Cage* (2016) and Religion." *Journal for Religion, Film and Media*, vol. 3, no. 1, 2017, pp. 123–55.

DeWeerd, Katherine. "Understanding How Sensory Input Affect Children and Helps Them Cope." *Social Skills Deficits in Students with Disabilities: Successful Strategies from the Disability Field*, edited by Helen Myers, Lanham, MD: Rowman and Littlefield, 2013, pp. 79–100.

Die Hard. Directed by John McTiernan, performances by Bruce Willis, Alan Rickman, and Bonnie Bedelia, Los Angeles: 20th-Century Fox, 1988.

Dr. Strange. Directed by Scott Derrickson, performances by Benedict Cumberbatch, Chiwetel Ejiofor, and Rachel McAdams, Burbank, CA: Marvel Studios, 2016.

Domingo, Myrrh, Carey Jewitt, and Gunther Kress. "Multimodal Social Semiotics." *The Routledge Handbook of Literacy Studies*, edited by Jennifer Rowsell and Kate Pahl, Abingdon, UK: Routledge, 2015, pp. 251–266.

Donehower, Kim. "Connecting Literacy as Sustainability." *Literacy, Economy, and Power: Writing and Research After "Literacy in American Lives,"* edited by John Duffy et al., Carbondale: Southern Illinois University Press, 2014, pp. 97–110.

Dooley, Karen. "Multiliteracies and the Pedagogies of New Learning for Students of English as an Additional Language." *Multiliteracies and Diversity in Education: New Pedagogies for Expanding Landscapes*, edited by Annah Healy, Oxford, UK: Oxford University Press, 2008, pp. 102–25.

Duffy, John. "Other Gods and Countries: The Rhetorics of Literacy." *Towards a Rhetoric of Everyday Life: New Directions in Research on Writing, Text, and Discourse*, edited by Martin Nystrand and John Duffy, Madison: University of Wisconsin Press, 2003, pp. 38–57.

Duffy, John, et al., editors. *Literacy, Economy, and Power: Writing and Research After "Literacy in American Lives."* Carbondale: Southern Illinois University Press, 2013.

Duffy, John, Julie N. Christoph, Eli Goldblatt, Nelson Graff, Rebecca S. Nowacek, and Bryan Trabold. *Literacy, Economy, and Power: Writing and Research After "Literacy in American Lives."* Carbondale: Southern Illinois University Press, 2013.

Easton, Lee. "Saying No to Hetero-Masculinity." *Cinephile*, vol. 9, no. 2, Fall 2013, pp. 38–44.

Elleström, Lars, and Jørgen Bruhn. *Media Borders, Multimodality, and Intermediality*. London: Palgrave Macmillan, 2010.

References

Ellis, Katie, and Mike Kent. *Disability and New Media*. Abingdon, UK: Routledge, 2011.
Exley, Beryl. "Communities of Learners: Early Years Students, New Learning Pedagogy, and Transformations." *Multiliteracies and Diversity in Education: New Pedagogies for Expanding Landscapes*, edited by Annah Healy, Oxford, UK: Oxford University Press, 2008, pp. 126–43.
Exner, Ulrich, and Dietrich Pressel. *Basics Spatial Design*. Berlin: Birkhäuser, 2017.
Expendables. Directed by Sylvester Stallone, performances by Sylvester Stallone, Jason Statham, and Jet Li, New York: Millennium Films, 2010.
Fairclough, Norman. "Multiliteracies and Language." *Multiliteracies: Literacy Learning and the Design of Social Futures*, edited by Bill Cope and Mary Kalantzis, Abingdon, UK: Routledge, 2000, pp. 162–81.
Farrell, Lesley. "Texting the Future: Work, Literacies, and Economies." *The Future of Literacy Studies*, edited by Mike Baynham and Mastin Prinsloo, London: Palgrave Macmillan, 2009, pp. 181–98.
Fawaz, Ramzi. *The New Mutant: Superheroes and the Radical Imagination of American Comics*. New York: New York University Press, 2016.
The Flash. Created by Greg Berlanti, Geoff Johns, and Andrew Kreisberg, performances by Grant Gustin and Tom Cavanagh, Atlanta: CW, 2014–2019.
Flower, Linda. *Community Literacy and the Rhetoric of Public Engagement*. Carbondale: Southern Illinois University Press, 2008.
Foresman, Galen. "Making the A-List." *Supervillains and Philosophy: Sometimes, Evil Is Its Own Reward*, edited by Ben Dyer, Chicago: Open Court, 2011, pp. 23–30.
Freire, Paulo. "The Adult Literacy Process as Cultural Action for Freedom." *Literacy Studies, Volume 1: Great Divides and Situated Literacies*, edited by Mastin Prinsloo and Mike Baynham, Newbury Park, CA: Sage, 2013, pp. 71–90.
Freire, Paulo. *Pedagogy of the Oppressed*. London: Continuum, 2000.
Frost, Alena. "Literacy Stewardship: Dakelh Women Composing Culture." *College Composition and Communication*, vol. 63, no. 1, 2011, pp. 54–74.
Gale, Bob, Dennis O'Neil, and Greg Rucka. *Batman: No Man's Land, Volume 1*. New York: DC Comics, 2000.
Garrido, Lea Espinoza. "*Luke Cage* as Postpost-9/11 TV: Spatial Negotiations of Race in Contemporary US Television." *Current Objectives of Postgraduate American Studies* vol. 19, no. 1, 2018, n. pg.
Gee, James Paul. *The Anti-Education Era*. London: Palgrave Macmillan, 2013.
Gee, James Paul. *An Introduction to Discourse Analysis: Theory and Method*. Abingdon, UK: Routledge, 1999.
Gee, James Paul. "Literacy, Discourse, and Linguistics: Introduction." *Literacy Studies, Volume 1: Great Divides and Situated Literacies*, edited by Mastin Prinsloo and Mike Baynham, Newbury Park, CA: Sage, 2013, pp. 225–38.
Gee, James Paul. *New Digital Media and Learning as an Emerging Area and "Worked Examples" as One Way Forward*. Cambridge, MA: MIT Press, 2010.
Gee, James Paul. "The New Literacy Studies." *The Routledge Handbook of Literacy Studies*, edited by Jennifer Rowsell and Kate Pahl, Abingdon, UK: Routledge, 2015, pp. 35–48.
Gee, James Paul. "New People in New Worlds." *Multiliteracies: Literacy Learning and the Design of Social Futures*, edited by Bill Cope and Mary Kalantzis, Abingdon, UK: Routledge, 2000, pp. 43–68.
Gee, James Paul. *Social Linguistics and Literacies: Ideology in Discourses*. Basingstoke, UK: Falmer Press, 1996.
Gee, James Paul. "Where We Are and How We Got Here." *New Digital Media and Learning as an Emerging Area and "Worked Examples" as One Way Forward*. Cambridge, MA: MIT Press, 2010, pp. 9–15.
Gilbert, Pam. "Personally (and Passively) Yours: Girls, Literacy and Education." *Oxford Review of Education*, vol. 15, no. 3, 1989, pp. 257–65.
Gillen, Julia. "Virtual Spaces in Literacy Studies." *The Routledge Handbook of Literacy Studies*, edited by Jennifer Rowsell and Kate Pahl, Abingdon, UK: Routledge, 2015, pp. 369–82.
Gilmore, James, and Matthias Stork. "Introduction." *Superhero Synergies: Comic Book Characters Go Digital*, edited by James Gilmore and Matthias Stork, Lanham, MD: Rowman and Littlefield, 2014, pp. 1–10.

Gilmore, James, and Matthias Stork. *Superhero Synergies: Comic Book Characters Go Digital.* Lanham, MD: Rowman & Littlefield, 2014.

Gladwell, Malcolm. *Blink: The Power of Thinking without Thinking.* New York: Back Bay Books, 2014.

Gledhill, Evan. "Twenty Percent of His Body: Scar Tissue, Masculinity, and Identity in *Arrow*." *Arrow and Superhero Television: Essays on Themes and Characters of the Series*, edited by James Iaccino, Cory Barker, and Myc Wiatrowski, Jefferson, NC: McFarland, 2017, pp. 78–94.

Goldblatt, Eli, and David Jolliffe. "The Unintended Consequences of Sponsorship." *Literacy, Economy, and Power: Writing and Research After "Literacy in American Lives,"* edited by John Duffy et al., Carbondale: Southern Illinois University Press, 2014, pp. 127–35.

Gooden, Kelly. "Superhero Physics: Eighth Graders Learn Physics Concepts From Superhero-Inspired Lessons." *Science Scope*, vol. 43, no. 5, Jan. 2020, pp. 32–41

Goodwyn, Andrew, and Kate Findlay. "Literacy Instruction." *Improving Literacy at KS2 and KS3*, edited by Andrew Goodwyn, P. Thousand Oaks, CA: Chapman Publishing, 2002, pp. 22–43.

Gordon, Jane Anna. "The Nature of Political Heroes: Some Aesthetic Considerations." *Discourse: Journal for Theoretical Studies in Media & Culture*, vol. 39, no. 2, Spring 2017, pp. 253–270.

Gotham. Created by Bruno Heller, performances by Ben McKenzie, Donal Logue, and David Mazouz, Los Angeles: 20th-Century Fox, 2014–9.

Graff, Harvey. "Epilogue." *Literacy, Economy, and Power: Writing and Research After "Literacy in American Lives,"* edited by John Duffy et al., Carbondale: Southern Illinois University Press, 2014, pp. 203–32.

Graff, Harvey. *The Labyrinths of Literacy.* Pittsburgh: University of Pittsburgh Press, 1995.

Graff, Harvey. "The Legacies of Literacy." *Literacy Studies, Volume 1: Great Divides and Situated Literacies*, edited by Mastin Prinsloo and Mike Baynham, Newbury Park, CA: Sage, 2013, pp. 147–62.

Graff, Harvey. *Literacy and Historical Development: A Reader.* Carbondale: Southern Illinois University Press, 2007.

Graff, Harvey. "The Literacy Myth at Thirty." *Journal of Social History*, vol. 43, no. 3, 2010, pp. 635–661.

Graff, Harvey. *The Literacy Myth: Literacy and Social Structure in the Nineteenth-Century City.* New York: Academic, 1979.

Graff, Harvey. *Literacy Myths, Legacies, & Lessons: New Studies on Literacy.* Livingston, NJ: Transaction Publishers, 2011.

Gray, Richard, and Betty Kaklamanidou. *The 21st Century Superhero: Essays on Gender, Genre and Globalization in Film.* Jefferson, NC: McFarland, 2011.

Greenwood, Jeremy, Nezih Guner, Georgi Kocharkov, and Cezar Santos. *Technology and the Changing Family: A Unified Model of Marriage, Divorce, Educational Attainment and Married Female Labor-Force Participation.* Cambridge, MA: National Bureau of Economic Research, 2012.

Haas, Christina. *Writing Technology: Studies on the Materiality of Literacy.* Abingdon, UK: Routledge, 2013.

Hackett, Abigail. "Multimodality and Sensory Ethnographies." *The Routledge Handbook of Literacy Studies*, edited by Jennifer Rowsell and Kate Pahl, Abingdon, UK: Routledge, 2015, pp. 295–307.

Hale, Bob, and Aviv Hoffmann. "Introduction." *Modality*, edited by Bob Hale and Aviv Hoffmann, Oxford, UK: Oxford University Press, 2010, pp. 1–20.

Hamilton, Mary. *Literacy and the Politics of Representation.* Abingdon, UK: Routledge, 2012.

Hamilton, Mary. "Moving Voices: Literacy Narratives in a Testimonial Culture." *The Routledge Handbook of Literacy Studies*, edited by Jennifer Rowsell and Kate Pahl, Abingdon, UK: Routledge, 2015, pp. 504–19.

Harries, Patrick. "Missionaries, Marxists, and Magic: Power and the Politics of Literacy in South-East Africa." *Literacy Studies, Volume 1: Great Divides and Situated Literacies*, edited by Mastin Prinsloo and Mike Baynham, Newbury Park, CA: Sage, 2013, pp. 331–61.

Harris, Muriel. "Writing Centers Are Also Reading Centers." *Deep Reading: Teaching Reading in the Writing Classroom*, edited by Patrick Sullivan, Howard Tinberg, and Sheridan Blau, Urbana, IL: NCTE, 2017, pp. 227–43.

Haslem, Wendy, Elizabeth MacFarlane, and Sarah Richardson. *Superhero Bodies: Identity, Materiality, Transformation*. Abingdon, UK: Routledge, 2019.

Hatfield, Charles, Jeet Heer, and Kent Worcester. "Introduction." *The Superhero Reader*, edited by Charles Hatfield, Jeet Heer, and Kent Worcester, Jackson: University Press of Mississippi, 2013, pp. xi–xxi.

Hawisher, Gail, and Cynthia Selfe. *Global Literacies and the World-Wide Web*. Abingdon, UK: Routledge, 2000.

Healy, Annah. "Expanding Student Capacities: Learning by Design Pedagogy." *Multiliteracies and Diversity in Education: New Pedagogies for Expanding Landscapes*, edited by Annah Healy, Oxford, UK: Oxford University Press, 2008, pp. 2–29.

Heath, Shirley Brice. *Ways with Words: Language, Life, and Work in Communities and Classrooms*. Cambridge, England: Cambridge University Press, 2009.

Heath, Shirley Brice. "What No Bedtime Story Means: Narrative Skills at Home and School." *Literacy Studies, Volume 1: Great Divides and Situated Literacies*, edited by Mastin Prinsloo and Mike Baynham, Newbury Park, CA: Sage, 2013, pp. 163–90.

Heath, Shirley Brice, and Brian V. Street. *On Ethnography: Approaches to Language and Literacy Research*. New York: Teachers College Press, 2008.

Henderson, Michael, et al. "Students' Everyday Engagement with Digital Technology in University: Exploring Patterns of Use and 'Usefulness.'" *Journal of Higher Education Policy & Management*, vol. 37, no. 3, June 2015, pp. 308–19.

Henderson, Robyn. "Mobilizing Multiliteracies: Pedagogy for Mobile Students." *Multiliteracies and Diversity in Education: New Pedagogies for Expanding Landscapes*, edited by Annah Healy, Oxford, UK: Oxford University Press, 2008, pp. 168–200.

Heydon, Rachel, and Jennifer Rowsell. "Phenomenology and Literacy Studies." *The Routledge Handbook of Literacy Studies*, edited by Jennifer Rowsell and Kate Pahl, Abingdon, UK: Routledge, 2015, pp. 454–71.

Horner, Bruce, and Min-Zhan Lu. "Towards a Labor Economy of Literacy." *Literacy, Economy, and Power: Writing and Research After "Literacy in American Lives,"* edited by John Duffy et al., Carbondale: Southern Illinois University Press, 2014, pp. 111–26.

House. Created by David Shore, performances by Hugh Laurie, Omar Epps, and Robert Sean Leonard, Los Angeles: Bad Hat Harry Productions, 2004–12.

Howe, Sarah. "Beyond Wounds and Words: The Rhetoric of Scarred Embodiment in *Arrow*." *Arrow and Superhero Television: Essays on Themes and Characters of the Series*, edited by James Iaccino, Cory Barker, and Myc Wiatrowski, Jefferson, NC: McFarland, 2017, pp. 95–110.

Huang, Cheng-Wen, and Arlene Archer. "Uncovering the Multimodal Literacy Practices in Reading Manga and the Implications for Pedagogy." *New Media Literacies and Participatory Popular Culture across Borders*, edited by Bronwyn Williams and Amy Zenger, Abingdon, UK: Routledge, 2012, pp. 44–60.

Iaccino, James. "The Arrow and His Villainous Counterparts." *Arrow and Superhero Television: Essays on Themes and Characters of the Series*, edited by James Iaccino, Cory Barker, and Myc Wiatrowski, Jefferson, NC: McFarland, 2017, pp. 46–60.

Indiana Jones: Raiders of the Lost Ark. Directed by Steven Spielberg, performances by Harrison Ford, Karen Allen, and Paul Freeman, Hollywood, CA: Paramount, 1981.

Iron Fist. Created by Scott Buck, performances by Finn Jones, Jessica Henwick, and Jessica Stroup, Los Gatos, CA: Netflix, 2017–8.

Iron Man. Directed by Jon Favreau, performances by Robert Downey, Jr., Gwyneth Paltrow, and Terrence Howard, Hollywood, CA: Paramount, 2008.

Ivanic, Roz. "Bringing Literacy Studies into Research on Learning across the Curriculum." *The Future of Literacy Studies*, edited by Mike Baynham and Mastin Prinsloo, London: Palgrave Macmillan, 2009, pp. 100–22.

Jacobs, Dale. *Graphic Encounters: Comics and the Sponsorship of Multimodal Literacy*. London: Bloomsbury, 2013.

Jenkins, Henry. *Convergence Culture: Where Old and New Media Collide*. New York: New York University Press, 2016.

Jennings, John. "Superheroes by Design." *What Is a Superhero?*, edited by Robin Rosenberg and Peter Coogan, Oxford, UK: Oxford University Press, 2013, pp. 59–64.
Jessica Jones. Created by Melissa Rosenberg, performances by Krysten Ritter, Rachael Taylor, and Carrie-Anne Moss, Los Gatos, CA: Netflix, 2015 and 2018.
Johnson, Genevieve Marie. "The Invention of Reading and the Evolution of Text." *Journal of Literacy and Technology*, vol. 16, no. 1, 2015, pp. 107–128.
Johnston, Jennifer. *Contemporary Issues in Australian Literacy Teaching*. Sydney, Australia: Primrose Hall Publishing Group, 2012.
Juliano, Stephanie. "Superheroes, Bandits, and Cyber-Nerds: Exploring the History and Contemporary Development of the Vigilante." *Journal of International Commercial Law & Technology*, vol. 7, no. 1, Jan. 2012, pp. 44–64.
Kakalios, James. *The Physics of Superheroes*. New York: Avery, 2009.
Kalantzis, Mary, and Bill Cope. "Changing the Role of Schools." *Multiliteracies: Literacy Learning and the Design of Social Futures*, edited by Bill Cope and Mary Kalantzis, Abingdon, UK: Routledge, 2000, pp. 121–48.
Kalantzis, Mary, and Bill Cope. "Language Education and Multiliteracies." *Encyclopedia of Language and Education, Vol.1*, edited by Stephen May and Nancy Hornberger, New York: Springer, 2008, pp. 195–211.
Karsai, Istvan, and George Kampis. "The Crossroads between Biology and Mathematics: The Scientific Method as the Basics of Scientific Literacy." *BioScience*, vol. 60, no. 8, 2010, pp. 632–8.
Keith, Heather, and Kenneth Keith. *Intellectual Disability: Ethics, Dehumanization and a New Moral Community*. Hoboken, NJ: John Wiley & Sons, 2013.
Kendrick, Maureen. "The Affordances and Challenges of Visual Methodologies in Literacy Studies." *The Routledge Handbook of Literacy Studies*, edited by Jennifer Rowsell and Kate Pahl, Abingdon, UK: Routledge, 2015, pp. 619–33.
Kinloch, Valerie. "Urban Literacies." *The Routledge Handbook of Literacy Studies*, edited by Jennifer Rowsell and Kate Pahl, Abingdon, UK: Routledge, 2015, pp. 140–56.
Kress, Gunther. *Before Writing: Rethinking the Paths to Literacy*. Abingdon, UK: Routledge, 1997.
Kress, Gunther. *Literacy in the New Media Age*. Abingdon, UK: Routledge, 2003.
Kress, Gunther, and Theo van Leeuwen. *Multimodal Discourse: The Modes and Media of Contemporary Communication*. London: Bloomsbury, 2001.
Kress, Gunther, and Theo van Leeuwen. *Reading Images: The Grammar of Visual Design*. Abingdon, UK: Routledge, 1996.
Kulick, Don, and Christopher Stroud. "Christianity, Cargo, and Ideas of Self: Patterns of Literacy in a Papua New Guinean Village." *Literacy Studies, Volume 1: Great Divides and Situated Literacies*, edited by Mastin Prinsloo and Mike Baynham, Newbury Park, CA: Sage, 2013, pp. 253–74.
Ladson-Billings, Gloria. "Liberatory Consequences of Literacy: A Case of Culturally Relevant Instruction for African American students." *The Journal of Negro Education*, vol. 61, no. 3, 1992, pp. 378–91.
Lathan, Rhea. "Testimony as a Sponsor of Literacy." *Literacy, Economy, and Power: Writing and Research After "Literacy in American Lives,"* edited by John Duffy et al., Carbondale: Southern Illinois University Press, 2014, pp. 30–44.
Lawless, Kimberly, and Scott Brown. "Developing Scientific Literacy Skills through Interdisciplinary, Technology-Based Global Simulations." *Curriculum Journal*, vol. 26, no. 2, 2015, pp. 268–89.
Lawrence, John. *The Myth of the American Superhero*. Grand Rapids: W.B. Eerdmans, 2007.
Lawrence, John, and Robert Jewett. *The Myth of the American Superhero*. Grand Rapids: W.B. Eerdmans, 2002.
Lee, Alison. *Gender Literacy & Curriculum: Rewriting School Geography*. Abingdon, UK: Taylor & Francis, 2014.
Legends of Tomorrow. Created by Greg Berlanti, Marc Guggenheim, and Phil Klemmer, performances by Brandon Routh, Caity Lotz, and Amy Louise Pemberton, Burbank, CA: Warner Bros., 2016–9.
Lemke, Jay, and Caspar van Helden. "Social Design Literacies: Designing Action Literacies

for Fast-Changing Futures." *The Routledge Handbook of Literacy Studies*, edited by Jennifer Rowsell and Kate Pahl, Abingdon, UK: Routledge, 2015, pp. 321–36.
Lethal Weapon. Directed by Richard Donner, performances by Mel Gibson, Danny Glover, and Gary Busey, Burbank, CA: Warner Bros., 1987.
Levine, Kenneth. *The Social Context of Literacy*. Abingdon, UK: Routledge & Kegan Paul, 1986.
Linge, Alex, and Henrik Muller. "Introduction." *Modality: Studies in Form and Function*, edited by Alex Linge and Henrik Muller, Sheffield, UK: Equinox, 2005, pp. 1–4.
Lopes, Paul. *Demanding Respect: The Evolution of the American Comic Book*. Philadelphia: Temple University Press, 2009.
Luke, Carmen. "Cyber-Schooling and Technological Change: Multiliteracies for New Times." *Multiliteracies: Literacy Learning and the Design of Social Futures*, edited by Bill Cope and Mary Kalantzis, Abingdon, UK: Routledge, 2000, pp. 69–91.
Luke Cage. Created by Cheo Coker, performances by Mike Colter, Simone Missick, and Alfre Woodard, Los Gatos, CA: Netflix, 2016 and 2018.
M., Jonita Aro. "Constructing Masculinity: Depiction of the Superheroes Superman and Batman." *IUP Journal of English Studies*, vol. 11, no. 1, Mar. 2016, pp. 32–8.
Madison, Ivory. "Superheroes and Supervillains: An Interdependent Relationship." *What Is a Superhero?*, edited by Robin Rosenberg and Peter Coogan, Oxford, UK: Oxford University Press, 2013, pp. 157–60.
Mahiri, Jabari. "New Literacies for a New Century." *What They Don't Learn in School: Literacy in the Lives of Urban Youth*, edited by Jabari Mahiri, New York: P. Lang, 2004, pp. 1–18.
Man of Steel. Directed by Zack Snyder, performances by Henry Cavill, Amy Adams, and Michael Shannon, Burbank, CA: Warner Bros., 2013.
Marazi, Katherine. "Superhero or Vigilante? A Matter of Perspective and Brand Management." *European Journal of American Culture*, vol. 34, no. 1, 2015, pp. 67–82.
Maruo-Schröder, Nicole. "'Justice Has a Bad Side': Figurations of Law and Justice in 21st-Century Superhero Movies." *European Journal of American Studies*, no. 4, 2019, n. pg.
Marvel's Agents of S.H.I.E.L.D. Created by Joss Whedon, Maurissa Tancharoen, and Jed Whedon, performances by Clark Gregg, Ming-Na, and Brett Dalton, Hollywood, CA: ABC Studios, 2013–9.
Maslon, Laurence, and Michael Kantor. *Superheroes!: Capes, Cowls, and the Creation of Comic Book Culture*. New York: Crown Archetype, 2013.
Maslow, A.H. "A Theory of Human Motivation." *Psychological Review*, vol. 50, 1943, pp. 370–96.
Mattingly, Carol. "Beyond the Protestant Literacy Myth." *Literacy, Economy, and Power: Writing and Research After "Literacy in American Lives,"* edited by John Duffy et al., Carbondale: Southern Illinois University Press, 2014, pp. 45–60.
McClenaghan, Douglas, and Brenton Doecke, "Multiliteracies: Resources for Meaning-Making in the Secondary English Classroom." *Multiliteracies in Motion: Current Theory and Practice*, edited by David Cole and Darren Pullen, Abingdon, UK: Routledge, 2010, pp. 224–38.
McKnight, John Carter. "The Mark of Cain: Bodies, Belonging, and the Bratva." *Arrow and Superhero Television: Essays on Themes and Characters of the Series*, edited by James Iaccino, Cory Barker, and Myc Wiatrowski, Jefferson, NC: McFarland, 2017, pp. 111–23.
McMillen, Cynthia M., et al. "Tackling Literacy: A Collaborative Approach to Developing Materials, for Assessing Science Literacy Skills in Content Classrooms through a STEM Perspective." *Language and Literacy Spectrum*, vol. 28, no. 1, 2018, Article 2.
Melia, Joseph. *Modality*. Montreal: McGill-Queen's University Press, 2003.
Miczo, Nathan. *How Superheroes Model Community: Philosophically, Communicatively, Relationally*. Lanham, MD: Lexington Books, 2016.
Miller, Sue, Hilary Janks, and James Stiles. "Literacy with Mobiles in Print-Poor Communities." *The Routledge Handbook of Literacy Studies*, edited by Jennifer Rowsell and Kate Pahl, Abingdon, UK: Routledge, 2015, pp. 634–48.
Mills, Anthony R. *American Theology, Superhero Comics, and Cinema: The Marvel of Stan Lee and the Revolution of a Genre*. Abingdon, UK: Routledge, 2014.
Mills, Kathy, and Barbara Comber. "Socio-Spatial Approaches to Literacy Studies." *The Routledge Handbook of Literacy Studies*, edited by Jennifer Rowsell and Kate Pahl, Abingdon, UK: Routledge, 2015, pp. 91–103.

References

Mirabelli, Tony. "Learning to Serve." *What They Don't Learn in School: Literacy in the Lives of Urban Youth*, edited by Jabari Mahiri, New York: P. Lang, 2004, pp. 143–63.

Mitch, David Franklin. *The Rise of Popular Literacy in Victorian England: The Influence of Private Choice and Public Policy.* Philadelphia: University of Pennsylvania Press, 1992.

Mitchell, Claudia, and Casey Burkholder. "Literacies and Research as Social Change." *The Routledge Handbook of Literacy Studies*, edited by Jennifer Rowsell and Kate Pahl, Abingdon, UK: Routledge, 2015, pp. 649–62.

Moore, David. "Some Complexities of Gendered Talk about Texts." *Journal of Literacy Research*, vol. 29, no. 4, 1997, pp. 507–30.

Moores, Shaun. *Media/Theory: Thinking About Media and Communications.* Abingdon, UK: Routledge, 2005.

Mor, Walkyria Monte. "Learning by Design." *A Pedagogy of Multiliteracies: Learning by Design*, edited by Bill Cope and Mary Kalantzis, London: Palgrave Macmillan, 2015, pp. 186–209.

Moss, Beverly, and Robyn Lyons-Robinson. "Making Literacy Work." *Literacy, Economy, and Power: Writing and Research After "Literacy in American Lives,"* edited by John Duffy et al., Carbondale: Southern Illinois University Press, 2014, pp. 136–54.

Murray, Mitch. "The Work of Art in the Age of the Superhero." *Science Fiction Film and Television*, vol. 10, no. 1, 2017, pp. 27–51.

Murray, Pippa. "Being in School? Exclusion and the Denial of Psychological Reality." *Disability and Psychology: Critical Introductions and Reflections*, edited by Dan Goodley and Rebecca Lawthom, London: Palgrave Macmillan, 2006, pp. 34–41.

Naqvi, Rahat. "Postcolonial Approaches to Literacy." *The Routledge Handbook of Literacy Studies*, edited by Jennifer Rowsell and Kate Pahl, Abingdon, UK: Routledge, 2015, pp. 49–61.

Narrog, Hieko. *Modality, Subjectivity, and Semantic Change.* Oxford, UK: Oxford, 2012.

National Academy of Sciences. *National Science Education Standards.* Washington, D.C.: National Academy Press, 1996.

Neville, Mary. "Improving Multimodal Literacy through *Learning by Design.*" *A Pedagogy of Multiliteracies: Learning by Design*, edited by Bill Cope and Mary Kalantzis, London: Palgrave Macmillan, 2015, pp. 210–30.

New London Group. "A Pedagogy of Multiliteracies." *Multiliteracies: Literacy Learning and the Design of Social Future*, edited by Bill Cope and Mary Kalantzis, New York: Macmillan, 2000, pp. 9–38.

Newfield, Denise. "The Semiotic Mobility of Literacy: Four Analytical Approaches." *The Routledge Handbook of Literacy Studies*, edited by Jennifer Rowsell and Kate Pahl, Abingdon, UK: Routledge, 2015, pp. 267–81.

Nichols, Sue. "Ecological Approaches to Literacy Research." *The Routledge Handbook of Literacy Studies*, edited by Jennifer Rowsell and Kate Pahl, Abingdon, UK: Routledge, 2015, pp. 104–23.

O'Neill, Megan. *Popular Culture: Perspectives for Readers and Writers.* Boston: Heinle & Heinle/Thomson Learning, 2002.

Ong, Walter. *The Presence of the Word: Some Prolegomena for Cultural and Religious History.* New Haven, CT: Yale University Press, 1977.

Ong, Walter. "Writing Is a Technology that Restructures Thought." *The Written Word: Literacy in Translation*, edited by Gerd Baumann, Oxford, UK: Oxford University Press, 1986, pp. 23–50.

Packer, Sharon. *Superheroes and Superegos: Analyzing the Minds behind the Masks.* Santa Barbara, CA: Praeger/ABC-CLIO, 2010.

Pahl, Kate, and Hugh Escott. "Materialising Literacies." *The Routledge Handbook of Literacy Studies*, edited by Jennifer Rowsell and Kate Pahl, Abingdon, UK: Routledge, 2015, pp. 489–503.

Pahl, Kate, and Jennifer Rowsell. *Literacy and Education: Understanding the New Literacy Studies in Classroom.* Thousand Oaks, CA: Paul Chapman Publishing, 2005.

Pahl, Kate, and Jennifer Rowsell, eds. *Travel Notes from the New Literacy Studies: Instances of Practice.* Bristol, England: Multilingual Matters, 2006.

Pattanayak, D. P. "Literacy: An Instrument of Opinion." *Literacy and Orality*, edited by David Olson and Nancy Torrance, Cambridge, England: Cambridge, 1991, pp. 105–8.

Radway, Janice. "Interpretive Communities and Variable Literacies." *Rethinking Popular Culture: Contemporary Perspectives in Cultural Studies*, edited by Chandra Mukerji and Michael Schudson, Berkeley: University of California Press, 2008, 465–86.
Rakes, H. "Crip Feminist Trauma Studies in *Jessica Jones* and Beyond." *Journal of Literary & Cultural Disability Studies*, vol. 13, no. 1, 2019, pp. 75–91.
Rennie, Jennifer, and Annette Patterson. "Young Australia's Reading in a Digital World." *Multiliteracies in Motion: Current Theory and Practice*, edited by David Cole and Darren Pullen, Abingdon, UK: Routledge, 2010, pp. 207–23.
Rheingold, Howard. "Stewards of Digital Literacies." *Knowledge Quest*, vol. 41, no. 1, 2012, pp. 53–5.
Rice, Jeff. *The Rhetoric of Cool: Composition Studies and New Media*. Carbondale: Southern Illinois University Press, 2007.
Richardson, Elaine. *African American Literacies*. Abingdon, UK: Routledge, 2002.
Richardson, Theresa R, and Erwin V. Johanningmeier. *Race, Ethnicity, and Education: What Is Taught in School*. Charlotte: Information Age Publishing, 2003.
Rogers, Rebecca, and Katherine O'Daniels. "Critical Literacy Education." *The Routledge Handbook of Literacy Studies*, edited by Jennifer Rowsell and Kate Pahl, Abingdon, UK: Routledge, 2015, pp. 62–78.
Romagnoli, Alex, and Gian Pagnucci. *Enter the Superheroes: American Values, Culture, and the Canon of Superhero Literature*. Lanham, MD: The Scarecrow Press, 2013.
Rose, Mike. *The Mind at Work: Valuing the Intelligence of the American Worker*. New York: Penguin Random House, 2004.
Rose, Mike. *An Open Language: Selected Writing on Literacy, Learning, and Opportunity*. Boston: Bedford/St. Martin's, 2006.
Rosen, Michael Louis. "The Lawyer as Superhero: How Marvel Comics' *Daredevil* Depicts the American Court System and Legal Practice." *Capital University Law Review*, no. 2, 2019, pp. 379- 433.
Rosenberg, Robin, and Peter Coogan. *What Is a Superhero?* Oxford, UK: Oxford University Press, 2013.
Rosenburg, Robin and Eller Winner. "Are Superheroes Just Supergifted?" *Our Superheroes, Ourselves*, edited by Robin Rosenburg, Oxford, UK: Oxford University Press, 2013.
Royster, Jacqueline, and Gesa Kirsch. *Rhetorical Voices: New Horizon for Rhetoric, Composition, and Literacy Studies*. Carbondale: Southern Illinois University Press, 2012.
Royster, Jacqueline J. *Traces of a Stream: Literacy and Social Change among African American Women*. Pittsburgh: University of Pittsburgh Press, 2000.
Ryan, Mary, and Tony Rossi. "The Transdisciplinary Potential of Multiliteracies: Bodily Performances and Meaning-Making in Health and Physical Education." *Multiliteracies and Diversity in Education: New Pedagogies for Expanding Landscapes*, edited by Annah Healy, Oxford, UK: Oxford University Press, 2008, pp. 30–57.
Sato, Chizu. "Rethinking Adult Literacy Training: An Analysis through a Third World Feminist Perspective." *Women's Studies Quarterly*, vol. 32, no. 1/2, 2004, pp. 73–89.
Saunders, Ben. *Do the Gods Wear Capes?: Spirituality, Fantasy, and Superheroes*. London: Continuum, 2011. Print.
Schroll, Mark A., and Claire Polansky. "Bridging Transpersonal Ecosophical Concerns with the Hero's Journey and Superheroes through Comicbook Lore: Implications for Personal and Cultural Transformation." *International Journal of Transpersonal Studies*, vol. 36, no. 2, July 2017, pp. 1–27.
Scribner's, Sylvia. "Literacy in Three Metaphors." *American Journal of Education*, vol. 93, no. 1, 1984, pp. 6–21.
Scribner's, Sylvia, and Michael Cole. "Literacy without Schooling: Testing for Intellectual Effects." *Literacy Studies, Volume 1: Great Divides and Situated Literacies*, edited by Mastin Prinsloo and Mike Baynham, Newbury Park, CA: Sage, 2013, pp. 91–106.
Selber, Stuart. *Multiliteracies for a Digital Age*. Carbondale: Southern Illinois University Press, 2004.
Shamos, Morris. *The Myth of Scientific Literacy*. New Brunswick, NJ: Rutgers, 1995.
Sherlock. Created by Mark Gatiss and Steven Moffat, performances by Benedict Cumberbatch, Martin Freeman, and Una Stubbs, London: BBC, 2010-7.

Shopova, Tatiana. "Digital Literacy of Students and Its Improvement at the University." *Journal on Efficiency and Responsibility in Education and Science*, vol. 7, no. 2, 2014, pp. 26–32.
Siebers, Tobin. *Disability Aesthetics*. Ann Arbor: University of Michigan Press, 2010.
Smit, David. *The End of Composition Studies*. Carbondale: Southern Illinois University Press, 2007.
Smith, Carlota. *Modes of Discourse*. Cambridge, England: Cambridge University Press, 2003.
Smith, Michael. "Seeking Sponsors, Accumulating Literacies." *Literacy, Economy, and Power: Writing and Research After "Literacy in American Lives,"* edited by John Duffy et al., Carbondale: Southern Illinois University Press, 2014, pp. 155–65.
Smith, Pamela. "Giving Voice to the Hand: The Articulation of Material Literacy in Sixteenth Century." *Popular Literacy: Studies in Cultural Practices and Poetics*, edited by John Trimbur, Pittsburgh: University of Pittsburgh Press, 2001, pp. 74–93.
Smith, Scott T, and Josei Alaniz. *Uncanny Bodies: Superhero Comics and Disability*. University Park: The Pennsylvania State University Press, 2019.
Snow, Catherine, and Kenne Dibner. *Science Literacy: Concepts, Contexts, and Consequences*. Washington, D.C.: National Academies Press, 2016.
Spider-Man. Directed by Sam Raimi, performances by Tobey Maguire and Willem Dafoe, Culver City, CA: Columbia Pictures, 2002.
Spider-Man: Homecoming. Directed by Jon Watts, performances by Tom Holland, Michael Keaton, and Robert Downey, Jr., Burbank, CA: Marvel Studios, 2017.
Stille, Saskia. "Participatory Methodologies and Literacy Studies." *The Routledge Handbook of Literacy Studies*, edited by Jennifer Rowsell and Kate Pahl, Abingdon, UK: Routledge, 2015, pp. 606–18.
Stornaiuolo, Amy. "Literacy as Worldmaking: Multimodality, Creativity, and Cosmopolitanism." *The Routledge Handbook of Literacy Studies*, edited by Jennifer Rowsell and Kate Pahl, Abingdon, UK: Routledge, 2015, pp. 561–72.
Strassel, Kimberley, Celeste Colgan, and John Goodman. *Leaving Women Behind: Modern Families, Outdated Laws*. Lanham, MD: Rowman & Littlefield, 2006.
Street, Brian V. "Autonomous and Ideological Models of Literacy: Approaches from New Literacy Studies." *Media Anthropology Network*. 24 Jan. 2006. Web. 12 Feb. 2014.
Street, Brian V. "The Future of 'Social Literacies.'" *The Future of Literacy Studies*, edited by Mike Baynham and Mastin Prinsloo, London: Palgrave Macmillan, 2009, pp. 21–37.
Street, Brian V. "Literacy in Theory and Practice: Challenges and Debates Over 50 Years." *Theory into Practice*, vol. 52, 2013, pp. 52–62.
Street, Brian V. *Literacy in Theory and Practice*. Cambridge, England: Cambridge University Press, 1984.
Street, Brian V. "New Literacies, New Times: Developments in Literacy Studies." *Literacies and Language Education*, 3rd ed, edited by Brian V. Street and Stephen May, New York: Springer, 2017, pp. 3–15.
Street, Brian V. "New Literacy Studies." *Language, Ethnography, and Education: Bridging New Literacy Studies and Bourdieu*, edited by Michael Grenfell et al., Abingdon, UK: Routledge, 2012, pp. 27–49.
Street, Brian V. *Social Literacies: Critical Approaches to Literacy in Development, Ethnography and Education*. Abingdon, UK: Taylor and Francis, 2016.
Stuller, Jennifer. "What Is a Female Superhero?" *What Is a Superhero?*, edited by Robin Rosenberg and Peter Coogan, Oxford, UK: Oxford University Press, 2013, pp. 19–24.
Sullivan, Patrick. "Deep Reading as a Threshold Concept in Composition Studies." *Deep Reading: Teaching Reading in the Writing Classroom*, edited by Patrick Sullivan, Howard Tinberg, and Sheridan Blau, Urbana, IL: NCTE, 2017, pp. 143–71.
Sullivan, Patrick. *A New Writing Classroom: Listening, Motivation, and Habits of Mind*. Logan: Utah State University Press, 2014.
Supergirl. Created by Ali Adler, Greg Berlanti, and Andrew Kreisberg, performances by Melissa Benoist and Mehcad Brooks, Burbank, CA: Warner Bros., 2015–9.
Tan, Jennifer. "Closing the Gap." *Multiliteracies and Diversity in Education: New Pedagogies for Expanding Landscapes*, edited by Annah Healy, Oxford, UK: Oxford University Press, 2008, pp. 144–67.

References

Teen Titans. Created by Michael Chang, voices performances by Scott Menville and Hynden Walch, Burbank, CA: Warner Bros., 2003–7.

Thistle, Susan L. *From Marriage to the Market: The Transformation of Women's Lives and Work.* Berkeley: University of California Press, 2006.

Thomas, Roy, Mike Gold, Jerry Ordway, and Robert Greenberger. *The Greatest Golden Age Stories Ever Told.* New York: DC Comics, 1990.

Thor: The Dark World. Directed by Alan Taylor, performances by Chris Hemsworth, Natalie Portman, and Tom Hiddleston, Burbank, CA: Marvel Studios, 2013.

Thweatt, Jeanine. "Origin Stories: Superheroes, Cyborgs, Artificial Intelligences (and Other Humans and Posthumans)." *Christian Perspectives on Transhumanism and the Church*, edited by Steve Donaldson, London: Palgrave Macmillan, 2018, pp. 197–207.

Tinberg, Howard. "When Writers Encounter Reading in the Community College First-Year Composition Course." *Deep Reading: Teaching Reading in the Writing Classroom*, edited by Patrick Sullivan, Howard Tinberg, and Sheridan Blau, Urbana, IL: NCTE, 2017, pp. 244–64.

Toliver, S. R. "Unlocking the Cage: Empowering Literacy Representations in Netflix's *Luke Cage* Series." *Journal of Adolescent & Adult Literacy*, vol. 61, no. 6, May 2018, pp. 621–630.

Tomovic, Cynthia, et al. "Scientific Literacy Matters: Using Literature to Meet Next Generation Science Standards and 21st Century Skills." *K-12 STEM Education*, vol. 3, no. 2, 2017, pp. 179–91.

van Leeuwen, Theo. "Looking Good: Aesthetics, Multimodality, and Literacy Studies." *The Routledge Handbook of Literacy Studies*, edited by Jennifer Rowsell and Kate Pahl, Abingdon, UK: Routledge, 2015, pp. 426–39.

Verano, Frank. "Superheroes Need Supervillains." *What Is a Superhero*, edited by Robin Rosenberg and Peter M. Coogan, Oxford, UK: Oxford University Press, 2013, pp. 83–7.

Vie, Stephanie, and Brandy Dieterle. "Minding the Gap: Comics as Scaffolding for Critical Literacy Skills in the Classroom." *Composition Forum*, vol. 33, 2016, n. pg.

Wandtke, Terrence R. *The Meaning of Superhero Comic Books.* Jefferson, NC: McFarland, 2012.

Warschauer, Mark. "Digital Literacy Studies: Progress and Perspectives." *The Future of Literacy Studies*, edited by Mike Baynham and Mastin Prinsloo, London: Palgrave Macmillan, 2009, pp. 123–40.

Warschauer, Mark. *Electronic Literacies: Language, Culture, and Power in Online Education.* Abingdon, UK: Routledge, 1999.

Williams, Bronwyn. "From Screen to Screen: Students' Use of Popular Culture Genres in Multimodal Writing Assignments." *Computers and Composition*, vol. 34, Dec. 2014, pp. 110–21.

Williams, Bronwyn, and Amy Zenger. "Introduction: Popular Culture and Literacy in a Networked World." *New Media Literacies and Participatory Popular Culture across Borders*, edited by Bronwyn Williams and Amy Zenger, Abingdon, UK: Routledge, 2012, pp. 1–14.

Williams, Bronwyn, and Amy Zenger. *Popular Culture and Representations of Literacy.* Abingdon, UK: Taylor and Francis, 2007.

Williams, J. Corey. "*Luke Cage* and Police Brutality." *American Journal of Psychiatry Residents' Journal*, vol. 12, no. 8, 2017, pp. 12.

Wimmer, Jennifer, and Benjamin Thevenin. "Media Art in the Elementary Classroom." *Arts Education and Literacies*, edited by Amy Jensen and Roni Draper, Abingdon, UK: Routledge, 2015, pp. 99–108.

Wonder Woman. Directed by Patty Jenkins, performances by Gal Gadot, Chris Pine, and Robin Wright, Burbank, CA: Warner Bros., 2017.

Wu, Siew Mei, et al. "Teaching Academic Literacy Using Popular Science Texts: A Case Study." *Teaching & Learning Inquiry*, vol. 6, no. 2, Jan. 2018, pp. 29–49.

Young, Morris. "Writing the Life of Henry Obookiah: The Sponsorship of Literacy and Identity." *Literacy, Economy, and Power: Writing and Research After "Literacy in American Lives,"* edited by John Duffy et al., Carbondale: Southern Illinois University Press, 214, pp. 61–78.

Index

ableism and superheroes 138–140, 217
accommodationist model of literacy
  210–212
Acu, Adrian 42
Addison, Joanne 100
aesthetics and literacy 195–197
Akinnaso, Niyi 102
Alaniz, José 138, 222
Allen, Barry (character) 8, 26, 34–35, 38,
  42,67, 70–72, 74–80, 123, 139, 159–160,
  168, 173–175, 191, 194, 196, 224
Archer, Arlene 112
Arkham Asylum 86, 124
Arkham City 136
Arkham Origins 161
Arnove, Robert 102, 118
Arrow 2, 7, 8, 36, 38, 40, 42, 48–62, 67–68,
  71, 85, 87, 91, 107, 142, 144, 148, 153–155,
  161–163, 168, 171–172, 179, 186, 189–93,
  202, 204–205, 212, 223
The Arrow Cave 56, 59, 172, 189–191, 195,
  197, 206, 224, 226
Avengers 3, 6, 136, 225

Baglieri, Susan 139, 149
Bahlmann, Andrew 221
Bainbridge, Jason 152
Bamford, Julia 169, 182
Barton, David 19, 23, 37, 55, 83, 145, 173,
  201, 203
Batman 12, 14, 42, 49, 53–54, 85–87, 91,
  93–96, 124,140, 161, 185, 196, 221, 225–226
Batman Begins 3, 86, 226
Batman V Superman 225
Bauerlein, Mark 89
Baynham, Mike 133, 183, 215
Bednarz, Sarah 186, 199
Belt-Beyan, Phyllis 90
Bergman, Daniel 81
Bezemer, Jeff 14, 98–99
Bianco, Joseph 111, 214–215
Black Lightning 221

Black Panther 226
Blau, Francine 102
Bloome, David 156
Blot, Richard K. 25
Bondi, Marina 169, 182
Boucher, Ian 176
Boudreaux, Armond 34
Boyd, Fenice 44–45, 56
Brandt, Deborah 14, 23, 25, 51, 55, 56–57,
  60, 70, 72–73, 88–89, 97, 144, 164, 166–
  167, 179–181
Brock, Cynthia 44–45, 56
Brooker, Will 1, 86
Brown, Jeffrey 37, 103, 130
Brown, Scott 69
Brownie, Barbara 222
Bruhn, Jørgen 137–138
Burkholder, Casey 125, 131
Burnett, Cathy 54, 187, 193
Burns, Gary 36

Cage, Luke (character) 2, 4, 34, 104, 117–
  132, 155, 163–164, 186, 207, 222, 225
Captain America: The First Avenger 3
Captain America: The Winter Soldier
  224–225
Carifio, James 48
Carillo, Ellen 194
Chambliss, Julian 221
citizens in superhero worlds 210–212
Clinton, Katie. 14, 23, 56–57, 97, 144,
  166–167
Cloonan, Anne 26
Coiro, Julie 191
Cole, David 17, 27, 34, 45, 119
Cole, Michael 183
Collins, James 25
Comber, Barbara 57, 185
Compton-Lily, Catherine 219
Coogan, Peter 115, 221
Cook, Kelli Cargile 89–90
Cook-Gumperz, Jenny 23

243

Index

Cope, Bill 25–26, 28–29, 39, 41, 46, 62, 78
Cornoldi, Cesare 140–141
Cortés, Guido 102
Cushman, Ellen 74

Dagostino, Lorraine 48
Daily, James 221
Damaske, Sarah 101
Dantzler, Perry 7
Daredevil (character) 2, 4, 7, 12, 20–21, 104, 136–147, 155, 158, 176–178, 186, 225
Daredevil (TV show) 2, 4, 9, 15, 21, 34, 40, 43, 85, 110, 119, 136–147, 158, 176–180, 183, 202, 225, 227
Daredevil (2003) 136
The Dark Knight 5, 86, 130, 136
The Dark Knight Rises 5
Davidson, Ryan. 221
Davis, Lennard 139, 142
Deadpool 226
The Defenders 7, 107, 118, 126
Delpit, Lisa 170
Derry, Ken 123, 135
detective skills 1, 11, 37–40, 48, 71, 103, 123, 126, 153, 173, 178, 191, 193–194
detective workspaces 185–187
DeWeerd, Katherine 149–150
Dibner, Kenne 69
Die Hard 61
Dieterle, Brandy 116
Dillard, Mariah 40, 119–121, 126, 130, 162–165, 206, 225, 226
discourse communities 18, 23, 90, 162, 169–171, 222
Dr. Strange 226
Doecke, Brenton 178
Domingo, Myrrh 46
Donehower, Kim 205
Dooley, Karen 208–209
Duffy, John 83, 87, 89, 98–99, 203, 206

Easton, Lee 153
Elleström, Lars 137–138
Ellis, Katie 147, 148
Escott, Hugh 185, 187
Exley, Beryl 64
Exner, Ulrich 199
Expendables 61

Fairclough, Norman 152
Farrell, Lesley 40
Fawaz, Ramzi 123
Findlay, Kate 223
The Flash 7, 34, 36, 40, 67–81, 85, 87, 91, 107. 142–144, 148, 159–160, 168, 173, 175, 186, 191–193, 202, 204, 205, 214, 223, 224, 226, 227

Flower, Linda 18, 128, 134, 152
Foresman, Galen 151
Freire, Paulo 52, 202
Frost, Alena 89

Garrido, Lea Espinoza 119, 124, 136
Gee, James Paul 18, 23, 25, 36, 50, 51, 63, 65, 130, 169–170, 193, 215, 222
Gilbert, Pam 113
Gillen, Julia 21
Gilmore, James 38, 221
Gladwell, Malcolm 41
Gledhill, Evan 154
Goldblatt, Eli 180
Goodwyn, Andrew 223
Gordon, Jane Anna 10–11
Gordon, Jim (character) 86–88, 91–93, 123–124, 174, 204
Gotham 2, 7, 8, 40, 42, 85–98, 124, 144, 153, 174, 176, 179–180, 186, 195, 202, 204–208, 212, 223, 224
Graff, Harvey 18, 89, 90, 99, 102, 118, 120, 127–129, 142, 166, 205, 209–210, 225
Gray, Richard 221
Graydon, Danny 222
Greenwood, Jeremy 101

Haas, Christina 187
Hackett, Abigail 121, 206
Hale, Bob 13
Hamilton, Mary 19, 23, 121, 145, 173
Harries, Patrick 215
Harris, Muriel 218
Haslem, Wendy 222
Hawisher, Gail 218
Healy, Annah 96
Heath, Shirley Brice 22, 133, 167, 222
Hell's Kitchen 12, 108, 136–137, 141–143, 155, 158, 176–177, 194, 225
Henderson, Michael 16
Henderson, Robyn 44, 99
Heydon, Rachel 180, 202
high-tech workspaces 189–193
Hoffmann, Aviv 13
Hogarth, Jeri (character) 100–101, 104–106, 108, 113, 157, 178
Horner, Bruce 210–211
House 104
Howe, Sarah 58–59
Huang, Cheng-Wen 112

Iaccino, James 58
Indiana Jones: Raiders of the Lost Ark 61
Iron Fist 7, 110, 126, 221
Iron Man 6, 11, 15, 94, 114, 223, 224, 225, 226
Ivanic, Roz 133

Index 245

Jacobs, Dale 89
Jaimovich, Nir 102
Jenkins, Henry 98, 174–175, 209, 219
Jennings, John 61
Jessica Jones 2, 7, 15, 85, 100–113, 119, 136, 153, 156, 183, 194, 202, 225
Jewett, Robert 142
Johanningmeier, Erwin 9
Johnson, Genevieve 130–131
Johnston, Jennifer 141
Jolliffe, David 180
Jones, Jessica (character) 2, 7, 9, 12, 20, 25, 34, 100–113, 118, 123, 139, 156–158, 169, 186, 93–194, 196–197, 224, 225, 226
Juliano, Stephanie 213

Kakalios, James 222
Kalantzis, Mary 25–26, 28–29, 39, 41, 46, 62, 78
Kampis, George. 70
Kantor, Michael 221
Karsai, Istvan 70
Keith, Heather 136
Keith, Kenneth 136
Kemp, Karen 186, 199
Kendrick, Maureen 223
Kent, Kent 147, 148
Kilgrave (character) 102–106, 109, 111–112, 118, 155–158, 162, 165, 224
Kinloch, Valerie 100, 120
Kirsch, Gesa 115
Knight, Misty (character) 117, 120, 124–126, 128–129, 132, 194–195, 197
Kress, Gunther 13–16, 18, 27–28, 45–46, 98–99, 171
Kulick, Don 127

Ladson-Billings, Gloria 128
Lathan, Rhea 119
Lawless, Kimberly 69
Lawrence, John 142
Lee, Alison 109
Legends of Tomorrow 7, 221, 227
Lemke, Jay 29
Lethal Weapon 61
Linge, Alex 14
literacy: acquisition 18, 20, 31–32, 74, 89–90, 100–102, 111–112, 118, 122, 126, 128, 130–132, 144, 176, 196, 211; definition 17–20; and disability studies 137–142, 144–147; equality 110–113; and ethnicities 117–122; events, definition of 19–90; and feminism 110–102, 113, 226; metaphors 93, 144, 147, 208–210; myths 18, 65, 117–118, 121, 126–130, 208–210; practices, definition of 22–26; and socioeconomics 55, 89, 102, 111–112, 127–130, 142, 146–147, 151, 154, 201, 204–208, 209, 218; sponsors 72–74, 80, 88–91, 94, 120, 142, 179–181, 224; stewards 60, 88–91, 94–96, 122, 180, 223, 224
Lopes, Paul 221
low tech workspaces 193–195
Lu, Min-Zhan 210–211
Luke Cage 2, 9, 15, 40, 85, 117–132, 136, 162, 186, 194, 202, 206, 208, 225, 226
Luke, Carmen 199–200
Lyons-Robinson, Robyn 118

M, Jonita Aro 93
Madison, Ivory 152
Mahiri, Jabari 184
Man of Steel 226
Marazi, Katherine 53–54
Maruo-Schröder, Nicole 34
Marvel's Agents of SHIELD 136
Maslon, Laurence 221
Maslow, AH 101, 109–110, 121
material literacies 187–189, 192, 197
Mattingly, Carol 122
McClenaghan, Douglas 178
McKnight, John Carter 58
McMillen, Cynthia 82
Melia, Joseph 13–14
mentors of superheroes 103, 160, 168–181, 207, 226
Miczo, Nathan 154
Miller, Sue 83
Mills, Anthony 221
Mills, Kathy 57, 185
Mirabelli, Tony 114
Mitch, David Franklin 90
Mitchell, Claudia 125, 131
modes, definition of 13–14
Moore, David 224
Moores, Shaun 218
Mor, Walkyria 215
Morris, Megan 36
Moss, Beverly 118
Muller, Henrik 14
multiliteracies, definition of 27–29
multimodal texts 16–17
multimodalities, definition of 14–16
Murdock, Matt (character) 34, 40, 43, 124, 136–147, 176–179, 186, 221, 225, 227
Murray, Mitch 182–183
Murray, Pippa 150

Naqvi, Rahat 52, 188
Nelson, Foggy (character) 140, 148, 176–179, 225
Neville, Mary 46
New London Group 27, 188, 202
Newfield, Denise 84

Nichols, Sue 28
NLS history 22–24

O'Neill, Megan 87
Ong, Walter 52

Packer, Sharon 225
Page, Karen (character) 36, 140, 143, 176–179
Pagnucci, Gian 10, 30–31, 51, 85, 221
Pahl, Kate 18, 28, 31, 185, 187
Pattanayak, DP 225
Patterson, Annette 196
Pennyworth, Alfred (character) 35, 42, 86, 88, 91, 93, 95, 180–181, 206
Polansky, Claire 50
Pressel, Dietrich 199
Prinsloo, Mastin 133, 183, 215
Pullen, Darren 17, 27, 34, 45, 119

Queen, Oliver (character) 8, 20–22, 25–26, 35–36, 38, 40, 42, 48–62, 67–68, 75, 92, 102–103, 139, 144, 146, 1154–155, 161–162, 165, 168–169, 171–173, 179, 188–191, 206, 212, 222, 223, 224, 226

Radway, Janice 20
Rakes, H. 155–156
Ramon, Cisco (character) 67, 70–72, 76–80, 160, 175, 191–192, 196
Rennie, Jennifer 196
Rheingold, Howard 89
Rice, Jeff 99
Richardson, Elaine 134–135
Richardson, Theresa 90
Romagnoli, Alex 10, 30–31, 51, 85, 221
Rosen, Michael Louis 11
Rosenberg, Robin 94, 115, 221
Rossi, Tony 61, 198
Rowsell, Jennifer 18, 28, 31, 180, 202
Royster, Jacqueline 90, 115, 152, 155
Ryan, Mary 61, 198

Sato, Chizu 112
Saunders, Ben 221
Schroll, Mark 50
scientific literacies 48, 67–81, 159, 174–175, 192
Scribner, Sylvia 146, 183
Selber, Stuart 101–102
Selfe, Cynthia 218
Shamos, Morris 67
Shapiro, Arthur 139, 149 139, 149
Sherlock 104
Shopova, Tatiana 189–190
Siebers, Tobin 139
Siu, Henry 102

Smit, David 170
Smith, Carlota 13
Smith, Michael 74
Smith, Pamela 187
Smith, Scott T. 222
Smoack, Felicity (character) 35, 41, 52, 54, 60, 91, 143, 168, 171–173, 189–191, 226
Snow, Caitlin (character) 67–72, 76–80, 160, 175, 191–192, 196
Snow, Catherine 69
specialized literacies 21, 26, 40–43, 48, 53, 57, 63, 68, 89–90, 100, 107, 125, 137, 144, 146, 148, 157, 159, 172, 174, 188, 195, 212, 217, 224
Spider-Man 10
Spider-Man: Homecoming 225
S.T.A.R. Labs 36, 67, 70, 72, 76–78, 159–160, 191–193
Stille, Saskia 209
Stork, Matthias 38, 221
Stornaiuolo, Amy 181
Strassel, Kimberley 101
Street, Brian 13, 18, 24, 44, 143, 144, 199, 210, 211, 214, 218, 222, 223
Stroud, Christopher 127
student activities: group 45–46, 64–65, 82–83, 98–99, 114–115, 133–134, 149–150, 166–167, 183, 198–199, 214–215; individual research 44–45, 63–64, 81–82, 97, 113–114, 132–133, 148–144, 165–166, 182–183, 197–198, 213–214; online projects 46–47, 65–66, 84, 99, 115–116, 134–135, 150, 167, 184, 199–200, 215–216
Stuller, Jennifer 115
Sullivan, Patrick 6, 158, 200
Supergirl 221, 227
superhero literacy 7, 24–26, 37, 48, 56
supervillains 12, 20, 67, 76, 78, 93, 103, 106, 108, 112, 123, 137, 151–165, 206–208, 225, 226

Tan, Jennifer 46
Teen Titans 161
Thawne, Eobard (character) 35, 39, 67, 70–71, 76, 79, 80, 153, 158–160, 165, 224, 226
Thevenin, Benjamin 63–64
Thistle, Susan 101
Thomas, Roy 12
Thor: The Dark World 5
Thweatt, Jeanine 166
Tinberg, Howard 200, 222
Toliver, SR 124, 128, 134
Tomovic, Cynthia 80
traditional literacy events 8, 26, 36, 40, 41, 85, 87, 93, 137, 141, 143, 146, 188, 195, 219, 223

urban literacies 118–122

van Helden, Caspar 29
van Leeuwen, Theo 171, 195–196
Vecchi, Tomaso 140–141
Verano, Frank 151
Vie, Stephanie 116

Walker, Trish 100–101, 103, 105–108, 110–113, 224
Wandtke, Terrence 221
Warschauer, Mark 20–21, 171
Wayne, Bruce (character) 2, 35, 40, 42, 49, 54, 86–66, 91, 93–96, 139–140, 180–181, 186, 188, 196, 204, 206, 208, 224, 226
Wells, Harrison (character) 67–68, 70–72, 76, 79–80, 159–160, 173, 191, 223, 224, 226
West, Iris (character) 34, 35, 173, 176, 204, 226

West, Joe (character) 35, 173–176
Williams, Bronwyn 19, 27, 33, 39, 69, 203–204, 212, 217
Williams, J. Corey 117
Wilson, Slade/Deathstroke (character) 35, 54, 58, 60, 103, 152, 154, 161–162, 165, 179, 223
Wimmer, Jennifer 63–64
Winkler, Anne 102
Winner, Eller 94
Wonder Woman 226
Wu, Siew 82

Young, Morris 83, 131

Zenger, Amy 19, 27, 33, 39, 69, 203–204, 212, 217